## About the author

Tim Di Muzio is a senior lecturer in international relations and political economy at the University of Wollongong. He currently edits the journal *Review of Capital as Power*.

# THE 1% AND THE REST OF US

## A POLITICAL ECONOMY OF DOMINANT OWNERSHIP

*Tim Di Muzio*

Zed Books
LONDON

*The 1% and the Rest of Us: A Political Economy of Dominant Ownership* was first published in 2015 by Zed Books Ltd, 7 Cynthia Street, London N1 9JF, UK

www.zedbooks.co.uk

Copyright © Tim Di Muzio 2015

The right of Tim Di Muzio to be identified as the author of this work has been asserted by him in accordance with the Copyright, Designs and Patents Act, 1988

Set in Monotype Plantin and FFKievit by Ewan Smith, London
Index: ed.emery@thefreeuniversity.net
Cover image © Gansovsky Vladislav/Getty Images
Cover designed by www.roguefour.co.uk

A catalogue record for this book is available from the British Library

ISBN 978-1-78360-143-1 hb
ISBN 978-1-78360-142-4 pb
ISBN 978-1-78360-144-8 pdf
ISBN 978-1-78360-145-5 epub
ISBN 978-1-78360-146-2 mobi

Printed and bound by Edwards Brothers Malloy

# CONTENTS

## TABLES AND FIGURES

**Tables**

**Figures**

# INTRODUCTION: TOWARDS A GLOBAL POLITICAL ECONOMY OF THE 1%[1]

Of all Classes, the wealthy are the most noticed and the least studied. (John Kenneth Galbraith 1977: 44)

The fact is that there is far more systematic information available on the poor, on farmers, workers ... than on the men and women of the rich and the well-born, on those who make up the 'upper strata' – if not the 'capitalist class' – of our society. Yet now it ought to be apparent ... that we must discover as much as we can about those who occupy the upper reaches of ... society if we are to understand ... the present as history. (Maurice Zeitlin 1974: 1112)

Study the rich and the powerful, not the poor and powerless ... not nearly enough work is being done on those who hold the power and pull the strings. As their tactics become more subtle and their public pronouncements more guarded, the need for better spade-work becomes crucial ... Let the poor study themselves. They already know what is wrong with their lives and if you truly want to help them, the best you can do is to give them a clearer idea of how their oppressors are working now and can be expected to work in the future. (Susan George 2010: 82)

One of the most interesting developments in the global political economy is our increasing awareness that a tiny minority of the world's population is growing obscenely wealthy. Of course, the fact that there is a gap between the rich and poor is hardly new or surprising. But two things appear to be novel in the present conjuncture: the magnitude of wealth held by the few and the intensification of inequality. Under conditions of what Stephen Gill has called 'disciplinary neoliberalism' and the 'new constitutionalism' – laws that protect and advance the rule of capital – this minuscule class of humanity has accumulated so much pecuniary worth that it is virtually impossible for them to spend it all (Gill 2008; Gill and Cutler 2014). Moreover, this tiny class set above humanity keeps getting richer and richer, and, as a consequence, more and more powerful. Even regular champions of capitalist markets are starting to get worried given the mounting evidence:

> For me the most convincing argument against the ongoing
> rise in economic inequality is that it is incompatible with
> true equality as citizens. If, as the ancient Athenians believed,
> participation in public life is a fundamental aspect of human
> self-realisation, huge inequalities cannot but destroy it. In a
> society dominated by wealth, money will buy power. Inequal-
> ity cannot be eliminated. It is inevitable and to a degree
> even desirable. But, as the Greeks argued, there needs to be
> moderation in all things. We are not seeing moderate rises in
> inequality. We should take notice. (Wolf 2014a)[2]

At the same time as wealth is accruing upwards, the majority of the planet's inhabitants experience varying degrees of auster-ity, precarity, indignity and exploitation in their daily lives. For many, life is little more than a permanent state of crisis and a daily struggle just to find shelter or put food and water on the table. Their material conditions of existence as well as their psychological well-being are severely affected by the deprivations and inequities they experience – particularly as images of opulent lifestyles become more widespread through international communications.

In the opening stages of the twenty-first century, the relationship between those at the top of the wealth hierarchy and everyone else has never been so stark. Indeed, both the magnitude and the concentration of wealth and income at the top are historically unprecedented. And if current patterns of production, consumption and accumulation continue, this massive canyon of disparity is likely to grow into an unbridgeable abyss. To provide just one example in this introduction, consider that Credit Suisse's Research Institute estimates that the richest 10% of adults own 86% of all global wealth, with the top 1% accounting for 46% of it (Credit Suisse 2013: 22). This means that just over 400 million people out of a population of 7 billion own most of the world's income-generating assets. Compare this with the bottom 3.2 billion people who own just 3% of all wealth between them.

This growing gap between the 1% and the rest of humanity was the central relationship to which the Occupy movement called our attention when they organised themselves to protest about the ruling 1% of the global economy under the banner 'We are the 99%'. As in earlier struggles for social justice, fairness and equality, the movement experienced police brutality and violence and its considerable encampments in cities worldwide were destroyed or dispersed. In the corporate for-profit press, the movement was largely ridiculed and even vilified for lacking a clear and simple message or for refusing to state its particular demands. But however we might fault the Occupy movement or critique its strategies and tactics, it did manage to shine a spotlight on one of the most pressing problems in twenty-first-century political economy: the concentration of wealth and income among the global 1%. And yet, as reflected in the quotes that open this introduction, there has been no comprehensive political economy of this tiny class of wealth-holders we will call dominant owners. In this light, the main aim of this study is to provide a critical and historically informed account of the rise and social reproduction of the global 1% and what its existence might mean for the rest of us and the future of the global political economy. It is written with the profound and utterly defensible belief that society is a shared project, but one that has been directed so far at enriching the very few.

## Political economy and the elite

The literature of sociological theory is of course familiar with the concept of a ruling or dominant class. In the twentieth century, perhaps the most famous text is C. Wright Mills' *The Power Elite* (2000 [originally published 1956]). Mills was concerned with the United States after World War II, and for him the power elite was the small minority of men who held key decision-making positions in the dominant institutions of American society. Mills argued that the interests of these men were largely interwoven and stemmed from their interchangeable positions in the military, the corporate sector and the state. These men make the most consequential decisions in society, and, while they are not always successful in achieving every one of their aims, they have, unlike the rest of society, the most significant institutions and resources at their disposal. Without owning these corporations and swaying politics, the power elite would not be wealthy. Indeed, Mills argued that personality, individual traits or meritorious ability can explain very little when it comes to accounting for the massive fortunes of private individuals and their families. He suggested that there were two major avenues to accruing wealth once corporations became the normal way of institutionalising capitalism. First, a 'big jump', meaning that an individual manages to obtain a position of strategic importance in the state, the military or a corporation. The second explanation for the accumulation of wealth is what he called 'the accumulation of advantages'.[3] Once one enters a strategic position and starts to accrue big money, more wealth, prestige and power typically follow due to the advantageous position one holds. But what of the rest of society?

Mills argued that the public is largely controlled or conditioned by the powerful – who also happen to shape the material and ideological culture through their control of mass media conglomerates. Thus, at the bottom of the social pyramid of wealth we find a politically fragmented and largely impotent mass of individuals and families largely caught up in the machinations of the powerful, but not omnipotent, few (ibid.: 9). Mills' analysis is still insightful today and was one of the first sociological attempts to theorise the accumulation and concentration of wealth and power in the United States. At stake for Mills was the death of democracy at the hands of the power elite. The United States would keep its shell of democracy but, in reality, policy outcomes would be shaped by a rich and powerful oligarchy to advance their particular class interests. Now, there is mounting evidence that Mills may have been exactly right. Two recent academic studies found that policy outcomes in the United States largely reflected the preferences of affluent Americans while the preferences of poor and middle-income Americans were virtually ignored (Bartels 2008; Gilens 2005; Gilens and Page 2014). This suggests, as the Noble Prize laureate Joseph Stiglitz (2011) put it, that the US government is of the 1%, by the 1% and for the 1%.

Mills' work inspired other scholars to study elite social forces from a sociological perspective (Domhoff 2006; Stanworth and Giddens 1974; Wedel 2009). In the field of political economy, studying the rich and powerful is typically the purview of critical scholars and a number of key concepts have been used to capture these agents and the institutions they own and/or control. For example, Stephen Gill (2008) uses the term 'globalising elites' while Kees van der Pijl (1998), Leslie Sklair (2001), William I. Robinson and Jerry Harris (2000) and William K. Carroll (2010) prefer to speak of a 'transnational capitalist class'. Susan George (2010) has labelled them the 'Davos class' after the yearly elite summit held in Davos, Switzerland known as the World Economic Forum. For their part, orthodox Marxists use the all-too-familiar term 'ruling class' or, often in shorthand, the term 'capital' to represent those who control the means of production and who profit from exploiting workers all over the world. For Nitzan and Bichler (2009), the focus of attention is on 'dominant capital', by which they mean the leading firms by market capitalisation and the government organs that enable and facilitate their pecuniary accumulation through various legal, technical and often violent mechanisms – all associated with the sabotage of human potential in one way or another. These conceptualisations are certainly helpful and have yielded significant insights into the interests, strategies and tactics mobilised by the globally powerful. The aim of this study is to contribute to this critical literature by focusing more narrowly on the global 1% or what I call dominant owners. If dominant capital can be conceived of as the largest corporations by market capitalisation and certain government organs, then those who own and profit from these institutions can be called dominant owners. Throughout this book I use dominant owners, the 1% and high-net-worth individuals interchangeably.

I do not approach this study unsympathetically or unaware of the significant methodological challenges involved in providing an enlightened historical and theoretical account of the global 1%. The major challenge, as Braudel recognised long ago in his study of capitalism and civilisation, is that the rich and powerful prefer to operate in the shadows. For example, Mitt Romney, the wealthy former Republican candidate for the presidency of the United States, refused to release any more than the last two years of his tax returns for public scrutiny. Of course, there was much speculation as to what his previous filings might show, but the point here is rather straightforward: secrecy is the handmaiden of capitalism and the global rich. So while the privacy of the 1% is a methodological limitation, it is also very much a part of the story: dominant owners need this privacy to operate. However, in spite of this limitation, there is sufficient information available to warrant a global political economy of dominant ownership.

The main contribution to the field of political economy is threefold. First, I source, assess and synthesise new quantitative and qualitative data that allows us to identify dominant owners and how they hold their wealth. Second, this book aims to contextualise our present moment of growing inequality, crisis and social struggle by situating the 1% in their historical context. The third contribution to the literature is that I bring to bear the new theory of capital as power to this study (Di Muzio 2014; Nitzan and Bichler 2009). In Chapter 2, I explain this critical approach to studying the global political economy in more detail and introduce the key concepts used by this emergent school of critical political economy. Here, I will merely mention that the 'capital as power' framework theorises capitalism as a mode of power rather than adopting the far narrower view taken by most Marxists that capitalism should be conceptualised as a mode of production. Production is, of course, important; but, as we will see, the concepts of ownership, power and differential capitalisation are far more significant for our investigation of dominant ownership. With this in mind, and before introducing the main arguments and content of this study, I would like to briefly highlight what this book is not and what is at stake in my analysis.

First, while many individuals will be mentioned, this book is not about individuals per se. As we will come to find, the massive chasm between the 1% and the rest of global society is not an individual problem but a political and structural problem of the highest order. If we fail to address this fact and focus on a few greedy and morally reprehensible individual actions, we will fail to truly understand 'the present as history' and how we might be able to challenge the prevailing social relations of power. These relations are unnecessary, unjustifiable and, in the final analysis, pathological. In other words, this book is about a global class dynamic and the social structure that has emerged over the last three centuries. Although they may stretch deeper back into human history, the current class dynamics of the global political economy have their roots in the violent creation of exclusive private property and its legal sanctification, European colonialism, the transatlantic slave trade, the discovery and use of fossil fuel energy and a never-ending class war over the generation and distribution of surplus wealth. In this sense, the accumulation of capital can very much be conceptualised as a permanent war.

Second, this study is not about vilifying wealth per se, nor is it motivated by envy. This study is primarily about critically exploring why so few have so much and why so many have so little. Is it a law of history, as Braudel suggested in his three-volume study of capitalism and civilisation, that 'the rich always be so few' (Braudel 1983: 466, emphasis original)? What could possibly justify the current distribution of income, wealth and ultimately life chances? How did it come to pass that the entire endeavour and primary goal in life of a small minority of humanity is to increase their differential wealth and power while the vast majority of humans are more concerned with a decent livelihood or eking out an existence? I call this deep-rooted yet compulsive behaviour pathological accumulation, not simply because it is habitual to the 1% and their army of political and financial helpers but because this addiction for wealth and power is destroying the planet for future generations.[4] Hervé Kempf expressed it best:

> the planet's ecological situation is worsening ... And that disaster derives from a system piloted by a dominant social stratum that today has no drive other than greed, no ideal other than conservatism, and no dream other than technology. This predatory oligarchy is the main agent of the global crisis – directly by the decisions it makes. Those decisions aim to maintain the order that has been established to favor the objective of material growth, which is the only method, according to the oligarchy, to make the subordinate classes accept the injustice of the social situation. But material growth intensifies environmental degradation (Kempf 2008: xvii).

So one of the fundamental contradictions the social justice movement will have to confront is the pathological drive to accumulate money and power held by the few versus the logic of livelihood, well-being and human security held by the many. This brings us to what is at stake in this work. As I see it, there are at least three things. First, if current trends continue, the tiny percentage of humanity that owns the majority of the world's wealth will continue to get wealthier at the expense of everyone else. The ethical dilemma here is that dominant owners do not, and indeed cannot, spend all of the income they accumulate. Instead, they continue to invest their money in more income-generating assets with the intention of making themselves even wealthier. So while the majority of the planet's inhabitants are subject to precarious or insecure conditions of existence – many of them easily addressed if the finance were forthcoming – a small fraction of humanity is accumulating vast fortunes not for the sake of well-being and livelihood but, as we shall discuss in detail in Chapter 2, for the symbolic accumulation of power and social status. For example, consider that the Organisation for Economic Co-operation and Development estimates that to achieve the Millennium Development Goals (MDGs) by 2015 it would cost US$120 billion (Stijns et al. 2012: 12). For many of us that might sound like a lot of money – and it is. But as a percentage of the US$200.5 trillion held by 8.4% of the global population it represents only 0.06% of their total wealth. Put another way, if we asked the 393 million people who own 83.3% of global wealth to pay for the MDGs, we would be asking each person to pay a whopping US$305.34 (my calculations using Credit Suisse 2013: 22). So the problem of achieving these goals is not that there is no money out there to possibly meet the targets. The major problem seems to be that those who actually have the most money have it invested in income-generating assets to make more of it for the sake of making more of it, which in turn is for the purpose of making more of it, ad infinitum. Put in the words of Adam Smith: 'the great affair, we always find, is to get [more] money' (Smith 2005: 342).

If this sounds a bit bizarre as an end goal for earthly existence, then you will enjoy this book. The second political problem, as we will find out, is that dominant owners also control the money supply through their ownership and/or control of commercial and central banks. This creates radically uneven access to money, with the majority of humanity experiencing a real scarcity of money. As I elaborate in Chapter 3, we will see that the reason for this scarcity of money is partially rooted in the power of commercial banks and their owners to create money by issuing interest-bearing loans. In other words, the power to create money is capitalised by investors. What this means is that, through their lending, banks help determine spending and investment priorities. Helping the world's most vulnerable populations has not been one of those priorities. As we shall discover later, reforming the way in which money is created should be a key priority for progressive activists who want to move beyond capital as a mode of human control.

The second thing at stake in this analysis is that we are starting to gather evidence suggesting that a high level of economic inequality leads to bad or undesirable social outcomes. This may sound intuitive to most people who have not been steeped in Ayn Rand's infantile fantasies of individual extremism. Indeed, the reverse hypothesis would be that high levels of economic inequality lead to desirable social outcomes – a proposition that, again intuitively, would sound absurd to most. Still, it is one thing to intuit that inequality causes social harm and another to demonstrate it in a scientific way that can be verified and replicated by other scholars. Wilkinson and Pickett's *The Spirit Level* (2009) does just that. The authors consider 11 health and social problems, such as drug abuse, imprisonment, obesity, social mobility and teenage pregnancies, and find that the more unequal a country, the worse it is likely to perform. So, if a political goal is healthier, happier and greener societies, then confronting current relations of force and power should be at the top of our agendas.

The third thing at stake in this analysis is whether or not we can find a convincing argument that definitively proves that the private fortunes of the few are deserved. The 'capital as power' approach used in this study and detailed in Chapter 2 will already suggest that they are not. This argument is elaborated at greater length in Chapter 5, when I consider the mounting empirical evidence that the vast majority of wealth is social and that individuals play a far smaller role in generating wealth than has been appreciated in popular discourse or capitalist fanfare. Indeed, the business press tends to lionise and worship wealthy individuals as though they were superhumans capable of feats that no one else on earth could even conceive of accomplishing. So there are three things at stake in this book: 1) a future of increasing inequality rooted in an unfair and corrosive monetary system; 2) the social harms of extreme inequality; and 3) the sociality of wealth and its radically unequal distribution among a minority of individuals.

## The main arguments and structure of the book

The arguments made in this book are presented over six chapters. Although each chapter introduces distinct arguments, my hope is that the reader will be able to appreciate the logic of their presentation and the value of the work as a whole. In the first chapter I argue that, while there is considerable scholarship on elite networks and the formation of a transnational capitalist class, there is a dearth of scholarly analysis focusing on the 1%, or what this study calls dominant owners or high-net-worth individuals. This group can be defined as individuals who have a minimum of US$1 million in investable assets – that is, assets intended to produce more money for their owners. This excludes their 'primary residence, collectibles, consumables and consumer durables' (Capgemini and RBC 2013: 4, note 3). According to the 2013 World Wealth Report there are about 12 million humans who belong to this category out of a global population of about 7 billion. So, while labelling the global wealthy 'the 1%' was politically expedient for the Occupy movement, when considered empirically from the point of view of wealth experts and leading financial institutions, the number of dominant owners is far smaller. In fact, high-net-worth individuals represent only 0.2% of the global population. The first chapter takes an analytical look at this minority and discusses the two major sources of income generation: labour and investments in income-generating assets such as stocks, bonds and real estate. The chapter also provides some examples of the geographical distribution of the 1% and details some of the key sources of their wealth. As this chapter is largely analytical, it is perhaps the driest chapter in the book. For this reason, I have tried to make the quantitative data as succinct as possible. What I hope emerges is a clear image of the disparity of wealth, and we have to ask what could explain such overwhelming inequality. Part of the answer lies in recognising that we did not arrive at this point in human history because of some conspiracy – although people often do conspire to pursue their private interests. Even the liberal Adam Smith argued that 'people of the same trade seldom meet together, even for merriment and diversion, but the conversation ends in a conspiracy against the public' (Smith 2005: 111). In this book, I argue that the current disparity in wealth can be explained by a logic of power that has been ruthlessly followed by high-net-worth individuals, the corporations they largely own, and their investment managers: the logic of differential accumulation (Nitzan and Bichler 2009). This logic is the subject of Chapter 2.

In Chapter 2 I outline the 'capital as power' approach used in this study. I explain why the neoclassical and Marxist understanding of 'capital' cannot explain prices and accumulation and therefore the distribution of wealth. I then argue that the 'capital as power' framework is more convincing in this regard since it understands capital in the same way as modern-day investors and their wealth management firms view it: as the capitalisation of expected future earnings adjusted for some factor of risk. I then offer an understanding of capitalisation as the dominant ritual of global investors and provide some examples to illustrate the theory of capital as power for the reader. In the final section, I sketch what could be called the architecture of capitalisation by exploring some of the key institutions and income-generating assets in the capitalist mode of power. Many readers will be familiar with these instruments and institutions, but many students new to political economy may not be. For this reason, I found it necessary to include them in this work since they are integral to understanding the capitalist mode of power. Overall, what I hope emerges from Chapter 2 is a keen awareness that the very logic of differential accumulation at the heart of modern capitalism is designed to intensify inequality, not overcome it.

The topic of Chapter 3 is wealth, money and power. I begin by contextualising modern wealth and its generation by looking at wealth historically. I then explore some of the main attempts to account for the generation of wealth that emerged from the eighteenth century onwards. Here, we consider mercantile thought,

William Petty, the French physiocrats, Adam Smith and the irascible Karl Marx. I argue that Marx's focus on social labour to explain wealth generation is convincing but only partially correct. What Marx largely missed is that the transformation in social property relations that created capitalist owners on the one hand and wage-labourers on the other also corresponded to a revolution in energy production and consumption in England and later elsewhere. The radical difference between the meagre wealth of the past and the abundance many experience today (and the 1% have a disproportionate share of this abundance) can be explained by humanity's uneven exploitation of fossil fuels: coal, oil and natural gas. In fact, the world's first billionaire – John D. Rockefeller – grew rich by monopolising the petroleum industry in the United States. But while real wealth has a material reality, it is also represented in money. What this means is that any explanation of wealth and the 1% must take into account not only energy but also the creation of money. So in the last section of this chapter I introduce a new general theory of money, energy and power. I explain how money is created and consider its role in the transition to capitalism as a new social relation of power. This is absolutely essential, since most people do not have any understanding of how money is actually created and most economists have generated an incredible amount of confusion on the matter (Häring 2013). If we fail to understand the generation of money, we fail to understand one of the central institutions of the capitalist mode of power and a primary reason for global disparity. As we will discover, our very money supply is capitalised by the few.

In Chapter 4 I explore the concept of differential consumption and the rise of what Citigroup refers to as a plutonomy – an economy driven by the consumptive practices of the 1%. I begin with the Gilded Age in the United States and by recognising that fossil fuels were a necessary, though not sufficient, cause of the new wealth – a fact that has been considerably overlooked by mainstream studies of wealth generation. I then move on to discuss differential consumption in what has been called the New Gilded Age. In the final section I consider Kempf's (2008) thesis that dominant owners and their quest for consumption, status and power are destroying the planet for future generations. What emerges from this discussion is that the global 1% have created not only a separate economy for themselves and their families but also a separate world view that prioritises the accumulation of symbolic power as represented in money above mere livelihood or any other ethical concern for the fate of humanity or the natural environment. Where ethical concerns can be discerned among this tiny minority, this is contradicted by their drive to accumulate ever more money, thus requiring more growth, the destruction of nature and the commodification and commercialisation of nature and human relationships. This drive to accumulate symbolically is in fundamental contradiction with the 99% who are largely concerned with a decent livelihood, security, and the well-being of future generations.

Moreover, the global 1% and their well-remunerated financial and political servants not only have created a separate economy and world view, but are increasingly insulating themselves from the rest of humanity. One major example is the growing number of fortified built environments (such as bullet-proof armoured vehicles, missile defence systems mounted on private yachts, gated communities and Armageddon survival bunkers).[5] What this suggests is that the more closed off dominant owners become, the less likely it is that they will be able to identify (let alone sympathise) with the everyday life struggles of the 99% and their politico-economic interests. This is a very worrying trend, as many earlier complex civilisations collapsed due to an insulated elite leadership blindly following a destructive path (Diamond 2005). The elites did not turn away from the destructive path, because they were the last to suffer the negative consequences of their own logic. What is troublesome today is that there is considerable evidence to suggest that our current leadership is almost completely unreliable and disconnected from the concerns of the 99% (Gill 2011).

Chapter 5 considers the major justifications for unequal wealth and seeks to challenge them based on new research on the origins of social wealth. We begin with Locke's natural rights defence of unequal property and the right to accumulate money without limit. I then show how Rousseau – also starting from the point of natural rights – overturned this argument based on the very logic Locke used to advance it. I go on to demonstrate how Bentham's disavowal of natural rights introduced a new justification for unequal property based on utility and the law. His explanation would go a long way in influencing the fantasy land of neoclassical economics. We then explore how mainstream economics justifies the rampant inequality of wealth. The final sections discuss Veblen's distinction between business and industry and explore serious research on the origins of social wealth and how this challenges the mainstream view of wealth being 'earned' on an individual and productive basis.

What I argue in Chapter 5 is that there is currently no convincing theory that can justify the level of income and wealth held by dominant owners. Indeed, I make the argument that the overwhelming surplus enjoyed by such a small section of humanity is not the result of individual 'effort' or 'productivity' alone but of a combination of factors: the uneven use of fossil fuel energy, a common heritage of compound human knowledge, the institution of ownership, access to resources, luck and socio-geographical positioning. As such, this study puts forward the critical argument that we need to start having a global conversation about social wealth and how we might conceive of fair and appropriate incomes within the context of the limits to growth and the need to develop a different societal logic premised upon well-being, livelihood and creativity. From the point of view of the 'capital as power' framework, a further challenge is to imagine what de-capitalised communities might look like. This is addressed more fully in the final chapter.

The sixth chapter of this volume is perhaps its most radical. It contextualises the Occupy movement that swept the planet after the global financial crisis and bank bailouts. I argue that while the movement did have some positive outcomes – such as drawing attention to the widening wealth gap – it was ultimately ineffectual in bringing about the serious change we need if we want to stop the gross inequality in income, wealth and life chances as well as to address our looming energy and environmental crises (Di Muzio 2012). As we will see, these crises are actually beneficial to certain portions of the 1% that stand to gain enormous amounts of money in the short term. I suggest that the only way to effect the change we need is not to create some movement of movements with a plurality of befuddled messages and horizontal leadership, but rather to establish a focused national political party of the 99% (linked transnationally) that has clear policy goals based on evidence, not conjecture. Leaderless leadership, as some radical democrats argue for, is a chimera and amounts to no leadership at all. The 1% can rule largely because the 99% are fragmented and following the logic of livelihood.[6] The 1% and their managers are playing a totally different game: capitalising the expected future income streams of society. They are following the logic of differential accumulation premised on the control of human creativity for profitable ends. I offer ten goals that a party of the 99% might discuss and organise around in order to challenge this reality. The chapter concludes with a brief discussion on creativity, power and the meaning of life.

What I think emerges from this discussion is that, if we do not overhaul the logic of differential accumulation and challenge the capitalist mode of power, we are likely to witness worsening political, economic, social and environmental conditions for the 99% and a severe crisis of legitimacy – already apparent in a number of places, such as Spain, Greece and Egypt. Such conditions could eventually lead to a politics of apathy and desperation, but they could also lead to more organised and intensified forms of resistance – including violent action. In this sense, the fate of the 1% is unmistakably tied to the fate of the 99%. The Canadian writer Margaret Atwood went so far as to suggest that events could spiral out of control:

> When distrust in a system becomes widespread among small players, it throws up something like Occupy Wall Street, or like the Tea Party. Or like, for instance, the French revolution. Before that game-changing event, a privileged class that made the rules – rules favoring itself – overspent on a foreign war and then tried to stabilize the nation by overtaxing the already ruinously taxed populace. Confronted with protest, the aristocrats responded with inflexibility and prevarication, and dedicated themselves to preserving their own advantages at the expense of everyone else. If this sounds in any way familiar, it may be bracing to recall that before long, heads were

being sliced from necks, blood was running in the streets, and France, riddled with internal dissension, lost its position as the most powerful country in Europe (Atwood 2012).

Let me be clear: I am in no way advocating violence as the solution to social justice issues. But as a political economist and social scientist it would be foolish, given past tumults and struggles, to deny the potential of violent outbreak unless we embark upon a radically different path to the one we are currently headed down. In the final chapter of this book, I try to carve out such a path in a suggestive manner. For now, we turn to an analytical account of the 1%, their geographical locations, and how they hold their wealth.

# 1 | THE UNUSUAL SUSPECTS: IDENTIFYING THE GLOBAL 1%

The distribution of wealth, therefore, depends on the laws and customs of society. (John Stuart Mill 2004: 86)

Domination means that the commands of a group or class are carried out with relatively little resistance, which is possible because that group or class has been able to establish the rules and customs through which everyday life is conducted. Domination, in other words, is the institutionalized outcome of great distributive power. (G. William Domhoff 2006: 199)

The accumulation of advantages at the very top parallels the vicious cycle of poverty at the very bottom. (C. Wright Mills 2000: 111)

## The professor and the prince

In 2010, a University of Chicago law professor created a mini-firestorm on the internet when he posted a blog entry lamenting a potential increase in the taxation rate of high-income earners. The professor wrote that he and his wife made a total of US$250,000 a year but that they were not 'wealthy' and therefore could not afford any increase in their income taxes. The mini-firestorm ensued for a number of reasons, but many commentators tried to put things in perspective by highlighting the fact that the professor's household income put his family in the top 1%. In actuality, his family was in the top 0.04% of global income earners.[1] Soon after the barrage of criticism, the professor deleted his blog and apologised for his insensitivity and the derision it caused towards his family. But despite these actions, and perhaps without knowing it, the professor demonstrated two very important points central to any global political economy of the 1%. The first is that, from a global perspective, making US$250,000 a year does indeed put you in the 0.04% of the world's richest citizens, although, and here is the paradox, nowhere near its wealthiest. In fact, if your income is US$31,100 or the equivalent in another currency, you are in the world's top 1% of income earners. This knowledge (or maybe lack thereof) did not stop another mini-firestorm from taking place about three years later. Saudi Prince Alwaleed bin Talal – who enriched himself through family connections, oil money and business acumen – filed a libel suit in a British court against *Forbes* for underreporting his wealth at a mere US$20 billion rather than (and this must matter a great deal to the prince) US$29.6 billion. One might think that a man who owns a 'marble-filled, 420-room Riyadh palace', a 'private Boeing 747 equipped with a throne' and a '120-acre resort on the edge of the Saudi capital with five homes, five artificial lakes and a mini-Grand Canyon' might overlook such trivial figures. But, like the good professor, he felt aggravated about his status in the social hierarchy. This is the crucial second point revealed by the professor's and the prince's mini-firestorms and the beginning of our study: how might we identify the 1% when wealth appears to be a relative or subjective judgement?

### Income and wealth: a primer

Despite his household's giant income compared with that of the global population, the professor is not considered wealthy because he and his wife derive most of their income from paid employment (wages and salaries) rather than their ownership of income-generating assets (typically called capital). And in the global hierarchy of life chances, ownership of income-generating assets is what generates additional or greater income and then wealth. The fact that the 1% own more income streams than the one they might get from their own labour is largely what sets the 1% apart from everyone else. To be clear about this, consider the fact that someone making US$200,000 a year and someone making US$10 million a year, or US$3 billion, a year are all included in the top 1% of the global population by income. We can immediately note that there is a giant difference between making US$200,000 a year and making US$3 billion a year. But this takes us into the heart of the matter and one of the primary reasons for this study. From a global perspective, the professor is one of the richest people on the planet because his and his wife's household can command much more of the world's goods and services than his counterparts who make far, far less. If we stop to consider that most of humanity survives on US$2 a day or less, then it becomes clear that the professor's family is considerably better off. His children will also likely have much better life chances than those born in a poorer country or those who have less affluent parents. But from his subjective and culturally embedded point of view, his household is by no means wealthy in a comparative financial sense. And the truth of the matter, despite his inability to recognise his household's global position, is that he's exactly right. From the perspective of the real 1%, he is not wealthy but surprisingly working class – however well remunerated for his work. And this is where we should pause and make a clear analytical distinction between income and wealth.

According to the *Oxford English Dictionary*, the etymology of 'income' can be traced to the Old English word 'incuman', which in the fourteenth century simply meant to enter or arrive or the beginning of something. By the seventeenth century, however, 'income' took on a more financial meaning: 'that which comes in as the periodical produce of one's work, business, lands, or investments (considered in reference to its amount, and commonly expressed in terms of money); annual or periodical receipts accruing to a person or corporation; revenue'. In accounting terms today, 'income' can have a number of meanings, but we can generally think of it as a flow or stream of earnings quantified and measured in European numerals (1, 2, 3, etc.) and divisible by time. This numerical system was adopted in Europe from the Hindu-Arabic system in the late fifteenth century. The term 'income tax' originated as a war tax in Great Britain in 1799. The tax became permanent after 1842. Readers would do well to remember that the source of the income tax in Britain has its roots in financing the organised violence of an emergent capitalist and slave-trading empire.[2] Last, the term 'national income' does not appear in the English language until 1878. Adam Smith's *Wealth of Nations* makes no mention of national income but he does speak about the 'general stock' of a country or society. We will discuss Smith's work at greater length in Chapter 3.

The term 'wealth' is about a century older than 'income' and derives from Middle English. In the thirteenth century, wealth could mean the existential condition of being happy and prosperous, a spiritual well-being or a blessing and/or an abundance of possessions or 'worldly goods'. In a world of what we would today call very little 'economic growth', it is small wonder that wealth was equated with the physical things one possessed. According to the *Oxford English Dictionary*, the turning point comes with John Stuart Mill's 1848 *Principles of Political Economy*.

In this work, Mill defined wealth as 'all useful or agreeable things which possess exchangeable value; or in other words, all useful or agreeable things except those which can be obtained, in the quantity desired, without labor or sacrifice' (Mill 2004: 11). This appears to suggest that wealth consists of things that have a price and cannot be acquired without labour or sacrifice, in keeping with classical political economy's idea that labour is a primary source of value. Marx, too, thought along similar lines: 'The wealth of those societies in which the capitalist mode of production prevails, presents itself as an immense accumulation of commodities, its unit being a single commodity.' Marx famously divided commodity wealth into two categories:

> use values become a reality only by use or consumption: they also constitute the substance of all wealth, whatever may be the social form of that wealth. In the form of society we are about to consider, they are, in addition, the material depositories of exchange value (Marx 1996: 26).

In this formulation, wealth is no longer simply an abundance of possessions or worldly goods but useful things associated with prices (exchange value). But it was Kirkaldy's study of wealth (1920) and its distribution that suggested that Mill's definition of wealth concealed abundant wealth from non-abundant wealth.[3] In other words, we can consider goods that can be traded for money as wealth, but what matters is the *proportion* of wealth in the hands of different classes. In many ways this is a throwback to the heart of classical political economy and its second preoccupation. The first preoccupation concerns the source of wealth, or what we today call economic growth, although the two cannot be fully equated. Once we know how wealth is generated, the second preoccupation is: how is wealth divided and why is it divided in this way and not in others? We will consider these questions in much more detail in Chapter 5, but for now we need to put forward a convincing definition of wealth from the point of view of modern finance. According to Investopedia, wealth can be defined as a:

> measure of the value of all of the assets of worth owned by a person, community, company or country. Wealth is found by taking the total market value of all the physical and intangible assets of the entity and then subtracting all debts.[4]

For individuals, financial wealth is equated with net worth – or the total monetary value of assets owned minus debts and obligations owed to others. For a country, wealth is measured as gross domestic or gross national product – a measure that is deeply problematic for reasons that we will explore in Chapter 3.

## A taxonomy of the global 1%

We have already uncovered that, at a certain level of income, many individuals who may not conceive of themselves as rich or wealthy are in the top 1% of global income earners. But to operate only in the register of income is to miss what this study considers the real global 1%: the tiny minority atop the pyramid of gross human inequality. To zero in on our unusual suspects – unusual since they make up only a tiny fraction of the world's population – we have to zero in on wealth, since 'wealth tends to be distributed less equally than incomes' (Allianz 2013: 49). We should also note that, as a rule, 'it is only when incomes have reached a certain level that systematic wealth accumulation is even possible' (ibid.: 49). As will become apparent below, what this means is that those individuals and countries who have had historically high levels of income will also have had historically

high levels of wealth. But our concern is with the distribution
of wealth within and between countries rather than wealth per
capita – a measure that is often used to obscure extreme patterns
of wealth inequality. For this reason, and for this reason alone,
our analysis will largely avoid per capita metrics. So how, then,
do we identify the 1%? In this book I will argue that the best way
to identify this minuscule class – despite some methodological
challenges – is to focus on how the leading financial institutions
interpret them. When we consider wealth ownership, accumulation and its distribution among the global population, there are
five major reports worthy of serious study – each with advantages
and disadvantages. For those unfamiliar with these reports, I
summarise the benefits and shortcomings of each below.

The original *World Wealth Report* was issued by Capgemini
and Merrill Lynch in 1996. After the global financial crisis, Merrill
Lynch was swallowed up by Bank of America and, since 2012,
the report has been co-authored with RBC Wealth Management.
These reports focus on what they call 'high-net-worth individuals'
(HNWIs), or those individuals with at least US$1 million or more
in investable assets. What this means is that the report excludes
'personal assets and property such as primary residences, collectibles, consumables and consumer durables' (Capgemini and
RBC 2013: note 1). In other words, if you own a multimillion-dollar
primary residence in Malibu, California (meaning you actually
live in it), have a Damien Hirst original worth millions and have
US$2 million worth of luxury private vehicles but only US$500,000
in financial assets, you are not an HNWI. Similarly, if you have
US$1 million in stocks and bonds and own a primary residence
worth US$300,000 and a single car valued at US$80,000, you are
in the category of an HNWI. The report also introduces the categories of mid-tier millionaires, who have US$5 million to US$30

million in investable assets, and ultra-high-net-worth individuals, or those with over US$30 million in investible wealth. As we can see, the cut-off of US$1 million is somewhat arbitrary, but it does at least give us a recognised benchmark for thinking about what wealth management companies, banks and consultancy firms think of when they think of the truly wealthy. The shortcoming of the report is that it considers financial wealth only from the perspective of HNWIs and therefore reflects less on how HNWIs compare with the rest of humanity and its meagre holdings.

The second oldest report began in 2007 and is issued by Knight Frank (a leading property consultancy) and, up until 2013, Citi Private Bank (a provider of banking services to the wealthy). Knight Frank's *The Wealth Report* considers HNWIs to be those with US$30 million or more in net assets. This means that, unlike the *World Wealth Report* mentioned above, an HNWI has US$30 million in assets (including all art, cars, homes, etc.) after subtracting all liabilities. For example, if I own a home worth US$25 million and have investments worth US$10 million but owe creditors US$15 million, then I would not be considered an HNWI by Knight Frank. Once again, the decision to classify HNWIs in this way is fairly arbitrary. However, since it sets the bar rather high, it does provide an alternative perspective to Capgemini and RBC Wealth Management's definition in the *World Wealth Report*. Moreover, Knight Frank boasts its expertise in assessing 'the attitudes of the wealthy towards property and investments', and its report for 2013 features a Prime International Residential Index and a Luxury Investment Index (Knight Frank 2013: 5).

A third report, entitled the *Allianz Global Wealth Report*, appeared in 2010. Allianz is a German multinational financial services company that specialises in insurance provision. Allianz offers no clear definition of HNWIs and instead focuses on the overall global wealth picture. In this sense it is useful, but for our purposes here – which are to provide a taxonomy of the global 1% – it is largely unhelpful. The reports from Allianz tend to focus on per capita measures as well as quintile analysis, which can be of use in some instances but in general they obscure an accurate picture of the global 1% in favour of focusing on aggregates.

A more useful approach is taken by Credit Suisse in its own *Global Wealth Report* series, which began in 2010. Credit Suisse works in collaboration with two well-known scholars of wealth – Anthony Shorrocks and Jim Davies. Working with these economists, Credit Suisse aims 'to provide the most comprehensive study of world wealth'. It boasts that, unlike other studies, its report analyses 'trends in wealth across nations, from the very bottom of the "wealth pyramid" to ultra high net worth individuals' (Credit Suisse 2013: 3). The Zurich-based company comes close to Capgemini and RBC's definition of HNWIs because the cut-off for consideration begins at US$1 million. However, this category extends all the way to US$50 million, crossing over into the US$30 million benchmark for ultra-high-net-worth individuals demarcated by Capgemini and RBC. For Credit Suisse, ultra-HNWIs have US$50 million and upwards (ibid.: 24). The problem is that Credit Suisse never clearly defines how it calculates wealth. For example, we do not know for certain whether art, collectibles, private vehicles, first homes and so on are included in its computation of wealth. In this sense, we are forced to take Credit Suisse at its word and consider net worth as its principal metric. Like Knight Frank, this would mean we can demarcate high-net-worth individuals (as the name suggests) by knowing whether their assets exceed their liabilities by US$1 million in the case of HNWIs or by US$50 million in the case of ultra-HNWIs.

The final report to consider is offered by a newcomer to global wealth metrics. Sponsored by UBS, the *World Ultra Wealth Report* was officially launched by Wealth-X in 2011. Wealth-X and its flagship yearly report aim to be the:

> definitive source of intelligence on the ultra wealthy with the world's largest collection of curated research on UHNW individuals. Our members identify, develop and enhance relationships with ultra affluent individuals as a direct result of working with Wealth-X.[5]

The benchmark for membership into the ultra-high-net-worth camp is a minimum of US$30 million in *net worth* – meaning, once again, that net assets come to US$30 million after all liabilities are subtracted.

What this brief overview of the existing world wealth reports reveals is that the attempt to analytically benchmark the extremely affluent by financial wealth or net worth is a bit of a subjective enterprise.[6] However, there does appear to be some consensus on defining the ultra-high-net-worth class – you would need financial assets or a net worth somewhere between US$30 and US$50 million to be included. What this review also suggests is that there is a hierarchy within the pyramid of the world's mega-affluent with those at the bottom no longer struggling to keep up with the Joneses but with the Gateses. Evidence for this claim is the billions of dollars in debt accumulated by those in the lower rungs of the hierarchy used to maintain or bolster their differential status vis-à-vis their wealthier counterparts (Frank 2007: 7).

But we do need some metric of the 1%, and it appears that we have two choices: to think of a pyramid of wealth based on financial assets or a pyramid of wealth based on net worth. Below I provide a sketch using both metrics and reveal that whichever metric we find more convincing, the real global 1% is much smaller than the Occupy movement's politically expedient label would suggest.

*The wealth pyramid by financial assets owned* According to Capgemini and RBC Wealth Management's report of 2013, there were 12 million HNWIs with a minimum of US$1 million in investable wealth in 2012. This is an increase of 1 million individuals or 9.2% from 2011. Collectively, the financial wealth of these individuals was US$46.2 trillion, which surpasses the pre-global financial crisis figure of US$40.7 trillion in 2007. The collective wealth of HNWIs is expected to grow to US$55.8 trillion by 2015. So, if all 12 million individuals had an equal share of the wealth in 2012, they would have financial holdings worth US$3.85 million each. But, of course, per capita figures tell us little about the actual distribution. Capgemini and RBC Wealth Management introduce three wealth bands, as illustrated in Figure 1.1.

The first band consists of what they call the 'millionaire next door' – a group demarcated by their ownership of financial assets

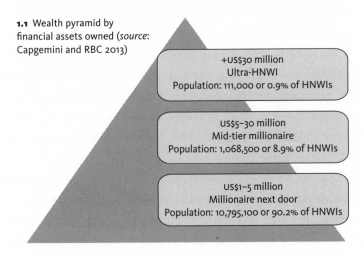

**1.1** Wealth pyramid by financial assets owned (*source*: Capgemini and RBC 2013)

+US$30 million
Ultra-HNWI
Population: 111,000 or 0.9% of HNWIs

US$5–30 million
Mid-tier millionaire
Population: 1,068,500 or 8.9% of HNWIs

US$1–5 million
Millionaire next door
Population: 10,795,100 or 90.2% of HNWIs

worth US$1 million to US$5 million. This group forms the base of the wealth pyramid and owns 42.8% of total HNWI wealth. In dollar terms, this translates into just over US$19.7 trillion. The next category consists of mid-tier millionaires with US$5 to US$30 million in capitalised assets. This group owns 22.0% of the total HNWI wealth or, in monetary terms, just under US$10.2 trillion. The top tier – the ultra-HNWIs – have 35.2% of the wealth share or just over US$16.2 trillion held as financial assets of one kind or another.

But this is within the wealth pyramid. What about their numbers in comparison with the global population of 7 billion people? The numbers are staggering: as a whole, the 12 million HNWIs by investible assets make up a meagre 0.2% of the global population. If we consider just the base of our pyramid, the millionaires next door represent 0.15% of the population. From there, the numbers really start to thin. Mid-tier millionaires make up 0.015% and ultra-HNWIs make up 0.0016% respectively.[7] Keep in mind that to be 1% of the global population, HNWIs would have to be a group of 70 million people. In other words, they would have to increase their numbers by 483%.[8]

*The wealth pyramid by net worth* A more inclusive way to classify the unusual suspects at the top of the global wealth pyramid is by net worth rather than just by investable assets (see Figure 1.2). Included in this calculation is everything a person owns after all their personal liabilities are subtracted from the total. Since this would include primary residence, art works, vehicles and so on, it allows for a more expansive field of players. Credit Suisse (2013: 22–5) estimates that there are 32 million people on the planet with at least US$1 million in wealth. If the figures are rounded, they represent a mere 0.5% of the global popula-

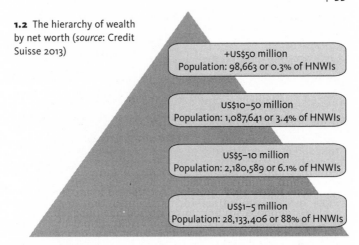

**1.2** The hierarchy of wealth by net worth (*source*: Credit Suisse 2013)

+US$50 million
Population: 98,663 or 0.3% of HNWIs

US$10–50 million
Population: 1,087,641 or 3.4% of HNWIs

US$5–10 million
Population: 2,180,589 or 6.1% of HNWIs

US$1–5 million
Population: 28,133,406 or 88% of HNWIs

tion, or 0.7% if we consider only the adult portion of the global population. Collectively, this class of wealth-holders owns 41% of all global wealth – US$98.7 trillion, or, on a per capita basis, just over US$3 million each.

But the truly remarkable story is how wealth is divided among them, and we see something immediately familiar to us from Figure 1.1: the base of the pyramid is massive, but, as we move up the wealth bands, numbers become as thin as oxygen at high altitudes. If, like Credit Suisse, we consider just the adult population of about 4.6 billion, then the base of our pyramid represents a mere 0.6% of all adults. The next three wealth bands represent 0.04%, 0.02% and 0.002% of the global adult population respectively. A tiny fraction of humanity, to be sure.

But once again, these wealth bands are somewhat arbitrary and serve to mask the extreme disparity within the HNWI class. For example, why use the cut-off of US$50 million for the highest band? Why include billionaires with those who have a net worth of at least US$50 million? Surely there are considerable differences between someone worth a billion dollars and

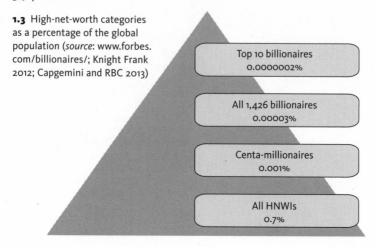

**1.3** High-net-worth categories as a percentage of the global population (*source*: www.forbes.com/billionaires/; Knight Frank 2012; Capgemini and RBC 2013)

Top 10 billionaires
0.0000002%

All 1,426 billionaires
0.00003%

Centa-millionaires
0.001%

All HNWIs
0.7%

a multimillionaire? So what would our global wealth pyramid look like if we stayed with net worth as the leading metric but altered the wealth bands to include billionaires and what Knight Frank called centa-millionaires (individuals with US$100 million in disposable assets) in its 2012 *World Wealth Report*? Figure 1.3 provides an illustration and considers each band as a percentage of the global adult population.

We already know that all 32 million individuals considered by net worth have wealth equal to US$98.7 trillion (Credit Suisse 2013: 22). Moving up the ladder, centa-millionaires make up a mere 0.3% of all HNWIs but have a net worth of US$39.9 trillion (Knight Frank 2012: 9). The billionaires make up a minuscule 0.005% of all HNWIs and have a collective net worth of US$5.4 trillion or a 5.5% share of all high-net-worth wealth. The top ten billionaires have a collective net worth of US$451.5 billion or 0.5% of the ultra-net-worth pie.

Based on these statistical observations, the human experiment with capitalism seems to confirm one of Braudel's key insights about capitalist civilisation:

Conspicuous at the top of the pyramid is a handful of privileged people. Everything invariably falls into the lap of this tiny elite: power, wealth, a large share of surplus production ... Is there not in short, whatever the society and whatever the period, an insidious law giving power to the few, an irritating law it must be said, since *the reasons for it are not obvious*. And yet this stubborn fact, taunting us at every turn. We cannot argue with it: all evidence agrees (Braudel 1983: 466, my emphasis).

Thus, whichever way we might seek to classify HNWIs, one thing is certain: while their class may expand yearly to encompass new entrants, HNWIs seem *always* to represent a minuscule share of humanity. As Braudel suggests, the reasons why so few have so much and so many have so little are not altogether obvious. In fact, one of the key tasks of our study will be to scrutinise Braudel's law so that we might start to give reasons for this incredible disparity in wealth, power and life chances. But for this we need a theory of capitalism. Providing a convincing theory of capitalism is the subject of our next chapter, whereas the conventional reasons given for wealth disparity are investigated in Chapter 5. But before moving on, we must consider how the 1% holds their wealth.

## Holding wealth

Those of us who have no financial assets, live pay cheque to pay cheque or have little or no knowledge of finance and investment are probably unfamiliar with how the rich hold and accumulate their wealth. The fact that most people are financially illiterate is already a substantial indication that finance is a language of power and domination. We should all recall that one of the most recognised articles in the various slave codes of the United States was the one that banned literacy and education to slaves. It was reasoned that if they could read and write, they could communicate and overthrow the system of slavery that virtually every slave abhorred (Cornelius 1983). To provide a quick example of the measure of our ignorance when it comes to modern finance, when asked what they would do if I gave them $5 million, many of my students at the University of Wollongong in Australia say they would spend some of it (typically on a home) and 'put the rest in the bank' to make more money. When I ask them why they prefer to make the lowest rather than the highest possible returns on their money, they are typically lost for words. It just seems natural that if you have surplus money you do not want to spend today, you keep it in the bank and the bank pays you interest. To some extent this is true: the 1% do keep some of their wealth as digital cash in the bank, earning interest. In 2013, according to Capgemini and RBC (2013: 16), about 28.2% of all financial assets were held as cash deposits. But the majority of high-net-worth holdings (71.8%) are in four additional asset classes, and this makes a big difference to how they accumulate more money and, by extension, power.

The first class is equities, or what are commonly referred to as 'stocks' or 'shares' in companies. Equities may represent an ownership interest over the company's assets and earnings potential but owners of equities may not have control over the company's day-to-day operations or future business strategy. Today's owners are largely what Veblen called absentee owners – they own but do not take care of the day-to-day running of the business. There are two ways to make more money by owning equities: 1) by selling them on to someone else for more money than you bought them for; and 2) by holding the equities and receiving periodic dividends from the company. Dividends are typically paid in cash per share and represent a portion of the company's earnings. In 2013, HNWIs held 26.1% of their financial assets in equities or stocks.

The second class of assets is real estate, sometimes referred to colloquially by the more expansive term 'property'. Typically, real estate means a given portion of land as well as any physical structures on that land. However, some countries have laws regarding who owns and can exploit the minerals or materials under the surface of the land. In many cases the true owner of sub-surface land is the government, which may exploit it by selling contracts to private companies. There are three types of real estate – residential, commercial and industrial – and three main ways to make money: 1) by selling the property for more than you bought it for; 2) by collecting periodic rent for allowing an individual or organisation to use the facilities; and 3) by collecting interest from people who need to borrow to buy or lease property. In 2013, HNWIs held 20% of their portfolios in real estate.

The third class of assets are called fixed-income securities. These financial instruments are typically corporate or government bonds on which returns are paid periodically and the full sum of money borrowed – the principal – is returned to the bondholder on a specific date. Unlike equities, where holding shares implies some degree of ownership of the firm, fixed-income securities are debt instruments. In other words, investors in fixed-income securities are creditors of the corporations and governments whose bonds they purchase. These are typically considered safer investments and, because of their low risk, usually yield lower returns than other asset classes. In 2013, the 1% held 15.7% of their wealth in fixed-income investments.

The last class of assets is considered to be alternative invest-ments. According to Capgemini and RBC Wealth Management, these assets include investments in hedge funds, structured products, derivatives, foreign currency, commodities and private equity. In 2013, HNWIs held 10.1% of their wealth in such alterna-tive investments. Let us now take each in turn.

Hedge funds are typically unregulated investment portfolios that are aggressively managed to generate higher than average returns. Whereas many workers will be familiar with regulated pension and mutual funds, hedge funds are typically reserved for very wealthy clients who have money in the millions to invest. Hedge fund managers can also borrow against their clients' capital, swelling their pool of funds and making it two to ten times larger (Mallaby 2010: 12). For example, if US$1 billion is deposited with a hedge fund manager, he or she can then lever-age this capital by borrowing US$10 billion from a bank. As of 2013, US$2.51 trillion were invested in hedge funds. The most fortunate managers – whom the BBC has labelled the Masters of the Universe – can make a yearly salary in the billions (Anderson 2011). For example, David Tepper of Appaloosa Management made US$4 billion in 2009, followed by George Soros, whose fund earned him US$3.3 billion. By comparison, the median salary of a registered nurse in the United States is US$56,165. We can express this as a ratio with Tepper's salary so we have some means to compare the difference in income between an average income earner and a billionaire: 1:71,219. This means that Tepper makes 71,219 times more money than a registered nurse. Thanks to a good deal of lobbying, he likely pays less in tax as a proportion of his income as well. The key question is whether Tepper is that much more productive in contributing to society than an average nurse. It is doubtful that Tepper's contribution to society is twice that of a nurse, let alone an absurd 71,219 times more, but we explore this question in greater depth in Chapter 5.

Structured products are tailor-made investment vehicles that typically package a traditional (safe) security such as a bond with an alternative payout schedule based on one or more underlying assets. Some claim that they can enhance an investor's portfolio by protecting capital while at the same time increasing the chances of better returns. Derivatives are financial instruments that derive their value from some underlying asset the investor does not own. The most common derivatives are swaps, options, futures and forward contracts. HNWIs also hold foreign currency to hedge against currency fluctuations and to take advantage of exchange rate differentials. The final two alternative investments are commodities, such as metals, agricultural goods and energy, and private equity. Private equity consists of equity securities (and often debt) that are not publicly traded on an exchange. Investments can be made by venture capitalists, angel investors or a private equity firm. Whereas the former may invest in young businesses or start-ups with the potential for strong earnings, private equity firms typically buy up publicly listed companies, delist them and then restructure them. Once they are restructured, the private equity firm usually relists them on an exchange to sell equity to the public. Money is made on the difference between what the company was purchased for and the value of the new shares issued to investors. Tidy profits have been made this way – typically to the detriment of workers and their income security.[9]

Now that we have a reasonable idea of how HNWIs hold their wealth, a look at their geography and their investments is in order. At first glance, this may seem like a trivial endeavour:

why should we care where the mega-affluent are from or where they invest? But, as we shall see, geography has a lot to do with how HNWIs accumulate their fortunes.

## The geography of the 1%

Human geography studies the places and spaces of human activities and social relations. It is a central argument of this book that the 1% continually create and inhabit a separate geography from the majority of humanity. We will explore the meaning of this claim in Chapter 4 on differential consumption. Here, however, we are concerned with the distribution of the 1% and their investments based on regions and countries.

If we define HNWIs by having a minimum of US$1 million in investable wealth, as Capgemini and RBC Wealth Management do, then the population of HNWIs can be divided by region as seen in Table 1.1 (Capgemini and RBC 2013: 5).

Moving from a regional to a country-level perspective, Figure 1.4 shows that the largest population of HNWIs is found in the

TABLE 1.1 High-net-worth populations by region

| Region | HNWIs | Regional population | Total wealth (US$ trillion) | HNWIs as a % of the population |
|---|---|---|---|---|
| Africa | 100,000 | 1,033,000,000 | 1.3 | 0.01 |
| Middle East | 500,000 | 394,409,001 | 1.8 | 0.1 |
| Latin America | 500,000 | 429,239,000 | 7.5 | 0.1 |
| Europe | 3,400,000 | 739,200,000 | 10.9 | 0.5 |
| Asia-Pacific | 3,700,000 | 4,200,000,000 | 12.0 | 0.09 |
| North America | 3,700,000 | 348,000,000 | 12.7 | 1.1 |

*Note*: I use the rounded numbers provided by the report so they do not necessarily add up to the exact figures given for the HNWI population or total investable assets owned.

*Source*: Capgemini and RBC 2013; World Bank population data.

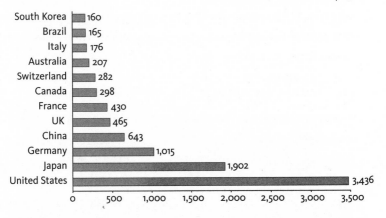

**1.4** Largest high-net-worth populations by country (thousands) (*source*: Capgemini and RBC 2013)

United States, followed by Japan, Germany and China (ibid.: 6). Perhaps not surprisingly, HNWIs prefer to hold wealth in their own home regions; only 20% to 35% is invested or held outside their home region. Figure 1.5 illustrates how wealth is allocated by region (ibid.: 17).

Using data from Wealth-X's 2013 report, we can also map the 199,235 individuals considered to be in the ultra-high-net-worth

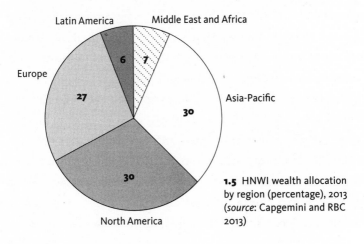

**1.5** HNWI wealth allocation by region (percentage), 2013 (*source*: Capgemini and RBC 2013)

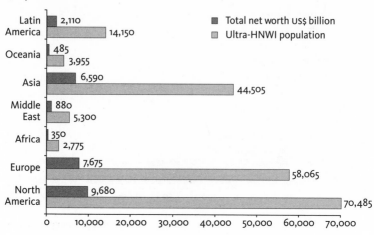

**1.6** Ultra-HNWIs by region (*source*: Wealth-X 2013)

category.[10] Collectively, the ultras have a net worth of US$27.8 trillion, the distribution of which is illustrated in Figure 1.6.

North America has the largest share of the ultra-high-net-worth population at 70,485 individuals, followed by Europe with 58,065 and Asia with 44,505. These three regions also have the highest net worth at US$9.7 trillion, US$7.7 trillion and US$6.6 trillion respectively.[11] Africa and Oceania have the smallest proportions of ultra-HNWIs with 2,775 and 3,955 respectively. They also represent the smallest share of net worth, with ultras claiming US$350 billion in Africa and US$485 billion in Oceania. The top five cities by ultra-high-net-worth population are New York (8,025), London (6,360), Los Angeles (4,945), San Francisco (4,840) and Paris (3,195) (Wealth-X 2013: 31, 39).

Of the entire ultra-high-net-worth population, 175,730 individuals, or 88%, are men who collectively own US$24.3 trillion of the US$27.8 trillion ultra-net-worth pie. Their average age is 58. Women make up a mere 12% or 23,505 of the ultra-HNWI population. Their average age is 54 and their total net worth a minuscule fraction of that of their male counterparts at US$3.5 trillion (ibid.: 20–4). Expressed as a ratio, this means that for every 1 ultra-high-net-worth woman there are 7.5 men. It is crucial for us to keep this vast disparity in mind when we consider one of the most important questions raised by this study: why is the world's wealth divided this way, and what, if anything, can justify it? Before considering this question in the chapters that follow, we have to make a stop in Billionaireville and then take a quick look at the rest of us (Frank 2007: 10).

## Billionaireville

In 1985 there were only 13 billionaires (Figure 1.7). In 2013, *Forbes* put the number at 1,426, with a total net worth of US$5.4 trillion – up from US$1.2 trillion in 2003 (Kroll 2005). So within the span of 28 years or about a generation in the world's wealthiest nations, the billionaire class increased by 10,869%. To put this increase in perspective, let's consider our nurse again with a median salary of US$56,165. An increase of 10,869% would mean

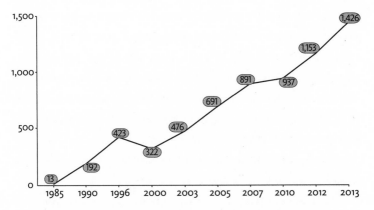

**1.7** Rise of the billionaire class, 1985–2013 (*source*: Data are from *Forbes'* billionaire list, archived at stats.areppim.com/stats/links_billionairexlists. htm (for 1996–2013); the figure of 13 in 1985 is given in Frank (2007: 10).

a yearly pay cheque of $6,104,573 – an incredible sum for any year's worth of work. What could possibly explain this rather abrupt spike in the numbers of the billionaire class? In 2005, *Forbes* chalked it up to 'improved global economic factors for their swelling fortunes. Bullish world stock markets, a weak dollar and surging commodity and real estate prices have all played a part. But so has old-fashioned entrepreneurialism' (ibid.). These may indeed be some contributing factors, but, as I will argue in the next chapter, they are not the decisive factors and therefore cannot convincingly explain this rapid increase in billionaires.

Geographically, billionaires are split between five regions. According to *Forbes*, the United States still boasts the most billionaires at 442, 'followed by Asia-Pacific (386), Europe (366), the Americas (129) and the Middle East & Africa (103)'.[12] Using data from Bloomberg's Billionaire Index, only 20 of the world's billionaires are women.[13] Put another way, for every 1 female billionaire there are about 71 male counterparts. As we noted above, we will have to keep this gender disparity in mind.

But once you become a billionaire, what are the chances of remaining on *Forbes*' list? According to Credit Suisse, the odds get better 'at the extreme upper-end of the world wealth distribution'. Of the top 100 billionaires from 2001 to 2012, an average of 17 left the list each year. This does not mean that they became destitute, just that they were no longer billionaires. If we consider a larger sample and compare lists from 2000 to 2010 for G7 and BRIC countries (where most billionaires reside), Credit Suisse found that 55% of billionaires remained on the list from 2000 to 2005 in G7 countries and 45% for the BRICs.[14] From 2005 to 2010, the odds increased from 76% in the G7 to 88% in the BRICs (Credit Suisse 2013: 28).

**The rest of us**

We now come to what the Occupy movement has called the 99%, or the 99.3% if we keep to the view that the so-called 1% are really the 0.7% of high-net-worth adults. We have already seen how this tiny class has more than they will ever need for a decent livelihood. But how wealthy are the rest of us? Credit Suisse estimates that in mid-2013, US$4,000 worth of assets would put someone in the wealthiest half of the global population. It would take US$75,000 worth of assets, however, to be included in the top 10% of global wealth owners. To be a member of the top 1%, it would take US$753,000, less than the US$1 million in net worth or financial assets to qualify as an HNWI. Overall, Credit Suisse estimates that 'the lower half of the global population possesses barely 1% of global wealth, while the richest 10% of adults own 86% of all wealth and the top 1% account for 46% of the total' (Credit Suisse 2013: 10–11). Marx's insight that capital concentrates in ever fewer hands appears to be confirmed by the evidence.

At the base of the 99.3% pyramid we find 3.2 billion adults, or 68.7% of the wealth-holding population. Collectively, this group is estimated to own US$7.3 trillion in wealth or just 3% of total worldwide wealth. The next group is a further billion adults who have somewhere between US$10,000 and US$100,000 in wealth. They make up 22.9% of adult wealth-holders and collectively own US$33 trillion or 13.7% of global wealth. The final group – those with wealth of US$100,000 to US$1 million – represents 7.7% of the wealth-holding adult population at 361 million individuals. Collectively, they have a net worth of US$101.8 trillion or 42.3% of the total. As we saw earlier, the 0.7% or 32 million individuals possess the remaining wealth: US$98.7 trillion or 41% of the total. But the base of the Credit Suisse pyramid is a bit misleading; for

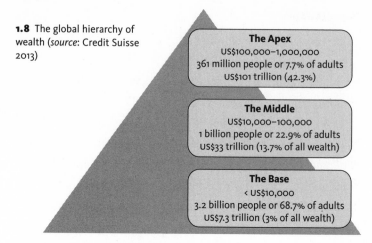

**1.8** The global hierarchy of wealth (*source*: Credit Suisse 2013)

**The Apex**
US$100,000–1,000,000
361 million people or 7.7% of adults
US$101 trillion (42.3%)

**The Middle**
US$10,000–100,000
1 billion people or 22.9% of adults
US$33 trillion (13.7% of all wealth)

**The Base**
< US$10,000
3.2 billion people or 68.7% of adults
US$7.3 trillion (3% of all wealth)

example, it hides the distribution among the 3.2 billion. While we do not know what the base of the pyramid would look like if the cut-off were less than the US$10,000 threshold, we do know that a huge swathe of the globe's population makes such a low income that it would be virtually impossible for them to accumulate any significant wealth. The World Bank estimates that 'more than 20 percent of the population in developing countries live on less than $1.25 a day, more than 50 percent on less than $2.50, and nearly 75 percent on less than $4.00' (World Bank 2013: 5). Since officialdom at the World Bank defines extreme poverty as living on less than US$1.25 a day, this means that 1.2 billion, or just over a third of the base of the pyramid, are officially extremely poor and unlikely to have any substantial material or financial wealth.

Figure 1.8 demonstrates that there is a considerable hierarchy within the 99.3%. This should hardly come as a surprise, since we already know that Credit Suisse estimates that 10% of all adults own 86% of all wealth on the planet. What this means is that 700 million people own the majority of the earth's wealth while the remaining 6.3 billion collectively own the remaining 14%. If we had set out to design a social order that is extremely efficient at inordinately rewarding a tiny fraction of human beings while ensuring that the majority endure low incomes and little wealth, we could scarcely have done a better job. But we cannot be satisfied with an analytical look at income and wealth distribution. We must now embark on a political economy of dominant ownership which in large measure means that we must provide a political economy of capital as power.

## 2 | CAPITAL AS POWER AND THE 1%

Power is not a means; it is an end. One does not establish a dictatorship in order to safeguard a revolution; one makes the revolution in order to establish the dictatorship. The object of persecution is persecution. The object of torture is torture. The object of power is power. (George Orwell 1949)

... if power is indeed the implementation and deployment of a relationship of force ... shouldn't we be analyzing it first and foremost in terms of conflict, confrontation and war? That would give us an alternative ... hypothesis: Power is war, the continuation of war by other means. (Michel Foucault 2003: 15)

Thus social power becomes the private power of private persons. (Karl Marx 1996: 85)

The key word is capital. (Fernand Braudel 1977: 47)

We have just been presented with a stark image of global disparity: the very few own incredible wealth while the vast majority own little to nothing. While the dominant owners worry about both preserving and accumulating more money, the vast majority of humanity experiences daily struggles for survival, dignity and livelihood. In this chapter we will encounter the reasons why such a massive chasm of inequality *can never be equalised let alone significantly narrowed in the present system.* The predominant argument in this chapter is that you cannot solve radical inequality – let alone global poverty – *by pursuing a logic founded upon the very idea of perpetuating ever greater*

*inequality* (Nitzan and Bichler 2009).[1] The goal of capitalists is
not to achieve greater equality of income and wealth but to make
income and asset ownership more unequal. This, no doubt,
comes up against barriers and various forms of resistance, but
that does not stop the logic from operating or triumphing. This
logic is what Nitzan and Bichler (ibid.) call differential accumulation and it is a pathological, albeit historical, drive pursued by
the few. Lest there is any confusion, what I mean by pathological
is that the differential accumulation of money, social status and
power is the ultimate end of capitalist endeavour. To be sure,
this logic is likely weaker in some capitalists than others, but
by definition – that is, to be a capitalist – they must obey the
logic of differential accumulation regardless of whether other
ideas and values they may hold are in direct contradiction with
the accumulation of money. To take one example: Thomas Jefferson's capitalisation of slave labour. The original composer
of the Declaration of Independence is said to have disliked the
effects of slavery on the social order. But Jefferson's estate, fortune – indeed, his wealth – depended on owning and forcing
other human beings to work for him. So while Jefferson may
have fulminated against the American slave system, his desires
and actions in another sphere – the sphere of gentlemanly living
founded upon the accumulation of money made on the backs
of slave labour – forbade him from transgressing that wretched
system of human oppression during his lifetime (Cohen 1969;
Davis 1999). In a similar way, we might find a number of hedge
fund managers concerned about global climate change or world
peace and they may even donate to organisations that advocate
for these causes. But if they suspect that higher returns could
be made from investing in companies that make a significant
contribution to climate change or in those that make what Kurt

Vonnegut called 'massacre machinery' in *Slaughterhouse-Five*, then it is a virtual certainty that those investments will be made.

To begin to explain this relationship of force between owners and the rest of us, we need to turn to political economy and, more specifically, to the work of an emergent school of critical political economy inspired by the work of Jonathan Nitzan and Shimshon Bichler (Nitzan and Bichler 2009; Baines 2014; Brennan 2012; Di Muzio 2007; 2014; Hager 2013; 2014; McMahon 2013). This new school of thought argues that capital is commodified differential power expressed in finance and only finance. In this view, capitalism is not a mode of production concerned with machines and labour alone, but a more encompassing mode of power. To unpack what this means, we have to go back to the origins of political economy and Braudel's key word from the quote above: capital. In other words, since most of us would agree that we live in capitalist societies – or perhaps more appropriately, a capitalist world order – we ought to know a little something about how political economists (and much later economists) have theorised capital. This is the subject investigated in the opening of this chapter. I then move on to discuss Veblen's recognition of *capitalisation* as the primary act of capitalists. Understanding capitalisation is essential in thinking about the political economy of dominant owners and to answer some of our questions regarding why wealth is divided in the way it is and whether or not this division is justified in some scientific way that we can evaluate and agree with. After looking at capitalisation, I then introduce the approach to political economy taken by the 'capital as power' school – in part inspired by Veblen's work. As we shall see, the key process we will concern ourselves with is the differential capitalisation of income-generating assets. In order to discuss this, we will introduce the concept of 'dominant capital' and what I have called 'dominant ownership' in the introduction. If these concepts are unfamiliar to some readers, rest assured that they will be explained in detail with examples provided in straightforward English. In the final section of this chapter, I sketch what could be called the architecture of capitalisation. This will help us connect the 'capital as power' approach to what we have already discussed in Chapter 1: how high-net-worth individuals (HNWIs) hold their wealth.

## A brief genealogy of the term 'capital'

What is today referred to as classical political economy emerged in the seventeenth century as a contested body of knowledge concerned with the nature, causes and distribution of wealth (Aspromourgos 1996; Milonakis and Fine 2009). It was also a language of battle. The 'science' of political economy could at once be mobilised for preserving or justifying present class relations or it could be used to challenge and overturn them. Either way, in societies divided by gender, class and sentiments about 'race', political economy can never be neutral. To paraphrase Cox, 'political economy is always for someone and some purpose' (Cox 1981: 128). The attempt at neutrality is largely what separates the early political economists from the neoclassical economists so dominant in our schools and universities today. Mainstream economists subscribe to a formal and mathematised scientific objectivity. For over a century since the marginal revolution of the nineteenth century, these economists have largely evacuated politics and power from their interpretation of economic reality. No earlier political economist, regardless of their aims or purpose in writing, understood politics and economics as two separate spheres. As Nitzan and Bichler caution:

It should be noted upfront that economics – or, more precisely, the neoclassical branch of political economy – is not an objective reality. In fact, for the most part it is not even a scientific inquiry into objective reality. Instead, neoclassical political economy is largely an *ideology in the service of the powerful*. It is the language in which the capitalist ruling class conceives and shapes society. Simultaneously, it is also the tool with which this class conceals its own power and the means with which it persuades others to accept that power (Nitzan and Bichler 2009: 2–3, emphasis original).

It is for this reason that this study is one of critical political economy: it does not separate politics from economics, and it theorises capitalism not as a benevolent mode of production concerned with making everyone better off but as a mode of power serving the very few. But before we discuss this in some detail, we must return to what the early political economists were concerned with.

On a general level it could be said that classical political economy concerned itself with four main problematics: 1) the problematic of the wealth of nations; 2) the problematic of wealth distribution among the population; 3) the problematic of justifying unequal wealth or property; and 4) the problematic of pauperism and poverty. The first of these problematics was concerned with how wealth – or what we would today call economic growth – was generated. The second problematic was to explain the distribution of wealth – how it was divided up between diverse classes or 'ranks' within society and, to some extent, how wealth was divided between kingdoms or principalities. Since wealth was clearly divided unequally for the classical political economists, a third problematic involved finding a justification for unequal wealth or property. Why did some accumulate more property and riches than others? And finally, the early political economists – some not very well known today – had to grapple with the rise of a new social actor: the poor, or, put another way, the pauper. As Polanyi explains:

> Pauperism, political economy, and the discovery of society were closely interwoven. Pauperism fixed attention on the incomprehensible fact that poverty seemed to go with plenty. Yet this was only the first of the baffling paradoxes with which industrial society was to confront modern man ... Where do the poor come from? was the question raised by a bevy of pamphlets which grew thicker with the advancing century (Polanyi 1957: 83, 90).

In one way or another, it could be argued that these four problematics animated the classics of political economy. It was not until much later that political economists would try to tackle a more foundational problematic: what is capital? Even today, scholars of all shades take the term for granted: 'Economists, political scientists, even literary theorists, freely employ the concept, yet few can say what the word "capital" truly signifies ... they continue to discuss "capital" as if it were conceptually unproblematic' (Cochrane 2011: 89–90). Yet, since it can be argued that capital is *the* central institution of our civilisational order, we ought to be clear about its meaning. Of course, we can identify with Shilliam's argument that 'no concept possesses an essential meaning'. In this sense, our purpose should be to draw out 'the concept's developmental trajectory in specific historical and socio-political contexts' (Shilliam 2004: 63). What, then, did capital mean historically, and how do we interpret it today? We can thank the French historian Fernand Braudel for

inquiring into the matter during his studies. Braudel found that
the term 'capital' derives from 'capitale', a Latin word based on
the expression for a head: 'caput'. It emerged in the twelfth to
thirteenth centuries and it meant 'funds, stock of merchandise,
sum of money, or money carrying interest' (Braudel 1983: 232ff).
According to Cannan's research, when applied to business, the
concept originally meant 'money to invest or ... money which had
been invested' (Cannan 1921: 478). But something happened that
would alter the meaning of capital and set it upon a new, more
materialist footing. In the hands of Adam Smith's insightful yet
confused political economy, the concept of capital underwent
two possible transcriptions: capital could mean either: 1) a store
of funds for investment (money); or 2) circulating or fixed capital
(material goods) (Smith 2005: 224).[2] In his investigation of the
early origins of the concept, Cannan put it thus:

> in Book 2, 'Of the Nature, Accumulation, and Employment
> of Stock,' he [Smith] divides the stock of an individual and
> of a community into two parts, the 'capital' and the 'stock
> reserved for immediate consumption.' This indicates a very
> serious departure from the conception of capital which had
> hitherto prevailed. Instead of making the capital a sum of
> money which is to be invested, or which has been invested in
> certain things, Smith makes it the things themselves (Cannan
> 1921: 480, my emphasis).

This reinterpretation had profound consequences for the
future of political economy. As decades turned into centuries,
neoclassical or mainstream economists came to focus on the
latter definition, grounding 'capital' in an unwavering materialism. In the new 'science' of economics, capital came to mean
*a physical factor of production such as plant, machines or equip-*

*ment.* For example, here's how one of the most popularly used textbooks on macroeconomics defines the term: '*Capital* is the set of tools that workers use: the construction worker's crane, the accountant's calculator, and this author's personal computer' (Mankiw 2005: 47). If this definition were true, then it follows that capitalists must be keenly interested in accumulating ever more equipment, plant and machinery, or, in Mankiw's formulation, tools, cranes, calculators and personal computers. Unknowingly, Mankiw is repeating Smith's confusion just as other economists instruct the neoclassical faith into impressionable young minds. Now imagine if we were to ask actual capitalists such as George Soros or Bill Gates whether they were interested in accumulating tools, equipment, calculators, personal computers and the like as the end goal of their endeavours. Our question would more than likely provoke ridicule. As Marx (and even Smith, despite his confusion) understood, capitalists are not interested in accumulating plant, machines and equipment as an end in itself. Capitalists are interested in accumulating ever more money, or, as Marx put it, 'use-values must therefore never be looked upon as the real aim of the capitalist; neither must the profit on any single transaction. The restless never-ending process of profit-making alone is what he aims at' (Marx 1996: 105). But when it came to providing an analytical definition of capital, Marx too remained trapped in a staunch materialism. Had he stayed with capital as money for investment or money invested in an income-generating enterprise and had theorised its actual and symbolic nature to command humans and natural resources, he might have come up with a different theory. Instead, Marx offered a theory whereby accumulation is *solely* rooted in the exploitation of surplus labour power during the production of commodities.[3]

For Marx, capitalism is both a mode of production and a social
relation of power between owners of the means of production
and workers who have no other choice but to rent their labour
power for a certain amount of time in order to gain access
to food, shelter and other necessaries of life. And while Marx
argued that the real goal of the capitalist was to turn money
into more money (M to M$^1$), his *scientific explanation* for why the
magnitude of money increased rested solely on the production
process, and the production process rested solely on his labour
theory of value.[4] In Marx's formulation, profit, or M$^1$, is the result
of workers producing more value during the working day than
they are paid for in wages. This unpaid 'surplus value' is the
source of the capitalist's profits. The problem, as summarised
by Nitzan and Bichler, is that:

> Marx's conception of capital – particularly his Smithian
> emphasis on production as the engine of accumulation and
> his Ricardian belief that labour values reflect the inner quanti-
> tative code of the process – was far too restrictive and, in the
> final analysis, misleading (Nitzan and Bichler 2009: 87).[5]

Marx's emphasis on production as the engine of capitalist
accumulation was indeed too restrictive, and, despite a litany of
attempts, Marxists have so far failed to convincingly demonstrate
how Marx's basic unit of socially necessary abstract labour time
can be transformed into market prices. Furthermore, Marx's
political economy also made a distinction – which originates
in the work of the seventeenth-century physiocrats – between
workers who create value and workers who merely circulate and
consume it. Yet, as Nitzan and Bichler have argued, 'there is
no objective basis, *a priori* or *a posteriori*, on which to decide
that the labour of a Volvo engineer or Fluor crane operator is

productive, while that of a government accountant or a stock broker is not' (ibid.: 87).

What this brief genealogy of the term 'capital' reveals is that we have two outmoded analytical definitions. The first is that of mainstream economics, which took the Smithian turn and accepted capital as 'the set of tools that workers use', to repeat Mankiw's formulation. The second stems from Marxist political economy, which has come to understand capital as unpaid surplus labour. But while scholars were busy pinning down the concept of capital and building research agendas around their interpretations, something else was going on in the world of actual capitalists. At the turn of the twentieth century, and with corporate finance being put on a steadier and perhaps more observable footing, an unconventional Norwegian-American working at the University of Chicago was investigating how actual businessmen (and they were overwhelmingly men) understood capital and modern business. His name was Thorstein Veblen.

## Corporate America and the rise of capitalisation

To some extent, Veblen had the good fortune of studying and writing at a time when the large corporation and the New York Stock Exchange (NYSE) were fast becoming norms of American life. The NYSE was founded in 1817 but the value and number of companies listed on the exchange expanded massively after the Civil War (1861–65) and the craze for railroads (Michie 2008: 73, 88). Standard Oil incorporated in 1870, Carnegie Steel Company and Coca-Cola Company incorporated in 1892, and Ford Motor Company did so in 1903. Corporate America was emerging and an explosion of capitalisation followed. By the 1920s, even ordinary Americans were fascinated by the prospects of making gains in the stock market. In this emergent order, Veblen could see what Marx perhaps could not and what the neoclassicals largely ignored: how businessmen understood 'capital'. Veblen argued that 'a theory of the modern economic situation must be primarily a theory of business traffic, with its motives, aims, methods and effects' (Veblen 2005: 4). As for other theorists, Veblen believed that the material structure of modern civilisation was the industrial system – this is what set the 'modern' apart from a pre-modern past of human endeavour. However, Veblen made a distinction between business and industry and argued that industry was not primarily run for human need but for business profit; or, put another way, 'industry is carried on for the sake of business and not conversely' (ibid.: 26). The end goal of business is not 'industrial serviceability' for the community but differential pecuniary gain and an 'increase of ownership' over income-generating assets (ibid.: 37). Veblen summarised it thus:

> The all-dominating issue in business is the question of gain and loss. Gain and loss is a question of accounting, and the accounts are kept in terms of the money unit, not in terms of livelihood, nor in terms of the serviceability of the goods, nor in terms of the mechanical efficiency of the industrial or commercial plant. For business purposes, and so far as the business man habitually looks into the matter, the last term of all transactions is their outcome in money values. The base line of every enterprise is a line of capitalization in money values ... The business man judges of events from the standpoint of ownership, and ownership runs in terms of money (ibid.: 84–5).

This focus on the modern business enterprise allowed Veblen to see that capital, to a modern businessman or investor, was

neither machines nor unpaid surplus labour, but the capitalisation of expected future profits:

> Under the exigencies of the quest of profits, as conditioned
> by the larger industry and the more sweeping business
> organization of the last few decades, the question of capital
> in business has increasingly *become a question of capitalization*
> *on the basis of earning-capacity*, rather than a question of the
> magnitude of the industrial plant or the cost of production
> of the appliances of industry ... As a business proposition,
> 'capital' means a fund of money values (ibid.: 89, 136, my
> emphasis).

There are two things of import in this passage. First, Veblen
notices that capital can no longer be talked about as a 'stock of
the material means by which industry is carried on'. Capital is
a fund of money values that capitalises a future flow of income
generated by the modern corporation (ibid.: 133). Second, unlike
the accounting practices of old, which registered capital as the
'aggregated cost of industrial equipment', the magnitude of a
firm's capitalisation does not reflect the cost of its assets but the
*earning capacity of the firm as a whole*. In this sense, capitalisation
is never fixed but subject to 'an ever recurring valuation of the
company's properties, tangible and intangible, on the basis of
their earning-capacity' (ibid.: 138).

Table 2.1 illustrates Veblen's point with examples taken from
the *Financial Times* Global 500 in 2012, the largest firms ranked
by market capitalisation or market value.

Market capitalisation or market value is calculated by multi-
plying the value of one share at any given point in time by
the total number of shares outstanding. So, for example, if we
opened a cookie company called XYZ and issued 100 shares at

TABLE 2.1 Selected firms, their assets and capitalisation, 2012

| Company | Total assets (US$ billion) | Market capitalisation (US$ billion) |
|---|---|---|
| Apple | 116 | 559 |
| Exxon Mobil | 327 | 409 |
| IBM | 113 | 242 |
| Nestlé | 119 | 207 |
| Google | 73 | 165 |

Source: *Financial Times* Global 500 2012.

US$10 per share, our market capitalisation or value would be US$1,000. If we were listed on a stock exchange, the value of our shares would fluctuate based largely on the future profit expectations of investors and our company's ability to meet or beat these expectations. Now, as we can see from Table 2.1, the value of a company cannot be determined by looking at its total assets. Rather, market capitalisation or the process of valuing a firm is subject to expected future earnings of companies. Put another way, 'in the business world the price of things is a more substantial fact than the things themselves' (Veblen 1923: 89). So, with Veblen, political economy was offered an alternative definition of capital as 'a fund of money values' that capitalises the expected future profits of income-generating entities such as corporations.[6]

However, while Veblen's political economy may have had the good fortune of being born at a time when capitalists were increasingly concentrating into corporations, he also had the misfortune of writing at the time when neoclassical economics was fast becoming the dominant school of economic thought. His own University of Chicago, founded by none other than John D. Rockefeller, would become a breeding ground for theorists schooled in neoclassical economics. They would keep to the

Smithian accident of making 'capital' material goods used in production. While not totally ignored, Veblen's keen observation of capital and the modern business enterprise was overshadowed by an uncritical, abstract and formal system of theory that has done much to obscure how power operates within the political economy of nations. Two radical political economists – Nitzan and Bichler – went on to build on Veblen's insights to give us a theory of capital not simply as a fund of money values invested or for investment, but as social power itself. In the next section, we explain this unique approach to the political economy of global capitalism.

## Capital as power

As we have discussed, not only are the two main analytical accounts of capital unconvincing from an academic point of view, but businessmen or capitalists could hardly care less about these debates. To overcome the shortcomings of the neoclassicals and Marxists, Nitzan and Bichler argue that we ought to theorise capital and capitalism by concerning ourselves with how actual capitalists understand them. And, as Veblen suggested, modern businessmen think of capital as a fund of money values used to capitalise expected future earnings. But that is not the end of the story. In an effort to understand the nature of capital, Nitzan and Bichler suggest that we must focus less on content (what is the specific business being capitalised) and more on form (the very act of capitalisation). And for this we have to uncouple capital from a strict materialism that focuses on capital solely as a mode of production and learn to see capital as a broader mode of power. From this point of view, we ask the following questions: what is being capitalised and for what purpose? We are already far advanced in answering these questions:

we know that capitalists are concerned with expected future earnings. But how are earnings generated? The easy answer appears to be by selling something and, on the face of it, this is correct. As Polanyi suggested some time ago, in a society dominated by capitalist markets, 'all transactions are turned into money transactions' and 'all incomes must derive from the sale of something or other' (Polanyi 1957: 41). But selling something can never be separated from the exertion of power over some part of – if not the entire – social process. What this means is that generating earnings from sales is a matter of business power. For this reason, in the 'capital as power' approach, we argue that what investors capitalise when they buy claims to future flows of income is the power of that business enterprise to shape and reshape the terrain of social reproduction relative to other firms trying to do the same thing. Nitzan and Bichler do not provide us with a clear definition of social reproduction in their work but a suitable description might be the way in which any society produces, consumes and reproduces its life and lifestyles, how it understands or conceptualises this mode of existence, and how it defends, both materially and discursively, its pattern of existence (Di Muzio in Gill 2011: 73–88). Now to some extent, the factors that influence social reproduction are over-determined. This is just another way of saying that many things influence the way we live, how we understand the way we live and how we defend ourselves from criticism – or, at worse, armed attack. No one is entirely powerless in shaping social reproduction. However, for power to exist at all it must be relative or differential and it must encounter resistance or opposition (Foucault 1977; Gill 2008). Since power is differential, this means that some have more power than others to produce effects and enact their will. For this reason, the 'capital as power' framework is concerned with what Nitzan and Bichler call dominant capital, which refers to those firms with the largest market capitalisation and the government organs that support them. Typically, this can be the top 100 firms by market value, or some percentage like the top 1% or 10% of all companies by market capitalisation. What data are used to represent dominant capital is at the discretion of the researcher and depends on the level, scale and scope of the analysis. But to give an example, there are 80,175 publicly listed companies on the stock exchanges of the world;[7] so, if we define dominant capital as the top 1% of firms, we would include the top 801 firms in our analysis, and if we used the 10% cut-off, the top 8,017.

Either way, we have to recall that in any given year only so much income and profit is made. How it gets distributed is a matter of ownership, power and the politics of class struggle. For example, gross world product was recorded at just under US$72 trillion in 2012.[8] The goal of firms is to redistribute more money to themselves than their counterparts, who are trying to do the same thing. This is why the 'capital as power' approach does not talk about just accumulation but *differential accumulation*. This is to say that some companies are able to redistribute more income to themselves at a faster rate relative to other firms trying to do the same. One indication of the differential nature of accumulation is the litany of benchmarks capitalists use to evaluate their performance. Typically, these take the form of an index that measures the percentage change in the value of a given basket of securities. Some 'baskets' can represent a small sector of the overall stock market while others can be more broad measures, such as Standard & Poor's (S&P) 500. The S&P 500 is an index of 500 corporations with high levels of capitalisation that are supposed to be representative of the broad market in the

United States; for example, Apple Inc., Exxon Mobil Corporation, General Electric Co., Chevron Corporation, Johnson & Johnson, and Google are some of the largest companies in the index. In 2012, the annual returns of the index were 16%. Now, suppose that during that same year we invested solely in Apple Inc. Since Apple opened in January 2012 at US$422.40 a share and a year later our share was worth US$527, our return would be just about 25%. Against our benchmark S&P 500 return of 16% we would know that we did far better than the overall market (by 9%). This, of course, is a very simplistic way of demonstrating the relative or differential nature of modern capitalism but it should be enough to highlight how important benchmarks are for investors and firms: it lets them know whether they are beating some average rate of return, meeting it, or falling behind it.

We have already introduced the concept of dominant capital and differential accumulation. We are now in a position to consider differential capitalisation and what I call dominant ownership. As Nitzan and Bichler point out, when we talk of accumulation we are talking about rising capitalisation or the increasing monetary value of owned income-generating assets. Differential capitalisation denotes a ratio of these assets. We can think of differential capitalisation at the level of the individual, the class or the firm. For example, consider Bill Gates, who at the time of writing had capitalised assets worth US$77.2 billion, and Eli Broad, with US$6.6 billion. Their differential capitalisation can be expressed as roughly 1:12 – or, put differently, Gates has capitalised 12 times the level of income-generating assets as Broad. Looking at Table 2.1 above, we can do this for Google and Apple – and indeed for the whole universe of firms. Expressed as a relationship, the differential capitalisation of these two firms is 1:3, or, put simply, Apple has just over three times the level of capitalisation as Google. To recall, in the 'capital as power' framework, higher levels of capitalisation mean that investors have more confidence in the firm's ability to shape and reshape the terrain of social reproduction in order to generate greater earnings. Lastly, from a class perspective, a ratio of differential capitalisation is more difficult to provide because the majority of the world does not own income-generating assets – this is the glaring difference between dominant owners and the rest of us. But if we consider the figures provided by Credit Suisse, we can get some idea of how the US$241 trillion in global wealth is divided. As already stated, Credit Suisse argues that the richest 10% own 86% of all wealth or just over US$207 trillion. The top 1% accounts for 46% of that ownership or about US$111 trillion. The remaining 90% of adults collectively own just under US$34 trillion. Expressed as a ratio, this means that the top 10% owns six times more wealth than 90% of the population while the top 1% owns just over three times more (Credit Suisse 2013: 11).

Whether we take the top 1% or the far smaller numbers of HNWIs at 0.2% (financial assets) or 0.7% (net worth) is of little consequence for our analysis or for real-world politics. What is significant and inescapable is the fact that a minuscule fraction of humanity owns virtually all of the income-generating assets across the world. They are the dominant owners. If dominant capital represents the firms with the highest level of capitalisation, dominant owners are those individuals – and often their families – who own the majority of capitalised assets, be they publicly listed firms on the stock exchanges of the world, government bonds, real estate or some other asset class. And everyone who has a paying job or buys their goods and services is working for them in one way or another. To illustrate what this means and how we might shed more light on the framework of capital as power, in the next section we consider some examples of capitalisation at work.

### The capitalist mode of power

Conceptualised as a mode of power, capital is understood as commodified differential power whereby the central acts of capitalists consist in: 1) commodifying aspects of nature, humans and knowledge, thereby subjecting qualitative things to a relatively malleable price system; 2) fighting for the legal ability to organise into firms or business units; and 3) capitalising the income streams generated from ownership, exclusion and commodification. The ability to capture income streams that are greater than what you might be able to get for your own direct labour is anchored in the creation of private property and the institution of ownership. As we will find, a number of factors have a bearing on the earnings of capitalised assets such as publicly traded firms or government bonds. This is why, in the 'capital as power' framework, we speak of a *power theory of value* rather than a labour theory of value or marginal utility. For dominant capital, supply and demand do not determine price in a competitive market; power does. Below, I consider a bank, JPMorgan Chase & Co.; a software and computer services firm we know as Facebook; and an aerospace and defence firm, Lockheed Martin.

*JPMorgan Chase & Co.* As of November 2013, JPMorgan Chase & Co. had a market capitalisation of US$206 billion. It was the twenty-fifth largest corporation in the world by market capitalisation and the fifth largest bank in the world after the Industrial and Commercial Bank of China, China Construction Bank, HSBC and Wells Fargo. Between January 1984 and November 2013 (the time of writing), the bank's capitalisation increased by 398%. Behind this quantitative leap is a qualitative story of how JPMorgan used its power to influence the social process to make earnings.

The earnings of JPMorgan are generated in a number of ways, including being legally able to: 1) create digital money out of thin air and collect interest on the debts created as assets for the bank; 2) assess and assign interest and fees to its customers for the use of various products such as credit cards; and 3) provide financial advice to clients.[9] But while this may be the core of its business, a whole series of additional power processes impact upon the company's profitability, from interest rates and the creditworthiness of its borrowers all the way to its offshore subsidiaries in tax havens. For example, according to its annual income statement, the overwhelming majority of the company's profits come from interest and fees on loans – the extension of credit being its major 'product'.[10] Therefore, we can assume that the bank will do everything within its power to ensure that interest and fees are protected from regulations that might encroach upon this massive profit-making centre. During the global financial crisis and the backlash against the big banks, a series of legislation was proposed to protect consumers and curtail the power of banks; this included the Consumer Overdraft Protection Fair Practices Act, the Mortgage Reform and Anti-Predatory Lending Act, the Credit Cardholders' Bill of Rights Act, and the Helping Families Save Their Homes in Bankruptcy Act. JPMorgan spent millions of dollars lobbying members of Congress (not to mention millions in campaign contributions) to influence these bills.[11] Additional factors that have a bearing on its profitability and therefore on its market capitalisation are the court cases, settlements and investigations related to a litany of alleged corporate malfeasance, including mortgage fraud, market manipulation, credit card and overdraft abuse, rigging the Libor and predatory lending. When it comes to morally questionable practices, JPMorgan's portfolio is highly diversified. But let us consider a closer example to demonstrate how redistribution takes place under the capitalist mode of power.

If one is born without an inheritance or significant family wealth, five options are typically available to achieve shelter and create a home: 1) construct one's own, if land and materials are available; 2) live with one's family in their dwelling; 3) rent from someone who owns real estate; 4) attempt to get a mortgage from a lender; or 5) move from place to place seeking various forms of illicit shelter (not a great option, particularly in colder climes). Where home ownership is valued and resources are available, average workers typically opt for renting their dwelling or obtaining a mortgage. Let's return to our registered nurse in the United States with a median income of US$56,165 or US$38,500 after federal income taxes are taken. Now, suppose our nurse approached one of JPMorgan's subsidiaries in Arizona for a loan to buy a home priced at US$150,000 and suppose he had a US$10,000 deposit to put down. According to Chase, for a 20-year fixed mortgage loan, our nurse would pay just over US$924 a month – over a quarter of his salary – with an annual percentage rate of 4.728%. Over the course of the loan, our nurse would pay about US$76,763 in interest, or US$3,838 a year, to Chase. In this way, the dominant owners of JPMorgan and its subsidiaries enrich themselves by capitalising a portion of our nurse's wages. Specifically, the bank will have taken 8.3% of his total after-tax income (excluding fees) over the 20 years it took to repay the loan. Put another way, at the end of this process our nurse would be forced to pay US$226,763 for a home originally valued at US$150,000 on the market. Of course, to those who have been through this process this may seem entirely normal – even desirable, since our nurse at least has the equity in his home. But when we realise that Chase assessed the application and invented the money to pay for the house as debt by inputting digits into a computer, the entire enterprise should be viewed with grave concern (Brown 2007; Collins et al. 2011). We will take a closer look at the creation of money in the next chapter.

The dominant owners of JPMorgan Chase, then, enrich themselves from people's need or perceived need to access credit, and its earnings are largely determined by protecting this profit centre from alternative forms of non-interest-bearing public credit, banking rivals and legal regulations that may help borrowers more than creditors. So who actually owns JPMorgan Chase? Who are the individuals or dominant owners who capitalise the extension of credit and the creation of debt? It is a fun exercise to try to find out, but, not surprisingly, it is difficult to tell. We know that at the time of writing its shares were held by 1,677 individuals and institutions – the vast majority, 74%, by institutional investors such as Vanguard Group Inc. and State Street Corp. But, as it turns out, while Vanguard Group Inc. is a privately owned investment management company, State Street Corp. is also majority owned by other institutional investors, including JPMorgan Chase. The most we can find on individuals relates to employees or former employees of the firm: James Dimon, James S. Crown, Douglas L. Braunstein, Daniel E. Pinto and Mary E. Erdoes. Collectively, they own US$217,782,856 worth of shares at the time of writing. These shares largely capitalise the interest-bearing debts of the firm's clients.

*Facebook* As of November 2013, Facebook had a market capitalisation of US$113 billion, ranking it, according to the *Financial*

*Times* Global 500 2013, 193 out of 500 companies by market capitalisation. Facebook is a software and computer services firm that the *Financial Times* called the 'world's dominant social networking site' (Budden et al. 2013). After Google, Facebook is the most accessed site in the world and has over a billion active users worldwide.[12] The company provides its users with a platform for social interaction and information sharing with individuals, organisations and for-profit companies. It also helps users capture 'life events' in the form of photos, status updates, likes and comments. According to Fuchs, Facebook users can be considered what Toffler called 'prosumers', or productive consumers, 'who work without pay' when they create content on their pages.[13] Since it does not charge its user base for the use of its software platform, the monetisation and capitalisation of Facebook compelled the company to rely on revenue from advertisers. This makes up the vast majority of the corporation's revenue stream. The second largest source of revenue comes from fees that allow users to buy digital and virtual goods and services from the companies developing its gaming platforms. Facebook will probably attempt to diversify its revenue stream over time, but the point now is to ask the following question: what is being capitalised when investors purchase shares in Facebook?

Once again, the simple answer is that investors capitalise the expected future earnings of Facebook adjusted for some risk factor. And since earnings come from revenue and revenue is primarily generated by advertising, then we are led to the conclusion that Facebook sells the human sociality and individual experiences of its user base to advertisers. So, in one sense, investors are capitalising Facebook's power to maintain the website, target advertisements to its users and ensure that the user base is stable or growing so that advertising firms have a target audience for their clients. Earnings obviously depend on active users and a paid workforce – from computer programmers and designers all the way to sales people and legal and financial advisers. But Facebook's earnings are contingent on far more than its paid and unpaid labourers and the desire to monetise user content. Facebook's owners and directors must be concerned with shaping politics, society and culture more broadly while dealing with potential competitors: for example, Facebook was found to have hired a well-known public relations firm to plant false stories about Google in major media outlets (Kucera 2011). Facebook is also in the game of lobbying and must seek to resolve legal disputes, fend off cyberattacks, influence privacy and data protection laws, acquire potential competitors, attract advertisers, influence the tax code and intellectual property legislation ... the list could continue.[14] These are just some of the ways in which the firm's earnings are contingent upon its power to shape and reshape politics, society and culture.

*Lockheed Martin* As of November 2013, Lockheed Martin had a market capitalisation of US$44 billion, ranking it 292 out of 500 companies by market capitalisation according to the *Financial Times* Global 500 2013. The firm is categorised as an aerospace and defence company, and, according to the Stockholm International Peace Research Institute, in 2011 it had the largest arms sales by value. Of its total sales, 78% comes from arms dealing.[15] The company's share price has also grown astronomically during the so-called War on Terror. Trading as low as US$17.44 a share in February 2000, shares in the arms dealer at the time of writing trade at US$138.97: this is a 697% increase over 13 years. Suppose back in 2000 you bought 1 million shares in the company, valued at US$17,440,000. Today, those same shares would be worth US$138,970,000 – a handsome return, and one that demonstrates that investing in the military industrial complex in a time of war can be an extremely profitable business, particularly for those on the inside shaping matters of war, peace and security. So what are investors capitalising when they purchase shares in Lockheed Martin?

Since earnings largely depend on arms sales revenues, innovations in military technology and the ability to sell the firm's weaponry to a global market *in the future* is surely being capitalised. But investors capitalise more than the 70,000 scientists and additional workers building and coming up with more effective ways to kill humans and destroy life-supporting infrastructure. Earnings and therefore capitalisation depend on the firm's power to shape and reshape the terrain of social reproduction as it pertains to questions of war, peace and security around the world. For example, Lockheed Martin has paid tens of millions of dollars to political campaigns. Tens of millions are also spent lobbying governments around the world on a full range of matters from nuclear policy to cyber-security. All of these actions have a bearing on the company's net earnings and its capitalisation. Without government contracts, the ability to export arms abroad, public investment in research and development, an enduring War on Terror and the potential for future world conflicts, Lockheed Martin's profits would plummet. The same is true for other 'merchants of death' (Engelbrecht and Hanighen 1934).

## The architecture of capitalisation

In the 'capital as power' framework, capital is neither productive equipment nor dead surplus labour, but commodified differential power quantified in money units. Since anything that generates an income stream can potentially be capitalised, there is little reason to theorise capitalism as specifically industrial or 'productive' capital. Instead, Nitzan and Bichler convincingly argue that capital is 'finance and only finance' (Nitzan and Bichler 2009: 262). This does not mean that production is unimportant. It simply means that capitalists are concerned with differential income streams they can commodify, own and, if need be, sell, not with industrial production per se.

In some ways this conceptualisation accords with Braudel's caution against thinking that capital is synonymous with the materialism of the Industrial Revolution:

> On a world scale, we should avoid the over-simple image often presented of capitalism passing through various stages of growth, from trade to finance to industry – with the mature industrial phase seen as the only true capitalism. In the so-called merchant or commercial capitalism phase, as in the so-called industrial phase, the essential characteristic of capitalism was its capacity to slip at a moment's notice from one form or sector to another, in times of crisis or of pronounced decline in profit rates (Braudel 1983: 433).

However, while there may be some points of contact between Nitzan and Bichler and Braudel's understanding of capitalism, there are significant differences. First, Braudel makes a conceptual split between the competitive marketplace and capitalism. He argues that, at one level, capitalism is actually competitive and prices will be set by some balancing of supply and demand. Yet capitalists, for Braudel, operate at the highest level, work in secret and largely dictate prices to consumers. Capitalism occupies a non-competitive space. But for Nitzan and Bichler it is difficult to make this conceptual split since the market and the price system are the very preconditions for capitalist power (Nitzan and Bichler 2009: 306–7). In other words, the price system forms the architectural base of capital as power – the quantitative matrix through which the accumulation and redistribution of income and wealth are accomplished. Second, Braudel has no theorisation of capital as commodified differential power that can be bought and sold on the market. Since dominant owners can sell their assets to one another, or even to members of the 99%, social power is commodified under capitalism.

But if capital is finance and only finance, understanding its architecture beyond the matrix of the price mechanism means taking a closer look at the financial market. The financial market consists of the bond market, stock market, real estate, com-modity market, derivatives market, foreign exchange market, money market, spot market, private equity, and the over-the-counter market. Combined with the price mechanism, credit rating and accounting agencies, institutional investors and central banks, regulatory agencies and offshore secrecy jurisdic-tions (commonly called tax havens), these markets make up the architecture of capital as power. They are the main avenues through which dominant owners accumulate their fortunes and organise and reorganise ownership patterns and the field of social reproduction. Since many non-specialists will be unfamil-iar with these instruments and institutions, below I do my best to explain them in a straightforward manner.

*The bond market* The bond market is the heart of the financial market. It consists of a primary market where new debt instru-ments are issued and capitalised by investors, and a secondary market where these debt issues are traded (bought and sold)

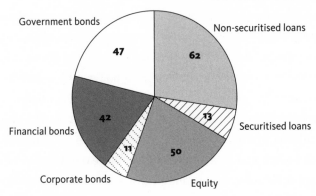

Government bonds

Non-securitised loans

47

62

Financial bonds

42

13

Securitised loans

11

50

Corporate bonds

Equity

**2.1** Global financial assets by category (US$ trillion, total US$225 trillion) (*source*: McKinsey 2013)

by investors. According to McKinsey Global Institute (2013: 2), in 1980 the financial assets outstanding (bonds, equities and loans) totalled a mere US$12 trillion. Today that number stands at US$225 trillion, or an increase of 1,775% in just 33 years (for a breakdown of current financial assets, see Figure 2.1). A full US$100 trillion of these assets are made up of bonds issued by financial corporations, non-financial corporations and governments. Government debt accounts for the largest proportion of the bond market at US$47 trillion, up from US$9 trillion in 1990 or an increase of 422%. Two countries – the United States and Japan – account for about half of all public debt.[16] Despite political incantations decrying government deficits and debt, the national debt is incredibly important for the financial market and the HNWIs we call dominant owners.

The first reason why government bonds are important is because interest rates on government debt set the benchmark for other forms of credit. As Doug Henwood explains:

Practically speaking, interest rates on public debts act as a

benchmark for the rest of the credit system; interest rates for
borrowers other than a central government – state and local
governments, households, corporations – are usually set in
reference to government rates at the same maturity. Markets
in general seem to need benchmarks like this (Henwood
1997: 23).

Interest rates on the national debts of the world provide lending institutions with a benchmark for additional credit instruments. Without public debt, dominant owners and their fund
managers would be lost at sea and a new benchmark would
have to be conjured up. The second reason why public debt is
important for dominant owners is that it provides them with
a 'no risk return' on their money. Traditionally, the sovereign
debts of Western governments have been considered 'risk-free'
or much safer vehicles of accumulation than, for example, the
stock market.[17] This is why dominant owners held about 15.7% of
their financial portfolio in instruments of this kind. While future
studies will have to be done for each country, Hager's research
has demonstrated that, in the United States, there was a massive
concentration of ownership of the 'national' debt in the hands
of the 1% (Hager 2014). A final reason why public debt issues are
important is because they provide the dominant owners of banks
an income stream of fees and interest when they underwrite
bonds of various kinds for governments and other organisations.
For example, Goldman Sachs 'serves as bond underwriter for
many state and local governments, nonprofit healthcare systems,
higher education institutions, public power and utilities, surface
transportation agencies, airports and seaports, housing agencies
and other public projects'.[18]

The big question is: what is being capitalised by these government debt instruments? Marx put his finger on it in his most famous volume:

> National debts, i.e., the alienation of the state [by sale] –
> whether despotic, constitutional or republican – marked with
> its stamp the capitalistic era ... As the national debt finds its
> support in the public revenue, which must cover the yearly
> payments for interest, &c., the modern system of taxation was
> the necessary complement of the system of national loans.
> The loans enable the government to meet extraordinary ex-
> penses, without the tax-payers feeling it immediately, but they
> necessitate, as a consequence, increased taxes. On the other
> hand, the raising of taxation caused by the accumulation of
> debts contracted one after another, compels the government
> always to have recourse to new loans for new extraordinary
> expenses. Modern fiscality, whose pivot is formed by taxes on
> the most necessary means of subsistence (thereby increasing
> their price), thus contains within itself the germ of automatic
> progression. Overtaxation is not an incident, but rather a
> principle (Marx 1996: 529–30).

What this passage suggests is that when the state borrows money from private individuals or financial institutions, it is effectively alienating or privatising a portion of its revenues. A small minority of creditors now have a claim on a future flow of income from state taxation. For Nitzan and Bichler, the government bond marked:

> the first *systematic capitalization of power*, namely, the power
> of government to tax. And since this power is backed by insti-
> tutionalized force, the government bond represents *a share in
> the organized violence of society*. This capitalization of power

marked the beginning of the end of the feudal mode of power.
Instead of a rigid structure of multiple personal 'protections'
and endless 'exceptions', there emerged the anonymous and
highly flexible capitalist 'bond' of private owners and public
governments. For the first time in history, organized power,
although still qualitatively multifaceted, assumed a universal
quantity (Nitzan and Bichler 2009: 294–5, their emphasis).

But dominant owners and their financial advisers are not
just after a share of government taxation. They will ruthlessly
capitalise any public asset that generates an income stream.
For example, in order to help Greece mask some of its public
debt, Goldman Sachs organised debt instruments that capitalised Greece's future airport fees and lottery system. In return
for short-term cash, the annual returns of these public assets
would be turned over to Goldman Sachs and its owners (Story
et al. 2010). What is interesting about these deals is that they
are not exactly the privatisation of government assets but of
government revenue. However, under the weight of mounting
public debt in Western governments, the *Economist* has called
for another rash wave of privatisations. Using figures from the
International Monetary Fund (IMF), the bastion of economic
liberalism reckons that there are US$35 trillion worth of public
assets across the 34 states that make up the Organisation for
Economic Co-operation and Development (OECD). The *Economist*
argues that at least US$9 trillion of these assets should be sold to
wealthy investors so that governments can raise cash to service
the interest on their public debts. Interestingly, the *Economist* is
partly owned by the Rothschild family of England, a family whose
wealth largely originates from indebting warring governments
and trading and manipulating government securities (Ferguson

1998). In return, a portion of European tax revenue went into Rothschild pockets. Whether we will witness another fire sale of public property in the coming decades is uncertain. What is certain is that previous governments in the Global South have been forced to sell public assets to service debt. For example, strongly encouraged by creditors fronted by the IMF, 'between 1990 and 2003, 120 developing countries carried out nearly 8,000 privatization transactions and raised $410 billion in privatization revenues' (Kikeri and Kolo 2005). In the Global North, Reagan and Thatcher began the drive in the 1980s but other members of the OECD soon followed:

> Over the past two decades, privatization has become a key ingredient in economic reform in many countries. In the last decade alone, close to one trillion US dollars worth of state-owned enterprises have been transferred to the private sector in the world as a whole. The bulk of privatization proceeds have come from the sale of assets in the OECD member countries. Privatizations have affected a range of sectors such as manufacturing, banking, defence, energy, transportation and public utilities. The privatization drive in the 1990s was fuelled by the need to reduce budgetary deficits, attract investment, improve corporate efficiency and liberalizing markets in sectors such as energy and telecommunications. The second half of the 1990s brought an acceleration of privatization activity especially among the members of the European Monetary Union (EMU), as they started to meet the requirements of the convergence criteria of the Maastricht Treaty (OECD 2001: 43).

The takeaway point here is that mounting debt and interest weaken public institutions and undermine social programmes that workers have struggled hard to achieve. Weakening these institutional barriers to the market and accumulation by advocating privatisation empowers corporations and their owners. Moreover, the global financial crisis added trillions of dollars to public debts in many OECD countries – debts that have to be serviced by ever more taxes, social spending cutbacks and privatisations. Back in 2006, a prescient Ann Pettifor suggested that we may be entering the era of a first world debt crisis. The signs all point in this direction and the worst may be yet to come. The only way out of this situation is to change our system of private credit creation. As we will see in Chapter 3, there are no philosophical or technical reasons why our governments have to be in debt to private social forces.

*The stock market* The market in tradable government debt was the first symbolic capitalisation of power. The money extended to monarchs and governments from private financial forces was largely used to pay for war while ever greater taxes from the public were redistributed to bondholders and traders (Webber and Wildavsky 1986). This market was so important that by 1840:

> the estimated value of securities outstanding on the London market was £1.3 billion. Of this figure, 89 per cent of securities traded were accounted for by the public debts of governments in Britain and abroad. In other words, the largest financial game in the world was the capitalization of the state's power to employ the organized violence of society and to tax its citizens to pay for the bill (Di Muzio 2014: 25).

Yet emerging alongside the market in government debt instruments were capitalised entities called joint-stock corporations. Originally these companies were given government charters to operate as a monopoly for a definite period of time. Once their specified activities were carried out – for example, building a canal for transportation infrastructure – they would be liquidated and disbanded. Today, however, the modern corporation can exist in perpetuity (Bakan 2005; Korten 2001).

When most people think of the stock market, they think that businesses list on an exchange to find the value of their firm in the marketplace (price discovery) as well as to raise money for future operations. This does indeed occur from time to time, but, as Henwood suggests, 'the stock market plays a very minor role in raising investment finance' for productive activity (Henwood 1997: 12). So if the stock markets are not primarily tools for raising finance, what purpose do they serve? The stock exchanges of the world largely serve as the state-protected markets by which dominant owners organise and redistribute ownership claims to money and power.

The first modern stock market emerged in Amsterdam around the Verenigde Oostindische Compagnie (VOC), or, translated, the Dutch East India Company. Originally the firm was given a 21-year charter by the States General of the Dutch Republic to 'send a fleet of ships regularly to the Far East for trading purposes, returning with goods for resale in Europe' (Michie 2008: 25). This is the sanitised way to put it. A more accurate way of stating it is to say that 'the principal goal of the organization was to establish an early and complete dominance over the production and distribution of spices' in Asia (Wolf 2010: 237). To do this, the company was given the complete monopoly of trade in the region, the right to make war and peace, the right to build fortifications and the right to administer the indigenous population for profit. As noted by Wolf, cornering the spice trade meant the destruction of local markets, the defeat or submission of local sultanates, the defeat of Portuguese traders operating in the region, the murder of indigenous social forces, forced labour and relocation, and the destruction of crops to ensure that locals would not infringe on company profits (ibid.: 238–9). In essence, the 1,143 investors who subscribed to the Dutch East India Company were capitalising the organised power of the company to wage war against adversaries in an effort to commodify local spices and exclude others from their trade. A share in the profits also meant a share in the imperial violence perpetrated on Portuguese competitors and local communities.

From these humble beginnings, more stock exchanges started to emerge:

> During the eighteenth century the global securities market grew in size and importance, with stock exchanges being established in several major European financial centres and in the 1780s extending overseas to the newly independent United States. *The basis of this market remained government debt created for military purposes*, whether for the incessant conflicts within Europe or the expenses incurred in gaining independence from colonial masters, as in the case of the United States (Michie 2008: 38, my emphasis).

From 1850 to 1900, 'stock exchanges evolved into central institutions of the capitalist world' (ibid.: 117). At the time of its report, McKinsey Global Institute found that of all global financial assets, US$50 trillion was held in stock markets around the world, or 22% of the US$225 trillion in capitalised assets. At the time of writing there are over 100 exchanges with the largest 57 accounting for US$62 trillion in market capitalisation – up US$12 trillion from when McKinsey performed its study in early

2013. Depending on the year, HNWIs hold about one-quarter of their financial assets in equities.

*Real estate* The market for real estate is another key component in the architecture of capital as power. HNWIs hold about 20% of their wealth this way. HNWIs can further enrich themselves by buying property low and selling high, borrowing on their existing properties to invest in other income-generating assets, renting out their property to non-home owners or vacationers, or collecting rents from leases on commercial real estate. For high-net-worth clients who desire more liquidity than sinking their capital into physical structures, there are real estate investment trusts that offer saleable securities that invest directly in the real estate market. There are no figures known to me on how large the world's commercial real estate market is, but McKinsey has estimated a value of US$90 trillion for global residential real estate (McKinsey 2009: 12).

*The commodity and derivatives market* HNWIs and their financial planners also capitalise commodities and derivatives. Commodities are considered primary products, as distinct from manufactured goods. There are two types: soft commodities, which typically represent things that are grown, such as sugar, coffee and fruit; and hard commodities, which tends to refer to things that are mined or extracted from the earth, such as crude oil, gold, silver, tin and copper.[19] Two indexes – the S&P Goldman Sachs Commodity Index (GSCI) and the Dow Jones-UBS Commodity Index (DJ-UBSCI) – provide investors in the commodity markets with a benchmark to assess returns. Investing in commodities makes up a relatively small portion of an HNWI's portfolio but commodities can still be quite lucrative.

One example is gold. For centuries, if not longer, capitalists, kings and traders have been fascinated with gold due to its unique properties as a metal (Bernstein 2000). For a time, the advanced capitalist nations tied their fate to the import and export of gold, until gold was abandoned as a form of currency able to lubricate an emerging global economy. In the early 1970s, fiat currency was normalised, backed by nothing other than a government's ability to enforce paper (and later digital) money as legal tender. But despite the rise of fiat money, HNWIs and their portfolio managers prefer to hold some gold – particularly in times of political and/or economic uncertainty. When gold prices rise, this is typically (but not always) an indication that investors are losing confidence in the stewardship of the global economy. And judging by the climb in gold prices since 2001, the loss in confidence seems to have been tremendous since the turn to more corporate-friendly policies that go under the broad banner of disciplinary neoliberalism (Gill 2008). It seems strange to ponder, but if the price of gold is anything to go by, what this suggests is that, at the same time as markets and financial actors gained more power, confidence and certainty in the economy eroded enormously.

Under the Bretton Woods system of fixed exchange rates, a country could theoretically take 35 paper US dollars and trade them for 1 troy ounce of gold. At the time of writing, 1 ounce of gold was trading at US$1,280. In other words, since 1971, when Nixon closed the gold window, the price of gold has increased by 3,557%. Had you invested US$140 in the 1970s, the same 4 ounces would now be worth US$5,120. Now imagine if you invested US$1 million at the time. The investment would now be worth US$36,571,428. But here is what is interesting. The price for an ounce of gold was only US$272 just before 9/11. After the War on

Terror was announced, gold skyrocketed to US$1,770 per ounce at its height in 2011. Whatever other factors influenced its price, clearly the War on Terror and the uncertainty it generated was excellent for owners and traders of gold. Those who understood the relationship between war, uncertainty and gold stood to make a killing.

Derivatives represent another nodal point in the architecture of the capitalist mode of power. A derivative is an asset whose value or price is derived (hence the term derivative) from one or more additional assets. Derivatives are popular with traders, and their notional – perhaps it is better to say theoretical – value relative to global gross domestic product (GDP) is enormous. Some analysts place their value at just over a quadrillion dollars, or just over 1 trillion multiplied by a thousand. The actual price of outstanding derivatives is impressive and they still have the ability to crash the economy, as the credit default swap debacle demonstrated during the opening stages of the global financial crisis. Still, whether they are simple or more complex, derivatives make up only a small percentage of an HNWI's portfolio.

*The foreign exchange market*  The gradual emergence of a foreign exchange market has facilitated the transnationalisation of dominant ownership and the capitalist mode of power. Without it, corporations and their owners would have to be content with local or national markets as well as local or national resources (unless acquisition was acquired by force or the trading of equivalently valued products was permitted). Ownership and profits would be confined to one territorial space. But the fact that money is not only a unit of account and a store of value but also a commodity that can be bought and sold has allowed groups of organised power we call corporations to operate transnationally.

As we saw earlier, the 1% mostly invest in firms from their home
territory, but if they want to own a part or all of a foreign firm,
the foreign exchange market facilitates their power to transact
globally. Of course, the foreign exchange market also facilitates
transactions for ordinary people. Yet the most important partici-
pants in this market are international banks; according to the
Bank for International Settlements, the daily turnover by the first
quarter of 2013 was US$5.3 trillion *a day* (BIS 2013: 4). Given the
transnationalisation of production chains, the diversity of trade
and a global tourist culture for the affluent, the magnitude of
these transactions should not come as a great surprise. But the
exchange does not simply facilitate the transfer of ownership
titles, the movement of goods and services and travel and tour-
ism. Since money is a commodity, it can also be traded for profit.
Perhaps the most famous case was when billionaire financier
George Soros bet against the British pound in 1992. Soros was
able to borrow heavily for months and converted his borrowed
pounds into French francs and German Deutschmarks. With
currency speculators selling the pound for other currencies, the
British Treasury tried to defend the value of sterling by using its
reserves to buy back pounds – to no avail. Soros became known
as the man who broke the Bank of England. The move cost
British taxpayers just over £3 billion. Soros walked away with
£1 billion, having added no value to human society whatsoever
(Litterick 2002). The question of value was also addressed by a
former hedge fund trader:

> I'd always looked enviously at the people who earned more
> than I did; now, for the first time, I was embarrassed for
> them, and for me. I made in a single year more than my
> mom made her whole life. I knew that wasn't fair; that wasn't
> right. Yes, I was sharp, good with numbers. I had marketable

talents. But in the end I didn't really do anything. I was a derivatives trader, and it occurred to me the world would hardly change at all if credit derivatives ceased to exist. Not so nurse practitioners. What had seemed normal now seemed deeply distorted (Polk 2014).

In the wake of a string of financial crises and protests in both the Global North and the Global South in the 1990s, Soros has since become critical of capitalist excesses and market fundamentalism. He is also a prominent philanthro-capitalist.

*The money and spot markets* Although their names can lead to confusion, the money market differs from the foreign exchange market in that it provides short-term debt instruments in a variety of forms such as US Treasury bills. These instruments typically have a maturity that lasts a year or less. The market largely exists to lubricate the wheels of capitalism by providing a market for those with excess cash to meet institutions' or individuals' need for short-term liquidity or cash. The money market is primarily used by governments, financial institutions and non-financial corporations, but HNWIs do hold a proportion of their portfolios in these instruments. They are typically low yield because they are viewed as less risky investments than equities and other assets. The last of the important financial markets that make up the architecture of the capitalist mode of power is the spot market. This allows owners of commodities and financial instruments to sell their goods for cash, with the buyer receiving these goods if not immediately then as soon as possible.

*Credit rating agencies* Due to the liberalisation of foreign direct and foreign portfolio investment since the 1970s, credit rating agencies have become more central to the architecture of capitalisation (Sinclair 2005). Credit rating agencies determine the creditworthiness of their clients and this in turn helps to determine asset values, potential asset values and interest rates. As a general rule, the more risky the asset, the lower the price will be. For example, if a credit rating agency assesses a firm's potential to earn future profits and finds it wanting, then the price of its corporate bonds will likely reflect the riskiness of the security. The same goes for government debt. If credit rating agencies downgrade a country's debt issues, the government can expect to pay more in interest due to the perceived riskiness in servicing its debt to private creditors. In this way, credit rating agencies can exert enormous power over publics that need to borrow from dominant owners and/or the institutions they own. The big three at the international level are an oligopoly – they control 95% of the market and assess trillions of dollars in debt every year. They are Moody's Investors Service, S&P and Fitch Ratings. The first two companies control about 40% of the market each while Fitch is left with 15% (Kingsley 2012).[20]

Credit rating agencies at the country level, such as Experian and Equifax, also help banks and other financial institutions capitalise the income of individuals by assessing the credit-worthiness of potential borrowers. The financial life choices of individuals as they pertain to credit and debt are quantified into an overarching credit score. Typically, the higher the score, the more creditworthy the borrower. Equally, the lower the score the more risky the client might be. The score is typically un-forgiving. It does not negotiate, sympathise with difficult life situations or desire to hear justifications or excuses for past deviances. It does not care if workers or their family members fall ill, whether the unemployment rate is particularly high in a given area of the country, or whether borrowers simply defaulted because their debt load was too high and a reasonable life could not be lived without walking away from debt. The number tells all: creditworthy, highly risky or somewhere in between. If credit is extended to the un-creditworthy, the borrower is typically condemned to do penance in the form of paying higher interest rates and often burdensome fees. For those without access to bank credit, there is a litany of corporate bottom feeders that are ready to capitalise on their misfortune. By and large, these institutions and their owners capitalise the future pay cheques of low-income workers. While they are willing to extend credit to those who do not have access to bank credit, they do so on far more punitive and often criminal terms (Powell 2009). Although it may not be as large as Wal-Mart or Exxon Mobil, one of the biggest players in the game is DFC Global Corp., with a market capitalisation of about US$411 million. Minimum wages that fall below the poverty line as well as low wages more generally feed the desperation of its clients and the wealth of its owners. And just who owns DFC Global Corp.? The ownership of the firm is largely masked by the institutional owners who own the majority of the company's shares. But Jeffrey Weiss, Norman Miller and Randall Underwood are part of the 1% that capitalise the future pay cheques of low-income earners, and they can do so only because there is a scarcity of income for the working poor.

Thus credit rating agencies and the firms they work for exert enormous power over the capitalist architecture of power since they are largely charged with assessing the risk of default or the length of potential default. This in no way means that they are good at their jobs. Plenty of evidence – in large measure due to conflicts of interest – suggests that the rating agencies are just as concerned with profits and prone to malfeasance and fraud as are the firms by which they are often employed. Sean Egan, a founding partner of a small rating company with no conflicts of interest with the companies it rates, gave the following United States Congressional testimony:

> The current credit rating system is designed for failure, and that is exactly what we are experiencing. AIG, Fannie Mae, Freddie Mac, Bear Stearns, Lehman Brothers, Countrywide, IndyMac, MBIA, Ambac, the other model lines, Merrill Lynch, WaMu, Wachovia, and a string of structured finance securities all have failed or nearly failed to a great extent because of inaccurate, unsound ratings ... Issuers paid huge amounts to these rating companies for not just significant rating fees but, in many cases, very significant consulting fees for advising the issuers on how to structure the bonds to achieve maximum triple-A ratings. This egregious conflict of interest may be the single greatest cause of the present global economic crisis. This is an important point which is often overlooked in the effort to delimit the scope of the across-the-board failures of the major credit rating firms ... there should be no doubt that none of this would have been possible were it not for the grossly inflated, unsound and possibly fraudulent ratings.[21]

Ratings can be viewed as 'inaccurate' only if we forget that the agencies responsible had a direct financial interest in pleasing their clients. It should also be recognised that the global financial crisis was not the first time the judgement of these firms faltered. But despite clear conflicts of interest and Congressional investigations, the rating agencies have used their power to curtail any effective reforms (Gordon 2013). Although many have lost fortunes due to their actions, the credit rating agencies have also served to enrich members of the 1%.

*Institutional investors* Institutional investors have become central to the architecture of capitalisation and some of the largest ones wield enormous power. Institutional investors are non-bank organisations that trade securities in large quantities. They act to collectivise or pool the investment contributions of individuals. Since their directors or managers are assumed to have sufficient financial training and experience, they are often lightly regulated; hedge funds are almost completely unregulated. Institutional investors comprise mutual funds, pension funds, insurance firms, hedge funds and sovereign wealth funds.

A mutual fund is an investment vehicle that pools the investment contributions of its members to make investments in stocks, bonds and other income-generating assets, such as commercial paper. Some privileged workers who are not capitalists or in the 1% may have money invested in mutual funds; if their money manager is successful, they will benefit from professional management and portfolio diversification. Total worldwide mutual fund assets amount to about US$27 trillion, with US funds making up roughly half the total.[22] Pension funds are also a pool of individual contributions but they are established by an employer and run by a professional money manager. Pensions are paid out as workers commence their retirement. The Government Pension Investment Fund of Japan is the largest pension fund in the financial world with about US$1.3 trillion in capitalised income-generating assets. Insurance firms can also be considered institutional investors since they collect premiums for various policies (for example on life or car insurance) and invest these premiums in money-making corporations. Berkshire Hathaway is the largest non-life insurance company with a capitalisation of US$284 billion.

Hedge funds are essentially mutual funds for the 1%. They

require a large initial investment that would be prohibitive for most workers. Managers of hedge funds typically use more aggressive investment strategies than their counterparts running mutual funds. Since they raise a massive pool of money from the 1%, they can use this initial fund as a basis to borrow additional capital, swelling their potential gains. The world's largest hedge funds by assets under management are in the United States and the UK. Collectively, the industry has about US$2 trillion in assets under management – a large sum but a small fraction of the wealth held by the global 1%.[23] According to the Sovereign Wealth Fund Institute, the assets of all sovereign wealth funds total just over US$6 trillion. By far the most significant source of investment money comes from states making money from oil and gas sales. Sovereign wealth funds are typically created to diversify a country's revenue streams and to benefit its economy and citizens. The largest fund belongs to Norway, which has US$818 billion in assets under management.

But far from just describing institutional investors, we must also consider them as institutions of organised power given that they control large pools of capital to be allocated throughout the global economy. In the international political economy literature, Adam Harmes (1998) has done a great deal to explore the impact of institutional investors on the global economy and the consequences for democracy and the 99%. His *Unseen Power* (2001) should be required reading for anyone who wants to understand the global political economy of institutional investors. Harmes argues that, with the rise of institutional investors since the 1990s, investment decision making has largely been centralised and capital allocated more collectively. Since fund managers are concerned with beating the average rate of return in their field and for their level of risk, they are highly competitive and prone to investing with a short-term horizon in view. But since they also control large holdings, the larger institutional investors can affect market prices. For example, suppose a fund has a considerable stake in the Ford Motor Company. If the fund manager is unimpressed with Ford's earnings targets and wants to exit by selling shares, selling them in bulk might trigger alarm bells among other fund managers and the price of the shares may quickly plummet. So size matters since it can affect share prices. Because of this, Harmes argues that fund managers have been keen to put pressure on corporate leadership to focus on boosting the share price. Some of the ways in which corporate managers have accomplished this goal are by offshoring employment to lower-wage countries with fewer if any environmental protections, by downsizing and flexibilising their existing workforce, and by selling company assets. The money saved or earned can be used in share buy-back schemes. When companies spend their cash on purchasing their own stock, they can boost the price of shares and make the owners of the firm wealthier. Another way in which fund managers exercise power is by lobbying governments to protect and/or advance their interests – for example, fighting to keep taxes low on income made from investments. Harmes also suggests that governments may lose policy autonomy because certain policy decisions – for example, trying to implement a universal healthcare system in the United States – may trigger the institutional investors to begin an investment strike that could send interest rates soaring.

But institutional investors do not just coerce corporations and governments. Harmes argues that there is a consensual moment of domination as well. This is because a portion of the 99% will have some money invested in these institutions. In this way, their long-term interests (the desire for a decent retirement) may line

up with the quest for profits. However, this relationship is not
without contradictions: for example, the now defunct energy
trading company Enron sabotaged California's energy grid by
forcing shutdowns. As millions went without power (including
hospitals), the price of electricity skyrocketed and Enron made
billions from the sabotage (Borger 2005). When its scheme eventually came to light, Californians were understandably upset,
but a former trader at the company told them to calm down.
He remarked that the California Public Employees' Retirement
System (CalPERS) was invested in Enron and therefore benefited
from the sabotage. In this way, CalPERS effectively capitalised
Enron's sabotage of California's electricity grid. Events like these
suggest that the relationship between workers and the 1% –
who do have some stake in the game, particularly through their
pension funds – is more contradictory than it might appear
on the surface. Another example would be workers invested
in companies that avoid taxes, downsize, offshore jobs, create
weaponry and destroy the environment for future generations.

*Central and commercial banks*  In some ways, central banks are
the most important institutions in the capitalist architecture of
power since they are supposed to help regulate the money supply.
It may be surprising for some to find out that the vast majority
of central banks are not operated by democratic governments
but operate at arm's length from elected politicians – even where
the government is said to 'own' them, as in Canada and Finland,
for example. In some cases, such as the US Federal Reserve, they
are owned outright by private banking corporations – and by the
dominant households who own those banks. What this means
is that the owners of publicly listed banks in the United States
effectively own the Federal Reserve and profit from the power

of commercial banks being able to increase the money supply by making interest-bearing loans. Owners of banks also have an ownership stake in the international central bank: the Bank for International Settlements (BIS) in Basel, Switzerland. The BIS claims to be the oldest international financial institution in the world, having been established in 1930 to deal with Germany's war reparations. Since then, it has become a central bank to the central banks of the world's richest nations. The BIS is largely owned by 55 central banks worldwide, while 14% of its shares are privately owned – by whom is not made public. All the owners receive dividends from the BIS.[24] The bank is somewhat remarkable for largely going unnoticed in the realm of international finance. The fact that its meetings are super-secret may help to explain why (Lebor 2013). As two reporters noted about the BIS:

> the building is largely bugproof, the goal being to prevent anything from leaking to the outside and any unauthorized individuals from penetrating into its interior. There are no public minutes of the meetings. Everything that is discussed there is confidential. The word transparency is unknown at the BIS, where nothing is considered more despicable than an indiscreet central banker ... These traits make the BIS one of the world's most exclusive and influential clubs, a sort of Vatican of high finance. Formally registered as a stock corporation, it is recognized as an international organization and, therefore, is not subject to any jurisdiction other than international law. It does not need to pay tax, and its members and employees enjoy extensive immunity. No other institution regulates the BIS, despite the fact that it manages about 4 percent of the world's total currency reserves, or €217 trillion (US$304 trillion), as well as 120 tons of gold (Balzli and Schiessl 2009).[25]

So the central banks – with some ultimately owned by the private households of the 1% – have their own international central bank. Through their control of interest rates they influence the dispensation of credit, which is primarily handled by commercial banks. The fact that most governments choose not to issue their own debt-free currency other than notes and coins is one of the main reasons why governments that do not raise enough money in taxation to meet their spending priorities must borrow from the private sector: private interests have separated the power to spend money (part of government fiscal policy) from the power to create it (central and commercial banks). For example, suppose an elected government wanted to build three new hospitals in an expanding urban centre. If it cannot raise enough money to finance the cost of these hospitals by taxing the population, it has to borrow at interest from the owners of capital. In other words, it has to go into debt to private owners to finance the hospitals. It must pay the cost of the hospitals *plus* interest to its creditors. Now, from the perspective of capital as power and a basic understanding of democracy, there is no technical reason why a government cannot just create the money to build the hospitals. But our elected governments do not use this power – the very power to create money has been capitalised and monopolised by the dominant owners who own significant shares in commercial banks around the world (Brown 2007; Collins et al. 2011).

For economic liberals, the fact that elected governments do not have control of the money supply is a positive good. The reason they give is that elected governments come and go and typically stay in power if they can promise their populations more goods and services and less tax. In this situation, economic liberals argue that governments will simply 'turn on the printing press' to placate the demands of their population for money and jobs. Put simply, it is reasoned that governments with control over the money supply spend as if there is no tomorrow. This, the economic liberals argue, will cause inflation, therefore reducing the value of money. For example, consider the Bank of Canada's boilerplate:

> If the Bank were to print money to repay the national debt or to finance government programs, it would be adding greatly to the amount of money in circulation. This would encourage people to spend and borrow more, and the economy would receive a temporary boost. But overall demand for goods and services would grow faster than the economy's ability to produce, and this would inevitably lead to higher inflation.[26]

This is not a fact but merely an assertion. We live at the most productive time in human history and businesses are not complaining about their ability to produce but about the limits of the market – limited by how much disposable income people have (Rowbotham 1998). There is little doubt that printing money en masse and at random *could* lead to higher rates of inflation. But this would be to assume that a public body in charge of issuing debt-free money would be incredibly inept and irresponsible. There is no good reason for believing that this assumption is a universal truth. Moreover, if economic liberals and central bankers do not trust elected officials, who, then, do they trust? Since the majority of money in circulation is created by commercial banks through loans, it must be that economic liberals deem bankers responsible stewards of the money supply. But as the recent global financial crisis, along with a series of historical 'asset bubbles', has demonstrated, many of the world's leading banks could hardly be said to have had the best interests of the public in mind. But the deeper point here is that most new money is created by commercial banks as loans, therefore making banks and their owners the primary allocators of credit and beneficiaries of interest payments. And since loans are largely premised on an individual's creditworthiness, the 1% (who already own most of the planet's income-generating assets) can largely borrow at their leisure. The few have easy access to society's most basic and needed resource: money. The many do not. There is a scarcity of incomes and money; the proof of this is mounting household debt in the OECD and elsewhere. This is highly problematic for democracy and challenges the notion that our elected governments are indeed sovereign. The banking families of the 1% control and profit from the creation of our money as debt and it is the mounting interest on this debt that pushes up the prices of goods and services (ibid.: 292–308).

*Offshore secrecy jurisdictions (tax havens)* The offshore system of finance is indispensable to the 1% and the corporations they own. Commonly known as 'tax havens', they are more appropriately called 'secrecy jurisdictions' for the services they provide to wealthy clients and multinational corporations (Shaxson 2011). Overall, there are about 80 such jurisdictions around the world (Henry 2012: 5). The IMF defines 'offshore financial centres' as jurisdictions that provide financial services 'by banks and other agents to non-residents' and noted that services such as 'low or zero taxation' and 'banking secrecy and anonymity' had rapidly expanded since the 1970s (IMF 2000). Shaxson argues that true offshore jurisdictions are politically stable because local politicians are largely controlled by outside financial interests in the major financial centres of the world such as New York and London:

But there is one feature of a secrecy jurisdiction that stands out above all: that local politics is captured by financial interests from elsewhere (sometimes these financial interests are criminal interests). This is why I include 'politically stable' in my definition: Meaningful opposition to the offshore business model will have been neutered in a serious tax haven, so that such irritants as local politics cannot interrupt the business of making money (Shaxson 2011: 9–10).

Using data from international financial institutions, the UN and central banks, a former tax expert from McKinsey, commissioned by the Tax Justice Network, estimated that in excess of US$21 trillion to US$32 trillion is squirrelled away offshore. A considerable portion is held by corrupt dictators and their families who accepted loans from Western banks and then deposited these same loans, or a significant portion of them, into a private account. The dictator's accountants would then record the loan as the 'national' debt of the country (George 1988; Henry 2003). It became impossible to service most of these loans – whether for corrupt governments or not – when US central banker Paul Volcker raised the interest rates to supposedly stamp out inflation in the United States. After saddling countries – many of them newly decolonised – with growing 'national' debts, the private bankers called on the IMF to coordinate how the political economy of entire communities could be reconfigured to service those debts. The result was a bevy of initiatives originally called 'structural adjustment programmes'. Three initiatives were particularly important for enriching the 1% of banking families while creating misery, poverty and unemployment for those in the lower quintiles of the 99%. The first initiative saw countries liberalise their foreign direct and portfolio accounts, which made it easier for Western creditors and corporations to invest and operate in the now financially subjugated countries (Perkins 2005). When it came to discipline and order, debt was a more effective technology of power than the sword. The second was a rash wave of privatisations that saw hundreds of millions in state assets sold to existing and newly minted dominant owners. Instead of these public assets being used as revenue-generating assets (or being run at cost) for the public, they now enrich a coterie of the 1%. And last but not least, the third initiative was to slash public spending on goods and services such as health and education (Chossudovsky 2003; George 1988). The 1% should know that these initiatives particularly affect women and children who tend to suffer most when austerity strikes (Sparr 1994). Thus, through the 'national' debt of foreign countries, the 1% in the Global North came to capitalise much of the labour force of the Global South, who were compelled to work for low wages in special economic zones producing exports for sale on the global market. Some of the proceeds of these exports go to service the 'national' debt. So while the families of the banking 1% have their yachts, designer clothes and soirées to celebrate their power, countless women and children will essentially be working a large portion of their lives servicing the debt owed to them and their class. Legalised chattel slavery did not die out because it was an abhorrent system but because the system of wage labour and debt money offered a more effective and useful economy of power for dominant owners.[27]

The offshore system has also been wonderful for the dominant owners of transnational corporations. Corporate tax avoidance is considered a serious issue of tax fairness and goes against the notion that members of a political community should contribute to the public spending priorities that help create better and stronger communities of healthy, safe and educated workers. Yet many pro-tax haven advocates stress that high taxes simply get passed on to consumers and so they argue for 'tax' competition (Shaxson 2011: 194ff). What this means is that political communities should be forced to compete with one another to offer the lowest possible taxes in order to attract investment and grow jobs. Such policies can lead to lower government revenues, increases in debt and ultimately cutbacks in services. There is already mounting evidence that US cities such as Stockton and Detroit are slashing services in light of insufficient taxes and mounting debt burdens. The social and economic consequences have been dire – particularly for the most vulnerable, typically women and children.

Illicit arms traders and drug runners also benefit from the offshore system, often getting their money 'cleaned' or laundered as it travels from one bank to another before ending up in government bonds, corporate bonds or even the stock markets of the world. As a US Senate investigation uncovered in 2001:

> U.S. banks, through the correspondent accounts they provide to foreign banks, have become conduits for dirty money flowing into the American financial system and have, as a result, facilitated illicit enterprises, including drug trafficking and financial frauds. Correspondent banking occurs when one bank provides services to another bank to move funds, exchange currencies, or carry out other financial transactions. Correspondent accounts in U.S. banks give the owners and clients of poorly regulated, poorly managed, sometimes corrupt, foreign banks with weak or no anti-money laundering controls direct access to the U.S. financial system and the freedom to move money within the United States and around

the world ... The failure of U.S. banks to take adequate steps to prevent money laundering through their correspondent bank accounts *is not a new or isolated problem. It is longstanding, widespread and ongoing* (Minority Staff of the Permanent Subcommittee on Investigations 2001: 1–2, my emphasis).

There is also evidence that a significant amount of drug money propped up the financial system with needed liquidity during the global financial crisis. Antonio Maria Costa, head of the UN Office on Drugs and Crime, noted that there was evidence to suggest that US\$352 billion in drug profits 'is now a part of the official system and had been effectively laundered' (Syal 2009). For its part, HSBC was caught laundering at least US\$881 million in drug trafficking money and forced to pay hefty fines (Treanor and Rushe 2012). So the offshore system cannot work without the help of an onshore system – a group of powerful and politically connected Western banks. But given the fact that the system promotes tax avoidance and transaction secrecy, we might wonder why it exists. A Nobel Laureate provided the obvious answer:

> You ask why, if you believe there's an important role for a regulated banking system, do you allow a non-regulated banking system to continue? The answer is, it's in the interests of some of the moneyed interests to allow this to occur. It's not an accident; it could have been shut down at any time (Stiglitz quoted in Komisar 2003).

Or, put in another way, the offshore system is the private economy of the 1%, the corporations they own and the illicit traffickers in arms and drugs. With our overview of the architecture of capital as power conducted, we are now in a position to discuss the links between wealth, money and power.

# 3 | WEALTH, MONEY AND POWER

The only wheels which political economy sets in motion are
greed, and the war amongst the greedy – competition. (Karl
Marx)[1]

For some time after the discovery of America, the first inquiry
of the Spaniards, when they arrived upon any unknown coast,
used to be, if there was any gold or silver to be found in the
neighbourhood? (Adam Smith 2005: 342)

Every tool is a weapon if you hold it right. (Ani DiFranco
'My I.Q.')

In this chapter I use the 'capital as power' approach to discuss
wealth, money and power. The chapter begins by offering a brief
history of wealth before the birth of political economy and the
fossil fuel revolution. Some readers may find my concern with
highlighting the role of energy out of place, but, as I hope to
make clear, it is impossible to explain the explosion in wealth
and capitalisation in any comprehensive way without recognising the surplus energy provided by the uneven consumption of
fossil fuels. With this established, I then explore how wealth
was understood by mercantilists, classical political economists
and the more radical Karl Marx. In the final section of this
chapter, I sketch a general theory of money, energy and power to
demonstrate their interconnections. The chief argument here is
that until we understand the capitalisation of the money supply
and how this is connected to surplus energy, we will understand
very little about the global economy, let alone about how we
might transform it.

**A brief history of wealth before political economy**

Before the mass exploitation of coal, oil and natural gas, what we today call 'economic growth' was never sustained (Wrigley 2010). From time to time communities could generate surpluses and grow, but since they were inevitably chained to the rhythms of photosynthesis, strict limits were imposed on what could be achieved. Moreover, as Jared Diamond (2005) and others have pointed out, some earlier societies were often prone to collapse chiefly due to their cultural and environmental practices (Tainter 1988). As Marx noted, reflecting on the entirety of human history, for most of it humans struggled for survival and social reproduction. The struggle involved not only an existential condition whereby nature had to be dealt with in some way but also a struggle against other groups trying to do the same. Violence and conflict were common in the human past, but mutual aid both within and between groups was also a part of the struggle for survival and social reproduction. But whether violent or working in cooperation, what remains a constant, argued Marx, was the social nature of human beings: they are always and everywhere to be found in groups, and it is this sociality – combined with our biology – that has allowed humanity to develop language, consciousness, technology and a conceptual apparatus for recognising patterns and solving problems (Ehrlich and Ehrlich 2008).

After the dawn of anatomically modern humans 200,000 years ago and their subsequent migration out of Africa to other continents 60,000 years ago, the first major transformation in human sociality after the mastery of fire was the Neolithic or Agricultural Revolution (Mellars 2006). Dating to 10,000 to 12,000 years ago, this transition involved humans domesticating animals and plants for use. Such practices led to more permanent human settlements and the rise of cities. This demographic shift away from hunting and gathering is believed to have first occurred in the Fertile Crescent and later spread by way of colonisation as hunting and gathering populations were devastated by settler violence and, in some cases, new diseases. There is an ongoing debate in the literature about this transition: why do hunters and gatherers transform into settled farmers (Weisdorf 2005)? Some believe that this shift was beneficial for the flourishing of human civilisation. In this view, farming must have been better than hunting and gathering for food and nutrition. But there is an alternative and more convincing hypothesis that emerges from the historical record: that the shift to agriculture and farming was the product of a struggle for power by elites. Richard Manning put it this way:

> For most of human history, we lived by gathering or killing a broad variety of nature's offerings. Why humans might have traded this approach for the complexities of agriculture is an interesting and long-debated question, especially because the skeletal evidence clearly indicates that early farmers were more poorly nourished, more disease-ridden and deformed, than their hunter-gatherer contemporaries. Farming did not improve most lives. The evidence that best points to the answer, I think, lies in the difference between early agricultural villages and their pre-agricultural counterparts – the presence not just of grain but of granaries and, more tellingly, of just a few houses significantly larger and more ornate than all the others attached to those granaries. Agriculture was not so much about food as it was about the accumulation of wealth. It benefited some humans, and those people have been in charge ever since (Manning 2004: 38).

Could the human need for food energy and the accumulation

of grain be the origin of the drive to accumulate money without concern for others or the planet? Was the first form of organised political power based on the control of the food supply derived from a defensive possession of the land? While they are interesting questions to ponder, we cannot say for sure. However, what does seem to be clear from the historical record is the fact that the transition to farming required the appropriation of ever more land – particularly as populations burgeoned and the soil was eroded by tillage. This appears to have occurred in two main ways: the deforestation of the earth (to convert forest to arable land) and the taking of it from others (Banner 2005; Weaver 2006; Williams 2006). As long as economic growth was chained to insolation and photosynthesis, as well as to some use of wind and water energy, having wealth above the norm of subsistence and basic shelter largely meant: 1) controlling the labour power of other human beings through force and/or custom; 2) monopolising trade and/or managing to acquire legal protection for an idea; 3) confiscating resources from others through wars and plunder; 4) acquiring some title or position that entitled the holder to a steady income from the taxation of others; and 5) gaining strategic control over necessary resources such as water, wood, food and later coal. For example, in 1066 the Norman conquest of England was achieved at the Battle of Hastings. Some years later, the Norman leader William the Conqueror instructed surveyors to roam the newly acquired land with the goal of creating a register of the population and the known stock of material wealth in the country. The register came to be known as the Domesday Book – which meant the Day of Judgment, a reference to the Christian God's final Day of Judgment on which there could be no appeal.[2] But the book was much more than a register. William's purpose was not simply to collect data on his newly conquered land and population. His real purpose was to find out how much his subjects possessed and therefore how much they could be taxed by royal authorities. And by what right did William now rule England as his own kingdom? The right of conquest – a rule imposed by the powerful in various legal and forceful gradations throughout the era of European colonialism. Today, such acts of conquest would be deemed wars of aggression in international law. Yet even today the politically powerful and the 1% they belong to or largely serve are often able to get away with wars of aggression. The fact that the entire Bush Jr. administration is not serving lengthy prison sentences for war crimes in Iraq is only the most recent example of how the powerful can politely ignore international law when it suits their interests.

But the complete conquest of the population of England was an overwhelmingly violent affair (Garnett 2009). The Normans slaughtered or exiled the old nobility and other rebellious sectors of the population. With a pacified populace, the conquering Normans gained a new kingdom of riches they could exploit for their personal benefit. To fortify this rule, William ordered a series of castles to be built in his new domain. The medieval 1% consisted of royals, nobles and church officials who held massive estates and taxed the population in one way or another. The violent power of war was transformed into the ceaseless structural power of the taxman and his punishments for failing to pay. The more prominent merchants and bankers would eventually join the ranks of the wealthy landholders. By the 1640s, increasingly capitalist landlords and some members of the merchant class would finance a war to advance and protect their interests against what they viewed as an encroaching monarchy (Braddick 2009; Brenner 2003). Out of this struggle between royal authority and the interests of lesser subjects would emerge the modern concepts of private property and individual ownership. With victory declared by parliament and institutionalised after 1688's Glorious Revolution, the Crown became subordinate to parliament. Those who held estates in land (largely descendants of the Norman conquest) by grant or pleasure of the monarch were now (for all practical purposes) owners of absolute private property (Pipes 1999: 30ff, 137). Land, which could be sold – and often was by English monarchs to raise funds for war – could now freely develop as the commodified private power of individual owners.

Up until this point, there were few if any theoretical accounts of the sources of wealth; life, to most, was spent exerting energy for the powerful few who controlled the land through conquest, land grants, purchase or custom (Engerman 1999). Indeed, Arthur Young, a British writer on agriculture and social statistics, thought that 'in 1772 only 33 million of the world's 775 million people actually lived in freedom. Servitude under monarchies remained the global norm' (Nikiforuk 2012: 12). But the fact that there was little thinking about what we would today call economic growth is perhaps hardly surprising when we discover that there was little conceptualisation of historical progress until about the mid-fifteenth century (Davies 2003). Even by the time of 1798, the fear of a lack of subsistence appeared to be very real to men such as the political economist and cleric Thomas Robert Malthus. Malthus, of course, is well known for his *An Essay on the Principle of Population*, in which he argued that food increases at an arithmetic rate (1, 2, 3, 4, etc.) while the population increases at a geometric rate (1, 2, 4, 8, etc.). Left unchecked, argued Malthus, the amount of mouths would outstrip the food available and lead to mass misery and death. Consider one of Malthus' passages in the second edition of the essay – a passage removed from later editions because of the considerable controversy it generated:

> A man who is born into a world already possessed, if he cannot get subsistence from his parents on whom he has a just demand, and if the society do not want his labor, has no claim of right to the smallest portion of food, and, in fact, has no business to be where he is. At nature's mighty feast there is no vacant cover for him. She tells him to be gone, and will quickly execute her own orders, if he does not work upon the compassion of some of her guests. If these guests get up and make room for him, other intruders immediately appear demanding the same favor. The report of a provision for all that come, fills the hall with numerous claimants. The order and harmony of the feast is disturbed, the plenty that before reigned is changed into scarcity; and the happiness of the guests is destroyed by the spectacle of misery and dependence in every part of the hall, and by the clamorous importunity of those, who are justly enraged at not finding the provision which they had been taught to expect. The guests learn too late their error, in counter-acting those strict orders to all intruders, issued by the great mistress of the feast, who, wishing that all guests should have plenty, and knowing she could not provide for unlimited numbers, humanely refused to admit fresh comers when her table was already full (Malthus 1992: 249).

As the reader can tell, this is hardly the language of a man celebrating a shared prosperity or looking forward to a future of wealth and abundance. For Malthus, there were strict limits imposed upon who could feast and who could not. If they grew too many in number, the poor were simply to starve.[3] In fact, throughout this period hunger was a key theme of the ruling 1% when they referred to their less-well-off counterparts, with Arthur Young declaring in 1771 that 'everyone but an idiot knows that the lower classes must be kept poor, or they will never be industrious' (Thompson 1966: 358). Being poor meant being constantly hungry, and, in a world where food was increasingly a commodity, it meant one had to find paid work to eat or rely on the beneficence of others. The physician and geologist Joseph Townsend (a major influence on Malthus), writing during the same period, argued much the same in his *A Dissertation on the Poor Laws*. As noted by Polanyi, Townsend's crucial point was that 'hunger will tame the fiercest of animals' and is the only thing that will spur the poor to labour (Polanyi 1957: 113). Polanyi argued that this was a turn away from more humanist forms of political theory to a vision of humanity more centred on treating people as animals:

> Hobbes had argued the need for a despot because men were like beasts; Townsend insisted that they were actually beasts and that, precisely for that reason, only a minimum of government was required. From this point of view, a free society could be regarded as consisting of two races: property owners and laborers. The number of the latter was limited by the amount of food; and as long as property was safe, hunger would drive them to work ... hunger was a better disciplinarian than the magistrate (ibid.: 114).

If hunger would spur the poor to work at home in Britain, the guns and whips of the plantation drivers proved more effective abroad.[4] It is estimated that between 1500 and 1870, 12 million Africans were taken from the western coast and transplanted to the 'New World'. Well over a million died on the journey across the 'Middle Passage' from Africa (Blackburn 2010: 3). More died within the first year of their arrival in lands far from their birth. Virtually from its beginning, the geopolitically competitive European colonial project was intimately tied to the transatlantic slave trade. There is little doubt that each colonial power offered different justifications for its advance, but the most powerful was the need for labour power to produce sugar, tobacco and cotton on colonial plantations (ibid.: 9, 234–5; Mintz 1986; Williams 1984; 1994; Wolf 2010). Sugar was by far the most profitable crop sold in Europe – one of the foodstuffs of those with disposable incomes. But as production increased and prices came down in the eighteenth and nineteenth centuries, the sweet substance was more accessible to working people – in particular as a fuel source for work. One of the primary reasons for this development was that – particularly in Britain at first – an emergent market society had been in the process of creation over centuries. Enclosure and the expropriation of customary rights combined with the monetisation of competitive leaseholds in the countryside led to waves of rural dispossession and over time an urbanised wage-labour society. We know this because urbanisation can be used as a proxy for the spread of the price system, since, by definition, city dwellers do not provide for their own social reproduction but instead must purchase goods on the market (Nitzan and Bichler 2009: 152). From 1500 onwards, England became far more urbanised than its European counterparts, suggesting to Wrigley that 'patterns of expansion and change in England reflect a different dynamic from those in continental Europe, especially after 1700' (Wrigley 2010: 64). This pattern was largely towards increasing market dependence and wage labour – two of the key ingredients of the capitalist mode of power.

This should be enough to demonstrate the point that in the

era before fossil fuels, for some to have more, others had to give something up: their labour, their land and resources, and, quite often, their lives. Even Adam Smith, who was far more optimistic about commercial society than Malthus, wrote that: 'Wherever there is a great property, there is great inequality. For one very rich man, there must be at least five hundred poor, and the affluence of the few supposes the indigence of the many' (Smith 2005: 580). The discussion above should also be sufficient to demonstrate that the primary drive to accumulate money does not have to wait for industrial capitalists: the search for wealth and riches among the powerful is already their principal logic. War, confiscation, plunder, violence, torture and the deployment of various forms of unfree labour were the common tools of accumulation in Europe and elsewhere (Sobel 2000).

In the pre-capitalist age, the Roman Catholic Church kept its European flock in awe through pomp, pageantry, rituals and the force of princely warriors and their retainers. Over time, however, the concept of surplus wealth started to enter the minds of early political economists, to the point where today entire nations are beholden to their gross domestic product (GDP), stock market indexes and the national accounts (Fioramonti 2013).[5] The key questions that lead to this development are the following: what constitutes wealth? And, more importantly, how was it generated (Vaggi and Groenewegen 2003: 7)? Where does surplus or wealth come from? What are its mainsprings and how should rulers govern to unleash the surplus-generating forces of society? In my reading of political economy, this thinking begins in Europe – perhaps for good reason.[6] It is this region – and in particular the tiny island nation of Britain – that will eventually exploit a new energy source that will break the chain of daily insolation: non-renewable but energy-dense coal will be used in huge quantities for the first time in human history. Since energy is generally defined as the capacity to do work, more energy (from coal, at first) leads to ever greater capacity for work. With some exceptions, most early political economists did not perceive the relationship between surplus energy and the surplus capacity to produce. Before what we today call the school of classical political economy, the nearest we got to thinking about wealth was called mercantilism. It was a variegated body of knowledge connected up with royal power, international trade and the merchant quest for profit from trade. This view would come to be challenged by early political economists, but to understand their critiques and their own vision of where 'surplus' originated, we must first consider the main tenets of mercantilism.

**Mercantilism**

The current of thought that has been labelled 'mercantilism' must be understood within the context of a rising European merchant class, European colonialism and the geopolitical competition for a share of international trade – including long-distance trade to the Americas and Asia. Moreover, during the Iberian colonisation of the Americas, large amounts of gold and silver had been imported to Europe from Mexico and Peru by Spanish conquistadors, which further emboldened geopolitical competition for colonial riches. Mercantilist thought also emerged at a time when gold and silver (called 'bullion') were the only trusted currencies for financing war and conducting international trade. In their overview of mercantilist thought, Vaggi and Groenewegen put it thus:

> Precious metals guaranteed the command over goods,
> resources and labor all over the world. The power of the state
> depended on the amount of gold and silver in its coffers,

because this international currency made it possible to build ships and to pay armies (ibid.: 16).

Since gold and silver were the main mediums of international exchange, early mercantilists such as Thomas Gresham and John Hales argued that encouraging more gold and silver to flow into the country than flowed out would enrich the nation. In this formulation, the wealth of any given country, as Vaggi and Groenewegen suggest, was conceptualised as a stock of bullion made on the sale of raw materials to other nations. The stock could be increased by raising interest rates (thereby attracting foreign capital), keeping the currency valuable by not debasing it with inferior metals, and organising a system of taxation to collect revenue for state coffers (ibid.: 17). Through the ideas of a one-time director of the East India Company, Thomas Mun, mercantilist thought underwent a further refinement, gaining greater specificity in the realm of policy. However, the source of wealth remained the same: a positive balance of trade and more money in the form of gold and silver. Whether the mercantilists were wrong or right about the exact source of wealth is perhaps less important than recognising that they were not issuing neutral knowledge but were positioned in a field of political power. Mun and other mercantilists were largely practical men involved in long-distance trade. When they talked about increasing the wealth of the nation, the 'nation' largely meant their own class. There is little doubt that they sought to encourage policies that would primarily benefit merchants and, to some extent, a royal treasury in constant need of war finance, to which they owed much for sovereign protections. This much Adam Smith would charge them with:

Such as they were, however, those arguments convinced the

people to whom they were addressed. They were addressed by merchants to parliaments and to the councils of princes, to nobles, and to country gentlemen; by those who were supposed to understand trade, to those who were conscious to themselves that they knew nothing about the matter. That foreign trade enriched the country, experience demonstrated to the nobles and country gentlemen, as well as to the merchants; but how, or in what manner, none of them well knew. *The merchants knew perfectly in what manner it enriched themselves, it was their business to know it. But to know in what manner it enriched the country, was no part of their business.* The subject never came into their consideration, but when they had occasion to apply to their country for some change in the laws relating to foreign trade. It then became necessary to say something about the beneficial effects of foreign trade, and the manner in which those effects were obstructed by the laws as they then stood. To the judges who were to decide the business, it appeared a most satisfactory account of the matter, when they were told that foreign trade brought money into the country, but that the laws in question hindered it from bringing so much as it otherwise would do. Those arguments, therefore, produced the wished-for effect (Smith 2005: 345–6, my emphasis).

In other words, the mercantilists helped themselves by masquerading their own particular interests as the general interests of the country. They also remained silent on the distribution of wealth. And given the fact that the majority of the population remained overwhelmingly rural and therefore not fully subject to the full dictates of the price mechanism or market imperatives, we can be sure that the merchants made up part of an early modern 1%.

## The birth of classical political economy

According to one scholar of political economy, the term 'classical political economy' was put forward by Marx to designate an emergent body of thought that broke from the mercantile tradition (Aspromourgos 1996: 2–3). The beginning of this new discourse on the origins of wealth began with Sir William Petty (1623–87) in England and Pierre le Pesant de Boisguilbert (1646–1714) in France. The tradition ends – at least according to Marx – with David Ricardo (1772–1823) and Jean Charles Léonard de Sismondi (1773–1842). Despite its advocates' considerable differences, what unites this branch of political economy is a concern to explain the generation of wealth or surplus not by merchant trade as evidenced by stocks of gold and silver, but in the production of material goods as evidenced by a flow of annual produce. But the search for the source of surplus value led to a further and perhaps more important question: if society was somehow creating more than its mere subsistence needs, how was this surplus divided in a class-based society and what justified this division? These questions would hardly be important if everyone in society received an equal portion of the surplus produced in any given year. But this was clearly not the case: some received a great deal more than others. The early political economists started to inquire why this was so.

*William Petty* In political economy, 'William Petty is the originator of the concept of an economic or social surplus', says Aspromourgos (2005: 1). To be clear, it is not as though surplus was never noticed before Petty came along and thought about it. It is simply the case that with Petty the concept of surplus was becoming a quantifiable object for political economy. Although the view is somewhat conjectural, it is likely that Petty developed his seminal idea of surplus through his engagement with the Hartlib Circle – a correspondence society concerned with advancing knowledge throughout Western and Central Europe. One of the key concerns of the time was agricultural improvement and the application of new techniques and technologies to agricultural production (ibid.). However, the focus of Petty and other agricultural improvers was not on agricultural production for need – that is, to supply nutritious diets to the population – but on production for profit. In his major work in 1662, *A Treatise of Taxes and Contributions*, there is a clear understanding that a surplus of goods could be generated from two primary sources of wealth: labour and land. Petty writes of an 'overplus', 'growth', 'superfluous commodities', 'surplusages' and 'supernumeraries' – the latter term meaning paupers. Surplus comes from ensuring that 'net output per worker [on the land] exceeds necessary consumption per worker' (ibid.: 12). Thus it could be said that Petty had an input theory of value: the price of a commodity was determined by the cost of supplying labour with subsistence wages and the cost of resources used in production (Vaggi and Groenewegen 2003: 33–4).

But whatever Petty's other intentions and conceptual innovations, the 1662 treatise is primarily a blueprint to advance a judicious system of taxation to pay for war (primarily) and other reasonable public expenditures – for instance, infrastructure. In the preface, Petty argues that his views can be applied widely but are certainly suitable for Ireland, where the Irish had been rebelling against English rule:

> Ireland is a place which must have so great an Army kept up in it, as may make the Irish desist from doing themselves or the English harm by their future Rebellions. And this great

Army must occasion great and heavy Leavies upon a poor
people and wasted Countrey; it is therefore not amiss that
Ireland should understand the nature and measure of Taxes
and Contributions.[7]

Translated, Petty means: 'the conquest of Ireland has been a
most brutal affair. Forcing the Irish to conform to our way of life
or dispossessing them of their land has caused their Catholic
leadership to rebel. In order to impose our Protestant rule and
way of life, we will require an army for some time before the
Irish are pacified and finally submit to our will. Since a permanent standing army will be expensive, it is best that Ireland's
Protestant governors understand how to raise taxes to support
their domination of the land and its people.' Petty is no neutral
or innocent witness standing outside society. As one scholar
has argued, his political economy was forged from his practical
experiences in evaluating expropriated land from Ireland (Fox
2009). From 1653 to 1687, when he died, he spent two-thirds of
his life in Ireland. His most important practical contribution
during this period was the Down Survey – a detailed survey
of land tenure and profitable and unprofitable tracts of land
throughout Ireland. The main purpose of the survey was to
provide a reasonably accurate picture of land occupancy so that
land could be redistributed to the soldiers and investors who
physically reconquered or financed the reconquering of Ireland
under Cromwell. Indeed, before it even left the shores of England,
the privately financed army sent to reconquer Ireland for the
English 1% was capitalised on the basis that 2.5 million acres of
Irish land could be confiscated. The capitalised land would then
be turned over to war financiers and soldiers as their 'return on
investment' (Bottigheimer 1967; Hazlett 1938).

In this way, we should understand Petty as embedded in certain relations of force that are pre-industrial but not pre-capitalist from the point of view of capital as power. It is not as if power and profit were invented with the Industrial Revolution (Marx's capitalism proper). In Petty's time, the accumulation of money and power was the primary goal of the few and Petty ended up squarely in the 1% through his ownership of expropriated Irish lands – his personal wealth increasing from £500 to £6,700 between 1652 and 1685 (Fioramonti 2013: 20). And while this period is certainly known for its discourse of agricultural improvement and the potential surplus to be had by such improvements, obtaining profitable land for a small class of 'gentlemen' farmers largely meant taking productive land away from others (Canny 1973; Ferro 1997; Rai 1993; Weaver 2006; Wood 2002). In England, this meant an internal war: enclosing land, dispossessing direct or peasant producers from common land and abolishing their customary right to it (Neeson 1993; Thompson 1991). Indeed, by 1850, 'Landlords owned 75–80 percent of the farmland of England' (Overton 1996: 204). Such measures would involve considerable violence and a growing penal code to deal with those who rebelled or struggled to survive by committing newly minted crimes against property (Hay 1980). Abroad, this more often meant the violent imposition of rule and the taking away of land by various means from native custodians. In more ways than one, we could read Petty's political economy as one of the first attempts to precisely quantify the power and worth of land appropriation. But Petty also desired to give people a monetary magnitude – to assess the worth of individuals so that they could more easily be taxed by royal authority (Fioramonti 2013: 21). This new knowledge being born – with its early attempts at mathematical exactitude and calculations of improvement and profit – continued to be refined as finance became more and more the language of power and appropriation. Numbers, maths, measurement, quantification, calculation and the price system all became the handmaidens of the capitalisation process – a process designed to reduce human sociality and creativity to the domination of private owners:

> Just as Hobbes's mechanical representation of political power inaugurated modern political thought, William Petty's quest for mathematical representations of national wealth provided the foundations of modern political economy. His attempt to turn the value of social phenomena (as well as human beings) into numbers was presented as a genuine effort at advancing knowledge and impartiality. In fact, it served the interests of the ruling elite and was amply adopted as an instrument of domination. And this has been true for all measures of economic performance, from that time to the present (ibid.: 23).

In its beginnings, political economy was not the discourse of paupers, just as it was not the discourse of subsistence farming. It was the discourse of a colonising power – both within countries and without. It was an emergent discourse of the 1% and its functionaries, who were developing tools to quantify qualitative social phenomena for the purpose of accumulation and – especially at this time, if not in the present – geopolitical war to accumulate more wealth and power. These origins already suggest to us that any progressive alternative to the capitalist mode of power will have to have, of necessity, its own system of quantification beneficial to society as a whole rather than to a tiny fraction of it.

*The physiocrats* From the shores of the agricultural revolution and expropriation in England and its emerging colonial empire, we move on to France to meet the physiocrats – a school of political economy inspired by the work of François Quesnay (1694–1774). Adam Smith's theory of wealth was directly inspired by the physiocrats, and they left a lasting impact on political economy – particularly with their conceptual distinction between productive and unproductive labour.[8] But, once again, we will not encounter a theory of wealth disconnected from power, political interests or social classes. We must place Quesnay and his followers, like Petty, within the matrix of a battle over the accumulation of money. As we shall see below, Quesnay's political economy was largely at the service of a new class of landowners who had the misfortune of joining an increasingly bankrupt royal and noble 1%.

Quesnay was born to a relatively privileged – if somewhat humble – position and studied medicine and surgery. Eventually he moved to Paris, where he worked for King Louis XV as his physician. He was made a noble by the king and given apartments in the Palace of Versailles. Quesnay, like the other physiocrats, was also an estate-holder – a key source of his wealth. Now with an estate of his own, Quesnay turned his mind to economic questions and, together with other interested elites, would discuss the economic matters of the kingdom (Ware 1931). By 1758, 31 years before the tumult of the French Revolution, he published his *Tableau Économique* or 'Economic Table'. The table purported to show that the prime source of wealth was productive agriculture, whereas all other economic activity was merely the consumption of it. Today, the table is celebrated as the first great analytical and systematic attempt to theorise the entire social reproduction of an economy. But once again, Quesnay's theoretical endeavour was connected to the class power of large estate owners.

At the time of Quesnay's writing, the kingdom of France was overwhelmingly a rural economy, with the 1% of estate-holders deriving their incomes from custom or from the kingly ordained right to tax peasants on their estates. Years of war and courtly extravagance had almost bankrupted the royal treasury and many of the nobility. A number of bureaucrats working for the king in *parlement* (more or less a council to the king) took advantage of the situation and bought up bankrupt estates. However, unlike the nobility who did not have a zeal for improving their lands, this new class looked to England's capitalist landlords and farmers to imagine how they too could make their newly acquired land yield more profit (ibid.: 609).

Since the physiocrats were not vested in merchant trade but in land, it is hardly surprising that they found the primary source of all wealth to be productive labour on the land. Or, more specifically, Quesnay and his physiocrats:

> saw that there is but one source on which men can draw
> for all their material needs – land; and that there is but one
> means by which land can be made to yield to their desires –
> labor. All real wealth, they therefore saw, all that constitutes
> or can constitute any part of the wealth of society as a whole,
> or of the wealth of nations, is the result or product of the
> application of labor to land.[9]

From this assessment, the physiocrats sought to advance their particular class interest as the general interest of the people of France. To do so they advocated free trade of grain within France and free export of grain from France, as well as a single tax on the agricultural surplus. Their goal was twofold: 1) to get out from under the heavy burden of taxes placed on the land; and 2) to achieve the highest possible price for agricultural goods (ibid.:

612). Free trade combined with a series of bad harvests escalated the price of bread. While landowners made larger profits, people starved. Those with energy rioted. As one observer noted:

> The fiscal program of the Economists [physiocrats] tends to relieve the rich and burden the poor; the execution of their agricultural programs benefits only the great proprietors and the majority of the inhabitants of the country gain only an increase of misery; the realization of their commercial program results in want or in the high cost of living from which all the consumers suffer cruelly (Weulersse cited in ibid.: 617).

But misery for the many and high prices for bread did not phase Quesnay. In fact, like the early English political economists, the potential for hunger (due to high prices) was interpreted as beneficial:

> It is thus a great mistake to accustom the people to buying their wheat at too low a price; they become less laborious, they feed themselves with little difficulty and thus become parasitic and arrogant; it is difficult to find workmen and domestic servants, and people are very badly served in the abundant years (Quesnay cited in ibid.: 618).

Once again we find that hunger is a better disciplinarian than the magistrate.

*Adam Smith* By the time Adam Smith published his *An Inquiry into the Nature and Causes of the Wealth of Nations* (1776), some of the key concepts of political economy were already in circulation. Smith built on these concepts to provide a more systematic account that largely challenged the discourse of mercantilism. But once again, Smith is no neutral or objective figure but an intellectual node in a more dynamic and emergent capitalist mode of power. His political economy was certainly critical of merchant business practices, but he ended up telling a story of wealth creation centred on the harmony of self-interested individuals pursuing gain in the market. Like Petty and the physiocrats, his work is directed at governors.

What is the engine of wealth creation for Smith? The simple answer is the division of labour, or the mere fact that many people work at different employments, thereby increasing productivity. Since individuals specialise in a given employment, they are compelled to exchange some of the products of their work on the market in order to receive the goods and services they do not produce for themselves. Smith was describing a society whose social reproduction was increasingly dependent on market exchanges. These new market relations of force, for Smith, were encouraged and protected by the constitutional framework inaugurated by the Glorious Revolution of 1688. Although there are debates about the significance of the revolution, it is generally thought to have subordinated the Crown to property-holders in parliament. From this point on, royal power could no longer be used arbitrarily; in legislative matters, parliament reigned supreme.

Yet Smith largely takes the social relations of his era for granted. He knows full well that certain individuals belong to different 'ranks' or classes and he has to have some theory to explain why it is that some people work for others. In other words, he has to address the glaring fact that a small minority of people have property and the majority do not. In fact, he even argues that government is instituted to protect the 1% of property owners against the struggling poor:

> The affluence of the rich excites the indignation of the poor,
> who are often both driven by want, and prompted by envy to

invade his possessions. It is only under the shelter of the civil magistrate, that the owner of that valuable property, which is acquired by the labour of many years, or perhaps of many successive generations, can sleep a single night in security. He is at all times surrounded by unknown enemies, whom, though he never provoked, he can never appease, and from whose injustice he can be protected only by the powerful arm of the civil magistrate, continually held up to chastise it. The acquisition of valuable and extensive property, therefore, necessarily requires the establishment of civil government ... Civil government, so far as it is instituted for the security of property, is, in reality, instituted for the defence of the rich against the poor, or of those who have some property against those who have none at all (Smith 2005: 580, 583).

To put this less politely: government is the organised power of the 1% of property owners who are entangled in a perpetual war with those who have no property at all. The problem with Smith's work, as Marx recognised, is that it does not provide a convincing account of how this relationship emerged historic-ally. This is where Smith's conjectural history overlooks the entire history of expropriation in the English countryside. He says that originally all the products of labour belonged to the labourer. However, at some unspecified time, some individuals appropriated land to themselves and built up a 'stock' (ibid.: 59). According to Smith, this stock or capital 'has been silently and gradually accumulated by the private frugality and good conduct of individuals, by their universal, continual, and un-interrupted effort to better their own condition' (ibid.: 283). It follows, then, that the waged workers or non-property owners come from ancestors who did not conduct themselves well, were wasteful and reckless, and had little interest in bettering their own condition. Historically, this of course is nonsense, but in order for Smith to advance his harmonious political economy he cannot admit that the true origins of unequal property stem from the violent exertion of power and the royal grant or sale of lands. Doing so would bring his analysis of the political economy closer to the radical position of the Diggers during the English Civil War of the 1640s, or even to Karl Marx a century and a half later. We will discuss Marx in just a moment, but consider this passage from the leader of the Diggers, Gerrard Winstanley:

> those that buy and sell land, and are landlords, have got it either by oppression or murder or theft; and all landlords live in the breach of the seventh and eighth commandments, *Thou shalt not steal nor kill.* First by their oppression: they have by their subtle imaginary and covetous wit got the plain-hearted poor or younger brethren to work for them for small wages, and by their work have got a great increase; for the poor by their labour lifts up tyrants to rule over them; or else by their covetous wit they have outreached the plain-hearted in buying and selling, and thereby enriched themselves but impoverished others: or else by their subtle wit, having been a lifter up into places of trust, have enforced people to pay money for a public use, but have divided much of it into their private purses; and so have got it by oppression (Winstanley quoted in Hill 2006: 85).

Winstanley is far from admitting that the rich are rich because of 'good conduct' and 'frugality'. A conquest did indeed occur in 1066, and the conquest did not stop operating when the initial war ended. The evidence is that the poor and oppressed have no property and no say in their own governance and are continually subject to masters for work, wages and survival. So whereas Adam

Smith considers wage labour unproblematic, the Diggers do not. They interpret it as an unnatural species of slavery imposed upon them through forceful means. Smith's is not the voice of the poor and oppressed but of the dispassionate scholar. His desire for harmony – what modern economists fetishise as 'equilibrium' – cannot admit violence, force or fraud in the making of a capitalist social order. Yet even in Smith there is recognition that immense wealth grows up alongside poverty and inequality. It was Karl Marx who perhaps most insightfully picked up on this contradiction to offer his own theory of surplus value.

*Karl Marx* The political economy of power and wealth takes a radical turn with the work of Karl Marx (1818–83). Marx can be thought to have made two major breaks with the liberal or classical political economists who largely supported the emergence of capitalism. The first is that Marx historicised capitalism as a unique way of producing commodities geared to generating ever more money for owners. If capitalism has a historical beginning and definite laws, then it can be understood politically and can have a historical end if it is shown that it is not in the interests of the vast majority of humanity. To Marx, this 'end' was a saner, more equitable, democratic and planned political economy geared to human need and well-being rather than to the profit of the 1%. This was a political goal, not an inevitable one, despite Marx's many assertions that capitalism had inexorable laws that gave it an expiry date. The second major break was Marx's fervent belief that the working class of productive wage labourers was economically exploited by its capitalist employers. To advance or justify a new social order, Marx had to convincingly demonstrate that the workers were indeed exploited by their paymasters. Without this demonstration, there would be little need for a revolution in social property relations; we would be squarely in a liberal political economy where wealth is generated by non-exploited workers. Avoiding this liberal interpretation is what is at stake for Marx's own radical political economy. To be sure, before Marx started to write *Capital*, he busied himself with a detailed examination of how all previous political economists approached the concept of surplus, or, perhaps more accurately, surplus value. There is no question in Marx, then, that the key problem of political economy is the source of surplus and its distribution. For Marx, surplus wealth is, and can only ever be, a social product. In the *Communist Manifesto*, Marx and Engels write: 'Capital is a collective product, and only by the united action of many members, nay, in the last resort, only by the united action of all members of society, can it be set in motion' (Marx and Engels 1848: 14). And unlike Smith, who could not see the full-scale turn to sustained industrial growth, Marx and Engels were writing at a time of tremendous, if uneven, growth and productivity:

> The bourgeoisie, during its rule of scarce one hundred years, has created more massive and more colossal productive forces than have all preceding generations together. Subjection of nature's forces to man, machinery, application of chemistry to industry and agriculture, steam navigation, railways, electric telegraphs, clearing of whole continents for cultivation, canalization or rivers, whole populations conjured out of the ground – what earlier century had even a presentiment that such productive forces slumbered in the lap of social labor? (ibid.: 7).

Marx and Engels clearly identify social labour as one of the key factors in the emergence of capitalist productivity, and, unlike Smith, Marx provides a historical sketch of how the social property relations of capital emerged. We saw earlier how for Smith wage labourers just appeared on the scene – the result of the prodigality and questionable conduct of their ancestors and ultimately their failure to accumulate 'stock'. The market also just appeared on the scene for Smith. It did not emerge because of the state, but in spite of it. Not so for Marx. Wage labour and the price-denominated market are creatures of state power in the service of capitalist landlords, merchants and industrialists. Marx calls the process by which people are forced into wage labour and market dependence 'primitive accumulation'. Since the wealth of the 1% is contingent on the price system and the market dependence of the many, we would do well to consider some insightful passages from Marx on how this situation developed.

In his section on primitive accumulation in *Capital*, Marx begins with the important – albeit commonsensical – recognition that people do not willingly expropriate themselves. This is simply to say that direct producers on the land do not – as a rule – give up their tenure on the land for nothing. In other words, they must be forced or incentivised out of this tenure in some way. Marx argues that this process lasted centuries in England and, after land was expropriated from Catholic Church estates, was mainly carried out by the privately funded violence of landlords seeking to create pasture out of arable land. The reason for doing this was the accumulation of riches to be gained by grazing sheep and harvesting their wool to sell on the world market – a key source of wealth for the landlord 1%. However, Marx argues that a new process began after the Glorious Revolution of 1688:

> The advance made by the 18th century shows itself in this, that the law itself becomes now the instrument of the theft

of the people's land, although the large farmers make use of their little independent methods as well. The parliamentary form of the robbery is that of Acts for enclosures of Commons, in other words, decrees by which the landlords grant themselves the people's land as private property, decrees of expropriation of the people (Marx 1996: 506).

These expropriations form the basis of the 'princely estates of the English oligarchy' (ibid.: 505). But the apparatus of domination over the peasantry and newly minted vagabonds unattached to the land was also facilitated by the creation of the Bank of England and the national debt. The national debt – even to this day – will become a key source of wealth for the 1%. It is worth quoting Marx at some length:

> At their birth the great banks, decorated with national titles, were only associations of private speculators, who placed themselves by the side of governments, and, thanks to the privileges they received, were in a position to advance money to the State. Hence the accumulation of the national debt has no more infallible measure than the successive rise in the stock of these banks, whose full development dates from the founding of the Bank of England in 1694. The Bank of England began with lending its money to the Government at 8%; at the same time it was empowered by Parliament to coin money out of the same capital, by lending it again to the public in the form of banknotes. It was allowed to use these notes for discounting bills, making advances on commodities, and for buying the precious metals. It was not long ere this credit-money, made by the bank itself, became the coin in which the Bank of England made its loans to the State, and paid, on account of the State, the interest on the public debt.

It was not enough that the bank gave with one hand and took back more with the other; it remained, even whilst receiving, the eternal creditor of the nation down to the last shilling advanced. Gradually it became inevitably the receptacle of the metallic hoard of the country, and the centre of gravity of all commercial credit (ibid.: 30).

What this passage suggests is that the Bank of England – which in the beginning was a privately owned institution – could not have survived without the power of the state. However, it is unclear whether Marx understood that the money lent to the 1% in parliament, while backed by precious metals, was created as credit out of thin air.[10] In other words, the bank did not lend the government all the money that it had on deposit but money created as debt, albeit anchored to a metallic hoard of silver and later gold. As one modern study demonstrates, implementing this exclusive system of money creation required a whole field of operations:

> Safeguarding the nascent culture of credit required debtors' prisons for the insolvent and the threat of execution for clippers and counterfeiters. Moreover, thousands of African slaves were carried in chains to the New World, so that profits from the South Sea Company might bolster people's trust in public credit. An unprecedented number of Englishmen were hurt or killed in wars with France that England would not have been able to conduct on the same scale without the employment of credit (Wennerlind 2011: 2).

Based on this fraud, the owners of the Bank of England went on to charge interest on the loans they extended to the government.[11] The money could also be loaned to capitalist landlords

and commercial enterprises and was intimately involved in funding English colonialism. In return for this finance, parliament
would then tax the population to raise revenue to service its
debt to the owners of the bank. Marx called this the 'alienation
of the state by sale', since the bank's owners were effectively
capitalising the government's ability to implement and enforce
taxes on the population.[12] And as we saw in Chapter 2, Marx
reasoned that taxation would balloon.

As was mentioned earlier, the majority of these loans went
to finance imperial wars. As Brewer asserts: 'the Fall of James II
in 1688 inaugurated the longest period of British warfare since
the middle ages. Britain was at war with France, and allies of
France, in 1689–97, 1702–13, 1739–63 and 1775–83' (Brewer 1989:
22). Such wars were not primarily fought for honour or national
glory but for the accumulation of wealth:

> War was an economic as well as military activity: its causes,
> conduct and consequences as much a matter of money as
> martial prowess. Nowhere in eighteenth century Europe was
> this better understood than in Britain. As Casanova, visiting
> London shortly after the Seven Years War, discovered in his
> conversations with Augustus Hervey, the captor of Havana,
> the British viewed war as far more than a matter of honor. It
> was also a question of property and profit (ibid.).

In order to finance war, an elaborate fiscal bureaucracy developed to collect taxes. Domestically, a mushrooming army
was tasked with enforcing tax payments and preventing discord
and insurrection erupting due to the increased levies on the
population (ibid.: 44). As Braddick confirms, Marx was indeed
correct: the national debt made the British the most overtaxed
people on the planet (Braddick 1996: 21–48). Excessive taxation,

according to Marx, was universally recognised as one of the most effective ways of expropriating 'peasants, artisans, and in a word, all elements of the lower middle class' (Marx 1996: 530). Those who could not pay their taxes entered into usurious and ruinous debt to moneylenders who would then take possession of the collateral (typically land) in lieu of payment. Taxation also served to bring the price system to the countryside and compelled labourers to work for wages or grow cash crops so that they could afford the tax. Evidence from the colonies demonstrates its wide application:

> In those parts of Africa where land was still in African hands, colonial governments forced Africans to produce cash crops no matter how low the prices were. The favorite technique was taxation. *Money* taxes were introduced on numerous items – cattle, land, houses, and the people themselves. Money to pay taxes was got by growing cash crops or working on European farms or in their mines (Rodney 1972: 165, emphasis original).

Failure to pay taxes was met with swift punishment at best, the loss of ancestral land at worst (Forstater 2005). A key aspect of expropriation by taxation was the system of tax protection for domestic manufacturers. Heavy taxes on imports protected domestic manufacturers by giving them a price advantage in the market. Britain would then encourage 'free trade' with its colonies so that its own goods could enter the colonial market at cheaper prices. For example, in 1814 the import tax on British woollens and cotton and silk goods was 2% to 3.5%, while the tax on imported Indian textiles to Britain was 70% to 80%. The consequences were devastating for the people and textile industry of India (Stavrianos 1981: 247).

So whereas Smith takes wage labour for granted and views the expansion of the market as a natural outgrowth of individual self-interest in spite of the state, Marx demonstrated the ways in which the creation of the market, modern ownership, great wealth for the few and the control of humanity through prices would have been unimaginable without state power. Polanyi summarises the situation aptly: 'the road to the free market was opened and kept open by an enormous increase in continuous, centrally organized and controlled interventionism. To make Adam Smith's "simple and natural liberty" compatible with the needs of a human society was a most complicated affair' (Polanyi 1957: 140). That was Polanyi being judicious. He later states: 'the market has been the outcome of a conscious and often violent intervention on the part of government which imposed the market organization on society' (ibid.: 250). The market and the price system were imposed on humanity not as a matrix of choice but as a mechanism of domination. The very precondition for capitalist power was market dependence and, for its universalisation, wage labour.

Marx's historical narrative of capitalism's emergence is far more convincing than Smith's. Yet Marx does not root his theory of value in the organised power he so clearly understood. Marx argued that *the sole* source of profit was unpaid surplus labour. In other words, workers were paid less during the working day than the value of what they actually produced. He held to his labour theory of value because, quite naturally, he saw humans as the only beings capable of producing extra or surplus value:

> It is only on this basis that the difference arises between the *value* of labour-power and the *value which that* labour-power *creates* – a difference which exists with no other commodity, since there is no other commodity whose use-value, and

therefore also the use of it, can increase its *exchange-value* or the exchange-values resulting from it (emphasis original).[13]

However, there is one commodity that can indeed be used to increase economic growth, or, in Marx's parlance, the level of virtually all exchange values: non-renewable fossil fuels. As long as the energy returned is greater than the energy invested to obtain fossil fuels, the energy released by using coal, petroleum and natural gas does indeed have the power to generate an incredible surplus (Goldstone 2002; Wrigley 2010). This is what made Britain, and later Europe and North America, so exceptional compared with the rest of the world: the exploitation of fossil fuels expanded the limits of the possible by *adding greater capacity to do work* (Hall and Klitgaard 2012). A contemporary of Marx's noted the relationship:

> Day by day it becomes more evident that the Coal we happily possess in excellent quality and abundance is the mainspring of modern material civilization ... It is the material energy of the country – the universal aid – the factor in everything we do. With coal almost any feat is possible or easy; without it we are thrown back into the laborious poverty of early times ... This question concerning the duration of our present cheap supplies of coal cannot but excite deep interest and anxiety wherever or whenever it is mentioned: for a little reflection will show that *coal is almost the sole necessary basis of our material power*, and is that, consequently, which gives efficiency to our moral and intellectual capabilities (Jevons 1866: 5, my emphasis).

Since Jevons, oil and natural gas have been added to the world's energy supply – albeit a supply that is unevenly shared throughout the world. The evidence for the link between energy and wealth is overwhelming and simple enough to verify in two ways: 1) all countries with high levels of GDP are large consumers of energy whereas those with low GDPs consume far less energy (UNDP 2000); and 2) the massive increase in global capitalisation (and therefore the accumulation of money) has corresponded with increasing energy consumption (Di Muzio 2014: 19–35). This does not mean that consuming fossil fuel energy is a sufficient condition for the production of immense wealth, but it is a necessary and decisive one. If we think back to Braudel's question about whether it is a law of history that the rich always be so few, one thing becomes crystal clear: what the 1% have been able to do remarkably well is to redistribute more energy wealth to themselves in the form of money. This was true of rulers in the past who usurped the energy and products of slaves, serfs, peasants and small pools of wage labourers before wage dependence and private property became ubiquitous. With the turn to fossil fuels, the main way in which incredible wealth is now achieved is through the ownership and capitalisation of organised power combined with the historically difficult task of shaping, disciplining, and quite often brutalising, a global labour force where the human capacity for work is commodified in wage form and capitalised by the owning 1%. As discussed in Chapter 2, the goal of capitalists is differential capitalisation – to accumulate more money faster than others. One important dimension of this is the capitalisation of the money supply and its links to energy and social power.

## The general theory of money, energy and power

There is a litany of modern books on the generation of wealth, but none so far has fully appreciated the deep connections between energy, money and power and how the current arrangement benefits the 1% (Bernstein 2004; de Soto 2003; Hall and Klitgaard 2012; Landes 1998).[14] Since capitalist power operates through and is registered by the price system, we should have a keen focus on money. There have been different forms of money historically but the more durable coins made from various metals were typically issued by sovereign authorities to finance war, trade and the affairs of state (Davies 2002). The big historical turn, however, came when private social forces gained control over the money supply so that commercial banks – with a central bank acting as regulator – now issue about 97% of the world's money supply through interest-bearing loans. Today, in richer regions of the world, most of the new money in circulation is due to banks creating number money on computer screens for mortgages and loans for big ticket items such as cars (Rowbotham 1998). But from the perspective of capital as power, we must ask what it is that bank owners are capitalising?

The first thing owners capitalise is the power of banks to issue money as interest-bearing debt. This, of course, is based upon an exclusion: no one else is permitted to issue money. Second, the bank's owners capitalise the borrower's ability to service the debt; the hope is that the debt is never fully repaid, so interest fees become perpetual. So a loan is essentially the capitalisation of earning or income capacity regardless of what form credit takes. However, access to money is radically unequal in our societies: banks deem that some people have greater capacity to repay than others (i.e. creditworthiness). What this means is that the distribution of money in the economy through loans will be skewed towards those who already have assets or a decent income stream from their labour. This might seem like an absurd proposition to some readers: if the rich really are rich, why would they need to borrow money? There seem to be three reasons: first, their money or investment managers often borrow large sums in an effort to make more money. So an asset pool of US$2 billion can become US$10 billion or so with borrowed number money from a bank. A 10% return on US$10 billion is more than a 10% return on US$2 billion. The second reason appears to be that people with considerable wealth, but not quite at the top of the high-net-worth pyramid, borrow so that they can keep up appearances with their more moneyed counterparts (Frank 2007). A final reason is that the corporations or businesses they own take on debt to expand or acquire other companies. At any rate, the unequal provision of money is crucial, but not the only important point to note.

The most important point is that, in a market-dependent economy, *money is a necessity for everyone* and there is never enough of it. As Smith even remarked: 'No complaint, however, is more common than that of a scarcity of money' (Smith 2005: 348). This was as true in the past as it is today.[15] But the supply of money is not democratically decided by our governments but premised upon people willing to go into debt to banks, *which are largely owned by private individuals and the families of the 1%*.[16] The banks do not have this money. It is not the savings of the owners or of depositors that is lent. They create it out of nothing.[17] It is fraud, pure and simple, but a highly guarded fraud.[18] Centuries ago, if you or I issued our own money we could have been blinded, have our hand cut off, been castrated, or a mixture of all three – or, what surely might sound better to some, given the options, put to death (Davies 2002: 140). In most countries today, counterfeiting would land us in jail for a good part of our lives. From bodily tortures and death to years in prison, such has been the progress of modern capitalism! Either way, a convincing argument is that no country can be declared democratic and no democratic people sovereign until that country controls its own money supply. Where the few capitalise the creation of credit in a money-starved economy, the rest of us are an interest farm for the bank-owning 1%. That this practice is such a lucrative business is confirmed by the fact that, after oil and gas companies, banks are the most heavily capitalised industry on the planet.[19] Put another way, investors and owners know that where there is not enough money in the economy for workers to purchase the goods and services they produce, there is a constant demand for interest-bearing credit.

But this is only part of our general theory. We now need to consider energy. We can define energy as the capacity to do work; thus, having more energy means – all things being equal – having a greater capacity to do work. Expressed differently, consuming more energy means that our societies have a greater capacity to shape and reshape the terrain of social reproduction. Because energy, like money in a market economy, is central to everything we do, it is a highly coveted resource. The source, quantity and quality of our energy supply has changed over time. Before the turn to fossil fuels, the energy historian Vaclav Smil called humans 'solar farmers' – that is to say, a people tending to, transforming and consuming the products created by nature through photosynthesis.[20] Of course, coal was known in antiquity, but it was used sparingly, most likely because wood was preferred where it was available and cheap. The transition to fossil fuels – with coal being the primary source of fuel well into the twentieth century – begins in Britain. As Nef (1977) points out, by the 1500s, Britain was suffering an acute energy crisis due to centuries of deforestation, enclosures of forests for the aristocracy and the high cost of wood. The use of coal and the technological developments that resulted from its use gave

Britain a decisive wartime advantage over its European rivals and contributed to it becoming the largest empire on earth. By 1922, the British Empire ruled over one-fifth of humanity. Coal and later oil energy created more capacity to do work in the economy and allowed bankers to expand the amount of interest-bearing debt money in that economy.[21] The result was the largest stock market capitalisation on earth until the United States started to exploit domestic oil deposits and overtook Britain in energy consumption and the extension of credit (Arrighi 1994).[22] Today, the New York Stock Exchange is the largest exchange by market capitalisation, while the United States consumes about 19% of the world's total primary energy supply. So, the general theory of money, energy and power can be summarised as follows:

1  Commercial banks have a monopoly on the extension of credit or money creation.

2  The power of banks to create money by issuing interest-bearing debt is capitalised by dominant owners.

3  The money supply is contingent on banks being able to find willing borrowers with the capacity to repay or service interest payments. This is facilitated by the monopolisation of money creation and its general scarcity (even where the money supply happens to appear massive).

4  Those with a greater capacity to repay have the ability to borrow more money and they can use this money to make more money through business or investments.

5  The capacity to repay debt or service interest payments is contingent upon access to energy, the majority of which now derives from fossil fuels in richer economies.

6  The capacity to repay debt or service interest payments is also contingent on energy-dependent economic growth.

7  The greater the amount of energy consumed in a society, the larger the money supply, the GDP, the market capitalisation of corporations and debt will be.

8  Since money is issued as interest-bearing debt, inflation is built into the capitalist mode of power.

9  The owners of the banks profit tremendously from their monopolisation of money creation.

10 The way we issue money has to be changed: instead of benefiting the few, it needs to benefit the many.

The full ramifications of this general theory will be discussed at length in a separate treatment (Di Muzio and Robbins 2015). I only note here that most scholars of political economy have largely ignored the link between energy and the way in which money is created and capitalised for the benefit of dominant owners. Whereas most people think of money as a medium to achieve stability and a decent livelihood – and the majority have no idea how it is created – for the 1% it is symbolic of their power to shape and reshape the natural and human order. It is not so much that money is power – although this is also true – as *their* money is *their* power. As the next chapter suggests, the supremacy of dominant owners is going from strength to strength despite some meagre signs of resistance to capitalist power. But the 1% do not understand their power only in monetary terms; they also display their power in acts of differential or conspicuous consumption. We turn to this topic and its consequences in the next chapter.

# 4 | DIFFERENTIAL CONSUMPTION: THE RISE OF PLUTONOMY

The central trend dominating ... has been the relentless growth of 'plutonomy' economics, a phenomenon that sees the wealth of the richest 1% growing far quicker than that of the general population. (Knight Frank 2012: 4)

Richistanis like to flaunt their wealth. And never before have so many flaunted so much. (Robert Frank 2007: 120)

History has rarely seen an era in which so much money has been made by so few people in such a short amount of time. (Jim Taylor et al. 2009: 4)

In my last year on Wall Street my bonus was $3.6 million – and I was angry because it wasn't big enough. I was 30 years old, had no children to raise, no debts to pay, no philanthropic goal in mind. I wanted more money for exactly the same reason an alcoholic needs another drink: I was addicted. (Sam Polk 2014)

In the previous chapter we considered wealth, money and power and argued that the historical concern of the 1% has been the differential accumulation of money *eventually* expressed in the rising capitalisation of income streams. Today, differential capitalisation is symbolic of their power over other humans and over the natural world. Moreover, the magnitude of their power/wealth in the modern period was made possible by private ownership, the surplus energy of fossil fuels, and organised corporate power – for example, over the creation of money as debt. Also symbolic is the differential consumption of dominant owners, which is evidence to others of their wealth, status and power. This chapter takes a closer look at how high-net-worth individuals (HNWIs) spend their money through the lens of what Veblen (2007) called conspicuous consumption.[1]

## The global plutonomy

The concept of a 'plutonomy' was penned by a team of global equity strategists in a 2005 report for Citigroup entitled 'Plutonomy: buying luxury, explaining global imbalances'. A subsequent report, 'Revisiting plutonomy: the rich getting richer', followed a year later and largely reiterated the first report. Taken together, the main aim of the reports is to provide an analysis of current economic trends capable of informing high-net-worth investment strategies. The thesis advanced in the report is twofold. The first argument is that 'the world is dividing into two blocs – the plutonomies, where economic growth is powered by and largely consumed by the wealthy few, and the rest'. The second argument is far simpler: 'the rich will keep getting richer' (Citigroup 2006: 10). The authors then read the concept of plutonomy back into history and argue that plutonomies have existed in 'sixteenth century Spain, in seventeenth century Holland, the Gilded Age and the Roaring Twenties in the U.S.'. Today, they argue that the United States, Canada, the UK and Australia (added in the second report) are all plutonomies powered by the differential gains made by the wealthiest 1% of income earners, or, in their words: 'the rich now dominate income, wealth and spending in these countries' (ibid.: 1). Their evidence for this claim is based on empirical research that shows the income share of the top 1% in these countries rising rapidly from the late 1980s to 2002 (Citigroup 2005: 6). But what is the main driver of this trend? According to the 2005 report, there are six: 1) technology enhancing productivity; 2) financial innovation; 3) cooperative governments favourable to capitalism; 4) immigration and 'overseas conquests'; 5) the rule of law; and 6) patented inventions. [2] They go on to argue that plutonomies have reshaped the global consumption map and therefore a change in our traditional thinking is required:

> In a plutonomy there is no such animal as 'the U.S. consumer' or 'the UK consumer', or indeed the 'Russian consumer'. There are rich consumers, few in number, but disproportionate in the gigantic slice of income and consumption they take. There are the rest, the 'non-rich', the multitudinous many, but only accounting for surprisingly small bites of the national pie (ibid.: 2).

What this passage suggests is that for the equity strategists at Citigroup, there are only two types of people: rich consumers and a 'multitudinous many'. Indeed, probably stealing a page from their hero Ayn Rand, the report claims that 'the earth is being held up by the muscular arms of its entrepreneur-plutocrats, like it, or not' (ibid.: 1). Meanwhile, the multitude has such a low share of overall income in plutonomies that they cannot be key drivers of increasing demand – particularly for most luxury goods. But the authors recognise that the extreme polarisation of income and wealth may not be sustainable and they question how societies may 'disrupt plutonomy' by expropriating wealth at the top of the income pyramid (ibid.: 22). The authors argue that expropriation can take two main forms: government taxation and tampering with property rights. However, while they understand the potential for a social backlash that may force politicians to raise taxes on the wealthiest 1% or infringe upon some of their property rights, the report largely discounts the immediate potential for such moves based on the evidence that, at the time they were writing, there were few political or social events that signalled rising popular discontent. One of the potential reasons for this, suggests the report, is that 'enough of the electorate' in plutonomies 'believe they have a chance of becoming a Pluto-participant. Why kill it off, if you can join it?' (ibid.: 24). Whether there is some truth to the idea that people consent to plutonomy because one day they fancy themselves joining the 1% of HNWIs is of course highly debatable. But the far more interesting point the report makes relates to what investors can do with their analysis of growing income inequality.

If the wealthy have much more to spend in plutonomies than their lesser counterparts on fixed or relatively stagnant incomes, the report reasons that equity investors should target those publicly listed companies that cater to the global wealthy. Or, in their colourful words: 'there is ... a more refined way to play plutonomy, and this is to buy shares in the companies that make the toys that the Plutonomists enjoy' (ibid.: 25). What is more, the authors of the report argue that the global rich prefer Giffen goods. Giffen goods are goods that people consume more of the more expensive they become. So, rather than soaring prices becoming a deterrent to demand, they are actually a powerful signal to the rich to acquire such goods. Towards this end, Citigroup identified a representative menu of equities from companies whose earnings are almost exclusively generated from HNWIs. Calling it the 'plutonomy basket', there are 24 suggested securities in the index (weighed equally), ranging from the automobile maker Porsche to the private banking house of Julius Baer.

By tracing the index back to 1985 and comparing it with the MSCI AC World Index, the authors found 'a handsome outperformance' (ibid.: 28).[3] Up until 1996, their plutonomy basket closely trails the MSCI AC World Index, meaning that investing in their basket of stocks would *not* have yielded significant differential returns. However, from 1996 to 2005, the luxury stock index starts breaking away noticeably and significantly. Overall, the index generated an average return of 17.8% per annum since 1985 – greater than the 14% return for the MSCI AC World Index.[4] So, returning to the example of investing US$1 billion, had we invested in the index for only one year, the return on investment would have been US$178 million. If we had invested the same amount over the entire 20-year period of the index and reinvested all the yearly returns, we would end up making US$26,479,257,870, or an overall increase of 2,548%.[5] We can perhaps see why one of the conclusions of the report is that 'there are rich consumers, and there are the rest. The rich are getting richer ... and they dominate consumption' (ibid.: 30). However, before exploring some dimensions of conspicuous consumption in the New Gilded Age, I want to briefly consider the age that gave rise to Veblen's concept.

### Conspicuous consumption in the first Gilded Age

What is the chief end of man? – to get rich. In what way? – dishonestly if we can; honestly if we must. (Mark Twain 1871)

The Gilded Age is well known to American history. The term was coined by Mark Twain and his co-author Charles Dudley Warner in their 1873 novel *The Gilded Age: A tale of today*. The title and aims of the book have been widely discussed, but in the American experience, the Gilded Age is now synonymous with a period of social transformation ushered in by the Civil War (1861–65), the mass exploitation of coal and oil and the concentration of capital into giant corporations. The era is known for its highly questionable business practices, rampant political corruption, labour violence, social unrest, corporate collusion, rising inequality and what went with it: an ostentatious display of conspicuous consumption among the newly wealthy (Carlisle 2009; Josephson 1934). The era is said to have lasted to the end of the nineteenth century but it could be argued that acts of conspicuous consumption continued on during the so-called progressive era and, of course, to this day. But whereas Twain and Warner satirised their generation, it was not until Veblen's *The Theory of the Leisure Class* that the consumptive practices of the wealthy few were subject to greater, if somewhat muddled, theoretical scrutiny.

Like Twain and Warner's novel, Veblen's concept of conspicuous consumption has been heavily debated by modern scholars, with one noted expert arguing that Veblen's writing on the subject is confused and difficult to confirm empirically. For example, Campbell (1995) argues that we can in fact find three different conceptions of conspicuous consumption in *The Theory of the Leisure Class*: a subjective, consequentialist and substantive formulation. While conceding that Campbell is probably right about the conceptual difficulties implied by Veblen's use of conspicuous consumption, Tilman (2006) has argued that an empirical analysis is entirely possible despite some methodological difficulties. My view is not to deny that there are different interpretations of 'conspicuous consumption' to be found in Veblen's first major study; nor is it my intention in this chapter to evaluate whether we can scientifically assess whether such practices exist in the minds of the affluent.[6] I merely take as a working hypothesis that dominant owners aim to consume differentially for status just as they aim to accumulate differentially for power. And just as there are benchmarks that let the rich know they are beating the average rate of accumulation, so we could make the argument that there are benchmarks when it comes to the consumption practices of HNWIs. For example, benchmarks could include the average size of a luxury yacht, the average square footage of a mansion, the average number of homes and their locations, the number of luxury cars in their possession, invitations to the right parties and auctions and so on.

From a historical vantage point, this may not appear as something wholly new: rulers in hierarchical and more complex societies have always sought to distinguish themselves through their material practices – typically by acts of exclusion that led directly or indirectly to the extraction of tribute or the control of human flesh as in slavery or sacrifices to the 'gods' (De Botton 2005; Wolf 2010). What was different in the Gilded Age was the scale on which fortunes were made as well as their concentration.[7] To be sure, by the end of the nineteenth century there were 4,047 millionaires in the United States out of an estimated population of about 65 million people (Beard 2009: 62).[8] If we use the millionaire mark as the cut-off point during this period, then the number of millionaires represented a meagre 0.006% of the total population. But, as we saw above, there are always hierarchies enfolded within the hierarchy of the affluent. If we use the popular 'top 400' that were considered to be members of 'Society' during the Gilded Age, then the truly affluent represented 0.0006% of every man, woman and child in the US. And as the affluent grew far richer than historically imaginable, they spent more and more of their money on conspicuous consumption. While a number of artefacts and practices – from yachts, art and furniture to vacations and lavish parties – could illustrate the differential consumptive practices of dominant owners, I use the example of housing since, according to Beard, 'houses were the most visible emblems of wealth' (ibid.: 62).

Mansions of unprecedented size were erected across the United States by the titans of wealth and symbolised their power and ability to sustain what Veblen (2007) called massive 'pecuniary damage'. Referring to wealthy New Yorkers, Josephson noted the following:

> 'nature's noblemen' all joined in the frenzied contest of display and consumption. Mansions and chateaux of French, Gothic, Italian, barocco and Oriental style lined both sides of upper Fifth Avenue, while shingle and jigsaw villas of huge dimensions rose above the harbor of Newport. Railroad barons and mine-owners and oil magnates vied with each other in making town houses and country villas which were imitations of everything under the sun, and were filled with what-nots, old drapery, old armor, old Tudor chests and chairs, statuettes, bronzes, shells and porcelains. One would have a bedstead of carved oak and ebony, inlaid with gold, costing $200,000. Another would decorate his walls with enamel and gold at a cost of $65,000. And nearly all ransacked the art treasures of Europe, stripped medieval castles of their carvings and tapestries, ripped whole staircases and ceilings from their place of repose through the centuries to lay them anew amid settings of a synthetic age and a simulated feudal grandeur (Josephson 1934: 234).

What this passage suggests is not only that the newly affluent competed to display their wealth by building private dwellings of gigantic and opulent proportions, but they also desired to emulate (and in many cases outdo) the grand mansions and estates of a feudal Europe. Names of Gilded Age mansions abound: The Breakers, Rosecliff, Beechwood Mansion, Marble House, Isaac Bell House, The Elms, Belcourt Castle, Harbour Hill, Chateau-Sur-Mer, Glessner House and Ochre Court to name some of the most renowned. But none of these mansions compares with George Washington Vanderbilt II's Biltmore Estate in Asheville, North Carolina. G. W. Vanderbilt II inherited all of his wealth and accomplished precious little with his leisurely life other than commanding the labour of those who designed and built his home.

Completed in 1895, Biltmore House (on Biltmore Estate) is the largest private home in the United States at 178,926 square feet, built on 4 acres of land.[9] By way of comparison, consider that the average home in the US in 2010 was 2,392 square feet.[10] In other words, Biltmore is about 75 times the size of an average modern dwelling. But in its own time, it was actually 300 times larger than an ordinary dwelling (Zanny 2012). According to the Biltmore's website:

> The celebrated architect Richard Morris Hunt modelled the house on three châteaux built in 16th-century France. It would feature 4 acres of floor space, 250 rooms, 34 bedrooms, 43 bathrooms, and 65 fireplaces. The basement alone would house a swimming pool, gymnasium and changing rooms, bowling alley, servants' quarters, kitchens, and more.[11]

The grounds of the Biltmore Estate – originally 140,000 acres, now 'only' 8,000 – were landscaped by Frederick Law Olmsted of New York Central Park fame. The estate also featured its own village housing 750 of the 2,000 inhabitants employed on the grounds or in the house. What was the cost of such a display of pecuniary damage? Biltmore cost US$5 million in 1895, or, in 2012 prices, about US$116 million to US$119 million (Foreman and Stimson 1991: 270–303). Today, the estate is still privately owned but operates as a tourist destination with an onsite luxury hotel and winery. The descendants of Vanderbilt's private empire of wealth continue to draw an income from this ostentatious exhibition of differential power and consumption. While Biltmore could hardly compare with great palaces such as the Royal Palace of Madrid or Buckingham Palace, it is a stunning example of materialism, power and symbolism in the Gilded Age of capitalism and concentrated private wealth. If we ignore palaces and castles, Biltmore was not to be outdone until a fortune was handed to Mukesh Ambani – discussed in the next section.

## Differential consumption in the New Gilded Age

If the first Gilded Age was distinctly American, the New Gilded Age can be considered far more global. Historians may differ on an exact date for its emergence, but Freeland has made the credible suggestion that we are in a twin New Gilded Age where a handful of emerging economies such as Russia, India and China are still going through their first Gilded Age while established plutonomies such as the United States and Canada are experiencing a second and perhaps far grander wave (Freeland 2012: 20ff; for a direct focus on the American case, see Bartels 2008; Frank 2007). By the New Gilded Age we mean a period of escalating inequality in income, wealth and life chances across a range of political communities. Although the germ of this era may extend further back, I date this period from the mid-1980s, when global gross domestic product (GDP) accelerated due to:

1) cheap fossil fuel energy after the 1973 and 1979 price spikes; 2) the introduction of new technologies – due largely to Cold War public research and development that was subsequently capitalised by the private sector; 3) the liberalisation of trade and investment regimes, which facilitated the movement of capital and commodities; 4) the creation of a more fully global labour market, which enabled firms to depress hard-won wage gains and discipline and control their workers with greater ease; and 5) the massive accumulation of debt at national, business and personal levels.[12]

According to the World Bank, in the 25 years from 1960 to 1985, global GDP increased from US$1.4 trillion to US$12.5 trillion, or an increase of 793%. But in the 51-year period from 1960 to 2011, the rate of change increased by 4,900% as global GDP reached US$70 trillion.[13] Thus a series of class practices that strengthened the power of capital within a generally favourable energy regime spawned a historically unprecedented boom in the generation of income and wealth (Gill and Law 1988). Such practices also generated a period of growing inequality. Not only has the 1% (and often smaller proportions) in certain countries been appropriating an ever greater share of the national income, but the number of billionaires and millionaires has been steadily increasing, offering further evidence that income is accruing at the top of the wealth pyramid. For example, in 1987 *Forbes* recorded 140 billionaires in the world. The figure now stands at 1,226 billionaires worldwide with expectations that this number will grow in the years ahead;[14] indeed, Wealth-X – a wealth intelligence firm – estimates that the number of ultra-HNWIs will increase by 3.9% over the next five years (Wealth-X 2013: 11).[15] To recap, of the US$225 trillion in outstanding net financial wealth in 2013, US$46.2 trillion was owned by 12 million HNWIs from around the world. Put differently, 0.2% of the global population own 21% of the world's financial assets (Capgemini and Merrill Lynch 2011; McKinsey 2011).

However, if we leave the realm of income distribution and consider the distribution of household wealth, global inequality appears far worse. The first estimates on this measure of inequality noted that 'the top 10 per cent of adults own 85 per cent of global household wealth' while the bottom 50 per cent 'collectively owns barely 1 per cent of global wealth'. Moreover, the study revealed that 'the top 1 per cent own almost 40 times as much as the bottom 50 per cent', with a massive gap between those in the top decile and those in the lowest decile. According to the authors of the report, the top decile has 13,000 times more wealth than those at the very bottom of the wealth pyramid (Davies et al. 2006: 26).

In the available literature, most attempts to account for this massive private accumulation of wealth rely on a number of explanations. However, while rationalisations abound, there appears to be little consensus on the precise origins of this wealth boom, let alone a convincing ethical or philosophical justification for such obscene levels of accumulation and inequality. Dominant explanations include the following – either isolated or in combination: the levering of technological change, the deregulation of finance, globalisation, effort, hard work and luck, rewards for special knowledge or skills, liquidity events and the growth in hedge funds run by 'super-intelligent' human beings. These explanations are all quite common in popular accounts (Frank 2007; Freeland 2012; Taylor et al. 2009: 21ff). But, at a more general level, some commentators make the distinction between the 'self-made' affluent and dominant owners who inherited their fortune. To some extent, the latter category is viewed as less deserving than their newly minted affluent counterparts who are said to have made their fortunes without assistance of any kind – for what else can 'self-made' mean? The tendency to believe that individuals are the sole source of wealth is deeply hardwired into many societies. For example, *Forbes*' own account of billionaires notes the following:

> We do not include royal family members or dictators who derive their fortunes entirely as a result of their position of power, nor do we include royalty who, often with large families, control the riches in trust for their nation. Over the years *Forbes* has valued the fortunes of these wealthy despots, dictators and royals but have listed them separately as they do not truly reflect individual, entrepreneurial wealth that could be passed down to a younger generation or truly given away.[16]

A full assessment of this culturally convenient argument using the 'capital as power' framework and additional evidence is explored in Chapter 5.[17] I believe an evaluation of this hypothesis is one of the most crucial arguments political economy has to come to terms with if it is to critically challenge the social reproduction of extreme wealth and gross inequality.

But here we are concerned with differential consumption, so let us begin with a prescient observation. One of the main arguments in the popular literature advanced by Kempf (2008: 50), Frank (2007) and Freeland (2012), and recognised by Citigroup's plutonomy thesis, is that dominant owners have created a 'self-contained world unto their own' (Frank 2007: 3). Frank calls this virtual world Richistan. In this world, the affluent have 'their own health-care system (concierge doctors), travel network (NetJets, destination clubs), separate economy (double-digit income gains and double-digit inflation), language (Who's your household manager?)' and ability to purchase permanent residency or even citizenship in choice countries (ibid.: 3; Parmar 2013). We could add to this 'virtual world' their own clubs and associations (such as Metcircle Networking, with a net US$100 million membership cut-off, the Emperor's Club, the Yellowstone Club, and so on). The high financiers of Wall Street even have their own super-secret fraternity: Kappa Beta Phi. A soirée held by the fraternity was infiltrated by a writer from the *New York Times* who caught a glimpse into 'the psychology of the ultra-wealthy' during one night of festivities. After watching how leading members of the club forced new recruits to dress in drag and mock the 99%, the reporter came to the conclusion that 'the upper ranks of finance are composed of people who have completely divorced themselves from reality' (Roose 2014).

The 1% also have unique psychological concerns (sudden wealth syndrome, spoiled children), built environments (mansions, private islands, sea-steading), vehicles (yachts, private submarines, Gulfstream jets, Aston Martin One-77s), security arrangements (panic rooms, bodyguards, billionaire super-security), financial and consumer advice (*How to Spend it*, *The Robb Report*, *Worth*), financial services (elite hedge funds, private bankers), restaurants (Masa, Aragawa, Ithaa) and dating services (MillionaireMatch, Sugardaddie). They also enjoy an entire buffet of luxury goods such as Franck Muller watches (the Franck Muller Aeternitas Mega 4™ Grande Sonnerie Westminster Carillon – the most expensive watch in the world sold – for US$2.7 million in 2009), pens such as the Aurora Diamante (price tag: US$1,470,600 – only one available per year) and the Algonquin Hotel's US$10,000 'Martini on the Rock', which features a diamond at the bottom of the glass. If you are wondering how the ultra-rich of the ultra-rich pay for such high-price items, you likely will not be surprised to learn that they have their own exclusive credit card. The Palladium Card, issued by JPMorgan, has no spending limit. The card is offered to their private banking clientele with US$25 million or more invested with the bank. The card itself is worth about US$1,000 as it is minted from palladium and 23 carat gold. The card also has a number of additional benefits such as a concierge service and access to private airport lounges and special events. Little wonder this unlimited charge card has been dubbed 'the credit card for the 1 percent of the 1 percent' (Cohan 2012).

According to Frank's study, within this world apart there is an ongoing consumptive arms race, with those lower on the Richistani rungs doing their best to keep up with their centamillionaire and billionaire counterparts – a competition for display and status that has seen these lower HNWIs take on ever larger mountains of debt (ibid.: 6–13). As previously mentioned, in Richistan the merely affluent do not try to keep up with the Joneses but with the Slims and Gateses of the world. One guide to such an endeavour is the CLEWI.

The Cost of Living Extremely Well Index or CLEWI was started in 1976 by *Forbes*. The index tracks 40 goods and services that are generally reserved for the ultra-wealthy. Not surprisingly, the index has been increasing in value since its inception.[18] While I will not reproduce the list of goods and services in its entirety here, a small sample of the index reveals what follows in Table 4.1.

The cheapest item on the full list is a subscription to *Forbes* at US$60, while the most expensive item listed is the Sikorsky helicopter at US$15.5 million. But while these items give us an idea of the luxury goods and services the affluent consume, many of the items listed are only benchmarks, while other goods and

TABLE 4.1  Selected items on the Cost of Living Extremely Well Index, 2012

| Item | Cost in 2012 ($) | Price change from 2011 (%) |
|---|---|---|
| Coat (natural Russian sable) | 265,000 | 10 |
| Facelift | 18,500 | 0 |
| Motor yacht (Hatteras 80 MY) | 5,125,000 | -3 |
| Washington Hospital Center (1 day) | 2,716 | 6 |
| Plane (Learjet 40XR) | 10,838,000 | 2 |
| Helicopter (Sikorsky S-76D) | 15,500,000 | 5 |
| Caviar (Tsar Imperial, 1 kg) | 13,600 | 0 |

*Source*: www.forbes.com/sites/scottdecarlo/2012/09/19/cost-of-living-extremely-well-index-our-annual-consumer-price-index-billionaire-style/.

services the mega-rich consume are not listed. As an example, I will consider the arms race in yachts, along with the boom in private submarine sales.

Without a doubt, the Hatteras 80 MY is a luxury yacht, boasting an overall length of 79 feet, 10 inches. But while the yacht may look impressive to most, it does not come close to the global fleet of mega-yachts. Writing in *Forbes* magazine, the editor of *Boat International* spelled out the current trend:

> When we at 'Boat International' first produced our Register, back in 1990, superyachting was still in relative infancy. Indeed, to get on the Top 100 list in 1990, your yacht needed to be just 147 feet in length (44.8 metres). Nowadays, your yacht would have to measure at least 240 feet in length (73 metres). That entry point is set to rise again in 2013, with 12 new yachts due to be delivered in the coming months, all of which will make the updated Top 100 list, knocking out a dozen smaller ones, and raising the bar to 246 feet (75 metres) (Thomas 2012).

How long the race to build the world's largest private yacht will go on is anyone's guess. When I first started writing this book, the world's largest super-yacht was the *Eclipse* at 533 feet and 2 inches long. It is only slightly bigger than the yacht called *Dubai*, measured at 531 feet, 6 inches and owned by Sheik Mohammed bin Rashid al-Maktoum – the head of the 'royal' family of Dubai and prime minister and vice president of the United Arab Emirates. *Eclipse* is owned by Russian oligarch Roman Abramovich and features two pools, a submarine, 18 luxury suites for up to 36 guests, three helipads, three launch boats, a working crew of 92, armour plating and bullet-proof glass. If this is not enough, the yacht also features a German-crafted missile defence system. And this is not Abramovich's only yacht; he owns four others.[19]

But just as *Eclipse* was being passed to its proprietor, the owner of *Dubai* announced that he would retrofit his yacht to regain the title of world's largest private yacht. The megalomaniac project was in vain. In April 2013, a 590-foot yacht called *Azzam* made its way out of its Hamburg port and into the world record book. The cost? US$605 million for the yacht and about US$60 million a year to staff and maintain the vessel.[20] The owner is the president of the United Arab Emirates, Khalifa bin Zayed bin Sultan Al Nahyan. And while not everyone can afford to command the construction of the planet's largest yacht, the number of yachts currently under construction gives us a considerable indication of how the newly rich are spending their fortunes.[21] Since 2006, 6,295 yachts have been purchased with 692 ordered for construction in 2013. The yachts range in size from 80 feet to 250 feet and above; the total length of all the yachts under construction in 2013 was 25.8 kilometres.[22] This figure does not include the Australian mining multimillionaire Clive Palmer's plan to build a replica of the *Titanic* (Harris 2013). So even in the midst of the global financial crisis and the age of austerity politics, the conspicuous consumption of yachts continues. And there are some early signs that it is moving on to private luxury submarines.

Currently, there are an estimated 100 private submarines cruising the world's vast oceans. They range in size, price and capability, with the cheapest model starting at US$1.7 million. A string of companies caters to their wealthy clients' demands: Hawkes Ocean Technologies, SEAmagine, Triton Submarines and US Submarines among others. The most elaborate 'Learjet of the sea' is currently the Phoenix 1000 proposed by US Submarines. It was commissioned by a wealthy client who later had to cancel the order. According to the company, the vessel 'would constitute the single largest private undersea vehicle ever built, and arguably, one of the most significant personal transportation devices of the century'. It boasts four floors and 470 square metres of interior space. The price tag: an estimated US$78 million. The marketers at US Submarines know their clientele:

> With 2300 megayachts operational around the world, some
> costing in excess of $150 million, the stakes in the game of
> one upmanship are rising. Some yacht owners like the idea of
> having a larger and more unique toy.[23]

Back on land, differential consumption continues in housing. We have already encountered the largest private residence built during the first Gilded Age: Biltmore House. Today, that record belongs to Mukesh Ambani, one of two brothers who inherited their father's business empire in textiles, petrochemicals and oil and gas. According to *Forbes*, as of 2014 there are 65 billionaires in India and Ambani is the wealthiest of them all.[24] With a population of 1.24 billion, this means that Indian billionaires represent a minuscule 0.000005% of a nation where 400,248,000, or 32.7% of the population, subsist on US$1.25 a day or less.[25] Still, Ambani saw fit to commission the largest private residence in the world.

Called Antilia, after a mythical island in the Atlantic, Ambani's 27-storey residence towers above Mumbai. It has 400,000 square feet of living space, three helipads, nine high-speed elevators, underground parking for 168 cars, a gym, swimming pool, movie theatre, spa, dance studio, balconies with gardens, an unknown number of guest rooms, a ballroom, snack bar and one entire floor dedicated to servicing Ambani's private fleet of luxury cars. Ambani's six-member family (including his mother) will inhabit the top six floors of the building. Antilia is staffed by an estimated 600 people catering to the needs of the family and their guests. At an estimated US$1 billion to US$2 billion, it is not only the world's largest private residence, but also its most expensive. The residence is also built in a country where the average Indian urban dweller occupies 504 square feet of space and 33% live in less space than US prisoners (Thakur 2008). In other words, Ambani's home has 794 times more living space than the average Indian dwelling. But then again, Ambani is not status-seeking with the average Indian but with the *global* billionaire class of which he is a part.

There are, of course, countless other examples of conspicuous consumption as dominant owners make ever greater returns on the income-generating assets they own. However brief, this sketch suggests that dominant owners aim to consume differentially and that these displays of consumption are primarily aimed at intraclass emulation and status-seeking. Having highlighted this secondary drive as equally important to the symbolic accumulation of money, I now move to the second part of my argument as first identified by Kempf – the argument that the consumptive practices of dominant owners are helping to lock global society into an unsustainable and indefensible quest for perpetual economic growth. This project not only alleviates calls for global redistribution but also threatens populations with environmental collapse.

### 'The rich are destroying the Earth'

From the effects of global warming to the recorded loss of biodiversity, the evidence of populations coming under stress or devastation due to unsustainable anthropocentric practices continues to mount (Barry 2012; Dauvergne 2008; Kolbert 2014; Newell 2012). Rather than retrace what other scholars have already demonstrated, this work sides with Kempf's assessment that 'the planet's ecological situation is worsening' and that 'we are entering a time of lasting crisis and possible catastrophe' (Kempf 2008: xvi).[26] But who is responsible for the acceleration of disaster? Kempf argues that the rich – what this book calls dominant owners – are destroying the Earth. He calls them the 'essential factor' in the biospheric crisis because they benefit from current social property relations and 'oppose the radical changes that we would have to conduct to prevent the aggravation' of the environmental situation (ibid.: 70). Kempf argues that this situation manifests itself directly and indirectly: directly since dominant owners control and benefit from the system of differential accumulation and indirectly in that their intraclass status-seeking urges others to emulate their insatiable and too often wasteful consumptive practices (ibid.: 70). Their mantra of economic growth is one of the ways in which the dominant owners are shielded from having to face up to the consequences of their actions and from having to confront a radical politics of rethinking how the global political economy might work towards a more fair and equitable distribution of resources and life chances:

> To escape any re-evaluation, the oligarchy keeps repeating the dominant ideology according to which the solution to the social crisis is production growth. That is supposedly the sole means of fighting poverty and unemployment. Growth would allow the overall level of wealth to rise and consequently improve the lot of the poor without – and this part is never spelled out – any need to modify the distribution of wealth (ibid.: 70).

The main problem with the growth hypothesis identified here is that it deflects our attention away from a local and global conversation about needed social and economic change. Other problems with the growth hypothesis include: 1) there is little evidence that beyond a certain point economic growth contributes to human happiness (Jackson 2009: 30ff); 2) economic growth has been tightly correlated with non-renewable fossil fuel consumption (Tverberg 2011); and 3) there are physical limits to many of the world's resources and evidence is mounting that we are reaching those limits (Heinberg 2007). As the polymath Kenneth Boulding asserted: 'anyone who believes that exponential growth can go on forever is either a madman or an economist' (United States Congress 1973: 248). Yet the political pursuit of facilitating investment climates in an effort to stimulate economic growth continues. As Clive Hamilton observed:

> In the thrall of the growth fetish, all the major political parties ... have made themselves captives of the national accounts. The parties may differ on social policy, but there is unchallengeable consensus that the overriding objective of

government must be the growth of the economy. The parties fighting elections each promise to manage the economy better, so that economic growth will be higher. The answer to almost every problem is 'more economic growth' (Hamilton 2004: 2).

Hamilton and Kempf argue that if the public and their governments are not willing to challenge this defensive armour of dominant owners, and if these same owners are unwilling to change their consumption habits or join a conversation about needed social change, then environmental collapse and accelerating inequality are virtually assured. From an ethical point of view that values human and natural life, this path appears indefensible, but it is one being forged daily by the 1% and the dominant capital they own.

A further problem with chasing GDP is that it is an *adding up* of all the price transactions in the economy. This means that things that are actually harmful to society boost GDP. For example, if a company pollutes a lake and has to spend money cleaning up their mess, this will be added to GDP rather than subtracted as being socially harmful. Similarly, if someone were to run around a neighbourhood smashing car windows, all the repairs would add to GDP. Every gun, tank and nuclear warhead adds to GDP. As the reader can tell, this is a terribly inaccurate indicator for assessing national or societal well-being. The point was not lost on Robert F. Kennedy:

> Too much and too long, we seem to have surrendered community excellence and community values in the mere accumulation of material things. Our gross national product ... if we should judge America by that – counts air pollution and cigarette advertising, and ambulances to clear our

highways of carnage. It counts special locks for our doors and the jails for those who break them. It counts the destruction of our redwoods and the loss of our natural wonder in chaotic sprawl. It counts napalm and the cost of a nuclear warhead, and armored cars for police who fight riots in our streets. It counts Whitman's rifle and Speck's knife, and the television programs which glorify violence in order to sell toys to our children.

Yet the gross national product does not allow for the health of our children, the quality of their education, or the joy of their play. It does not include the beauty of our poetry or the strength of our marriages; the intelligence of our public debate or the integrity of our public officials. It measures neither our wit nor our courage; neither our wisdom nor our learning; neither our compassion nor our devotion to our country; it measures everything, in short, except that which makes life worthwhile. And it tells us everything about America except why we are proud that we are Americans (cited in Fioramonti 2013: 81).

# 5 | SOCIETY VERSUS THE SUPERMAN THEORY OF WEALTH

The value or worth of a man is, as of all other things, his price; that is to say, so much as would be given for the use of his power, and therefore is not absolute, but a thing dependent on the need and judgment of another. (Thomas Hobbes 1651: 54–5)

... men have agreed to a disproportionate and unequal possession of the earth. (John Locke 2005: 27)

I am convinced there is only one way to eliminate these grave evils, namely through the establishment of a socialist economy, accompanied by an educational system which would be oriented toward social goals. In such an economy, the means of production are owned by society itself and are utilized in a planned fashion. (Albert Einstein 2009)

We have already provided a sketch of some of the views on the origin of social surplus – the master question of political economy. In this chapter, I will consider the main justifications for its unequal distribution. In contrast with Hobbes' view of sovereign ownership, I begin by considering Locke's interpretation of ownership and his justification for an unlimited accumulation of property in the form of money. As we shall uncover, it is Locke's ideas that underpin what I call the superman theory of wealth. This is the view that dominant owners have become incredibly wealthy because of their individual, superhuman talents. Given the scale of their wealth today, these talents, whether the result of DNA or acquired through learning, must far surpass those of non-dominant owners and our human ancestors to justify their pecuniary fortunes.

## From Hobbes to Locke's theory of ownership

In trying to convince English subjects of the need for an absolute sovereign, Hobbes invited them to imagine a condition before civil government. He suggested that the pre-state condition was one of general war: a never-ending battle of each against all. In this existential condition, no one's life was safe and all were equally subject to the potential terror of others. Let us push to one side the fact that Hobbes is not talking about a real war such as the Norman Conquest, but an imaginary war he conjures up for the sake of his argument. How does he derive this fictional war? Hobbes makes the claim that war is possible only because individuals are more or less equal in power, ability and talent. Of course, Hobbes did admit that there were differences between subjects, but these were subtle and largely inconsequential. To demonstrate the equality of humans (or, for Hobbes, men), he says that if men really were radically unequal then one of two situations would take place. First, the strongest would simply subjugate the weak and either enslave them or decimate them. Second, the weak would realise that they were too feeble to fight and would simply surrender to the strong. So, in the thinking of Hobbes, 'differences lead to peace' and equality to constant war (Foucault 2003: 91). Since Hobbes ultimately wanted peace, this is the reason why he argued for a monarch with absolute *differential* power over his subjects. This overarching power, reasoned Hobbes, would ensure the security of commercial transactions and the lives of men.

At first glance, the position taken by Hobbes seems strange.

Why start with the natural equality of subjects when Hobbes is clearly living in a time of widespread inequality in the distinction of class, rank and privilege? The answer has to be the context in which Hobbes was writing: the tumultuous times of the English Civil War (1642–51) and the republican Commonwealth. During the tumult, radically democratic positions were advanced about the natural rights of Englishmen that challenged the traditional view of royal society and princely order. These more radical ideas came to the fore in pamphlet after pamphlet by the Levellers and the Diggers, among other recalcitrant groups in society.[1] Not only did the people have the right to resist illegitimate forms of power, men also had the right to participate in the political community as enfranchised citizens – a radical idea for the times.[2] These men held that rights were not something granted to them by the king of the realm but originated in the very fact that they were born in England. Ellen Meiksins Wood illustrates how the notion of popular, rather than royal, sovereignty challenged English political thought:

> these people would exert their 'popular sovereignty' not just by reclaiming their rights in tyrannical emergencies but regularly and repeatedly, in the normal exercise of their everyday political rights as citizens. After this theoretical innovation, and after the historic events that brought it into being, English political theory was never the same again. Theorists of a far less radical disposition, including even a defender of royal absolutism like Hobbes, felt obliged to meet the radical argument on its own ground, even to show that their preferred, and less democratic, forms of government met this new test of political legitimacy (Wood 2012: 240).

Ideas of rights and equality had come into conflict with the existing distribution of political power and property in England, and, as Wood suggests, once in circulation, they were difficult to remove from the body politic. A new set of empowering, if radical, ideas had entered the human consciousness: the right to have a say in one's own governance, the right to rebel against illegitimate authority and, for the Diggers above all, the right to resist wage labour and work in cooperation with others for common benefit. Thus political economists and moral philosophers in support of the emerging capitalist mode of power would have to wrestle with, and indeed justify, inequality amidst these new and challenging ideas. The fact that history or God has made it so was no longer acceptable to an increasingly literate population undergoing profound changes in their daily lives. The problem became particularly acute with a greater social surplus to distribute and growing recognition that there was a perpetual shortage of money in the economy (Wennerlind 2011). Into the fray stepped John Locke.

Before Locke's intervention, what little political philosophy existed understood property as the grant of a sovereign. In other words, private individuals held property at the pleasure of the monarch and this pleasure could always be rescinded. In Locke's *Two Treatises of Government* we get an altogether different interpretation: one that serves to justify not only the existing inequality of property, but also the right of the few to accumulate without limit. Locke was an Oxford-educated philosopher and physician in the employ of Anthony Ashley Cooper, First Earl of Shaftesbury (1621–83), an English politician and wealthy landowner through inheritance. Shaftesbury also sought to profit from English colonialism – a position that Locke defended (Arneil 1994; 1996; Jahn 2013: 45ff; Wood and Wood 1997: 116ff).[3]

Locke begins his section on property by relying on the Chris-

SOCIETY VERSUS WEALTH | **169**

tian Bible. He agrees that in the beginning God gave the Earth to all men as a commons. If this is so, reasons Locke, how do we arrive at private property? Yet answering this question is not his only goal. If we pay close attention, what Locke wants to demonstrate is 'how men might come to have a property in *several parts* of that which God gave to mankind in common, and that *without any express compact of all the commoners*' (Locke 2005: 18, section 25, my emphasis). Thus there are two things of importance that Locke has to convince us of: 1) a man can own several different types of property; and 2) he can come to own that property without the express consent of everyone. The burden of his argument is a large one. How does Locke make his case?

Locke's first move is to say that everyone has a property in their own capacity to labour, and while nature seems to provide an abundance of useful products for all, it is only by mixing labour with the products of nature that a man may claim a portion of this abundance as his own to the exclusion of all others. The first restriction, however, is that taking away from the commons cannot be done unless there are sufficient provisions for others. Locke imagines a man picking apples and acorns in the forest and asks whether we would find it reasonable for this man to go around asking everyone for consent for their appropriation, or whether just the fact of his taking possession of the apples and acorns through labour is enough. Put differently, from this abstract example, Locke wants to show that it would be absurd to ask everyone for consent for the mere reason that this would be incredibly inconvenient. He then goes on to say, in one of his most telling passages, which reveals his and Shaftesbury's political interests:

And the taking of this or that part, does not depend on the

express consent of all the commoners. Thus the grass my horse has bit; *the turfs my servant has cut*; and the ore I have digged in any place, where I have a right to them in common with others, become my property, without the assignation or consent of any body. The *labour that was mine*, removing them out of that common state they were in, hath fixed my property in them (ibid.: 19, section 28, my emphasis).

Astute readers will wonder how we go from a situation where someone in the forest is picking apples and acorns to one where all of a sudden a servant appears on the scene. Locke equates the forest-gathering scenario (personal labour picking apples and acorns) with the labour of a servant (not the direct labour of the person claiming property or ownership). But this is precisely the move Locke has to make if he wants to justify individual private property and exclusive ownership. The labour of the servant has to be the private property of the servant's master – no further explanation is required as to how the servant arrived on the historical scene.

Locke then moves on to say that people may object to this appropriation from the commons as private property because what is to stop someone from gaining possession of as much as he or she can? Locke's answer is that God did not give the Earth to man to let portions of it spoil or go to waste. This is Locke's second limitation on ownership: one cannot appropriate so much of the commons that portions of it are allowed to spoil. This sounds reasonable enough, but Locke goes even further in his case for exclusive private property. He takes us out of the forest and on to a farm. His argument is simple: improving the land through cultivation is a God-bound duty, and as long as there is enough land for others to cultivate, the improver of land has a right to claim exclusive rights over the acreage he has worked. Improving and cultivating land that was previously lying waste is not only the path to property ownership but actually adds to society, since the land yields more products than wasteland. What is important to note is that the products of the land are not for direct consumption but produced for exchange value or profit. Locke is very clear about this when he discusses 'wasteland' in America.

So, after demonstrating that labour is the real source of value in improving the land, Locke has to explain how it can be that some own much more than others, since, while there may be differences in talent and skill among men, they would hardly be so drastic as to justify massive disparities in property ownership. It turns out that money is the great decider:

> And as different degrees of industry were apt to give men possessions in different proportions, so this invention of money gave them the opportunity to continue and enlarge them ... Where there is not some thing, both lasting and scarce, and so valuable to be hoarded up, there men will not be apt to enlarge their possessions of land (ibid.: 26, section 48).

In the same section, Locke goes as far as to say that enclosing the land would be senseless without the incentive to make money – and, by extension, to augment one's power. So how does money lead to an increase in possessions or greater wealth or property? Locke's answer is that selling surplus goods on the market for money does not allow them to spoil. For example, I may sell surplus potatoes I cannot eat and in exchange receive some silver coins. The transaction satisfies Locke's own limitation on property because it does not lead to spoilage: my customer can eat my potatoes that I could not eat and I have silver coins that I can then use to buy something I need. As this continues, some cultivators will amass more and more coins and therefore more power to command labour and resources, leading to the accumulation of more money. For Locke, this disparity is justified because by using money, people have tacitly consented to the resulting distribution of property. And there we have it all wrapped up in a tight bow: ownership confers the right to accumulate money without limit.

Of course, this was all philosophical fantasy detached from the actual processes of private property appropriation and the accumulation of money.[4] But it did not stop it from being popular among the powerful and propertied. Until Rousseau's critique of property and Bentham's response that influenced mainstream economics, Locke's theory of property supported the rise of what Macpherson called 'possessive individualism' (Macpherson 1978: 200). This extreme form of individualism laid the groundwork for what I have called the superman theory of wealth: the radically antisocial belief that wealth is *the sole result* of individual efforts and talents – biological or acquired.

### Rousseau, Bentham and mainstream economics

For Locke, the property that a person had in their own personal labour gave them the natural right to appropriate the products of the Earth as private property. As long as money is around, people have the right to accumulate it without limit. Today, modern economists celebrate private property as one of the key explanatory variables for the rise of the West and its unequal wealth. They forget that, starting from Locke's premise, alternative interpretations are available.

Like Locke, Jean-Jacques Rousseau (1712–78) also started from a natural rights tradition but demonstrated the exact opposite conclusion: the right to accumulate without limit sanctified by Locke's theory led to a situation whereby the majority of men were without property or the chance of ever acquiring any. In such a situation, Locke's natural right to property was contravened for the majority:

> What a strange and fatal condition – where accumulated riches facilitate still greater riches, but where men with none can acquire none; where the good man knows no way out of his misery; where the most roguish are the most honored and where virtue must be renounced for men to remain honest (Rousseau quoted in Wood 2012: 192).

In other words, Lockean natural rights and the right to accumulate without limit led to a property-owning minority and a property-less majority. Rousseau also condemned the practice of working for others for wages and argued that 'no one should be able to appropriate the labor of others or be forced to alienate his own' (ibid.: 209). He imagined a society where no one was poor enough to have to rent their labour to someone else and no one was rich enough to purchase the labour power of others (Macpherson 1978: 29ff). For Rousseau, property was power, and thus those without property had no power. At any rate, Rousseau, like the Diggers, abhorred wage labour and understood government as an organised force protecting the propertied against the struggling property-less. By starting from the premise of natural rights, Rousseau's analysis exploded Locke's justification for radically unequal property relations. To safeguard unequal property, a new justification would have to be found. Into this fray stepped Jeremy Bentham.

Bentham (1748–1832) was a British philosopher born to wealth. As we have already discussed, other than philosophy his main business venture – which was never realised and for which he remained forever annoyed – was to capitalise the labour of poor workers in a prison built for a perfect economy of surveillance and discipline: the Panopticon.[5] But rather than dwell on his prison creation and his many writings, what concerns us here is how Bentham approached the concept of unequal property from a new perspective: that of utility. Like most political economists, other than perhaps Marx, Bentham addresses his thoughts to statesmen and particularly legislators. He begins by saying that the goal of every legislator should be the happiness of the society they are governing. Happiness, for Bentham, is a product of four additional but subordinate ends: subsistence, abundance, equality and security. However, of the four, security is chosen as the most important because Bentham believes, as do some moderns, that the other three goals cannot be accomplished without security. There are two things that are interesting about Bentham's justification for unequal property. The first is that he avoids the concept of natural rights and conceives of property as being created by the law. In this sense, there can be no appeal to a 'birthright' when it comes to acquiring property. The law is what the law is, and over time some have managed to accumulate vast fortunes while others have not. Second, Bentham claims that most people are confused when they associate property with material goods. Property for Bentham is an *expectation regarding the future*, and the future is primarily a matter of security. In part, this is an early recognition that property owners capitalise *expected* future income and that part of their asset prices is conditioned by an assessment of risk or insecurity.[6]

But Bentham was writing at a time when the non-propertied were continuing to question the inequality of wealth, power and property, and so he was forced to deal with the call for equality despite his fervent belief that some should be subordinate to others. He admits that equality of property might be a worthwhile goal in the long run; but, in the short term, taking away property from the rich to give to the non-propertied would pose a greater harm to the ultimate goal of achieving happiness: that of providing security. There is no question in Bentham that the existing distribution of property was to be protected by the law, so any calls for equality, in Bentham's formulation, must always yield to the security of existing property relationships. Bentham comforts himself by saying that the poor do not really know how the rich live, so they do not experience any torment or pain because they have nothing with which to compare their situation. This is unlike the rich, who can experience pain when their property is confiscated. They have experienced luxury and expect luxury, so redistribution would simply make them unhappy. In the end, Bentham asks himself whether equality and security must be perpetually at war. In perhaps the most mistaken prediction of all time, Bentham answered that to some degree they are incompatible but that, over time, property ownership would tend towards equality.

It was one thing to wax philosophical about uneven wealth. It was quite another to try to scientifically demonstrate why the 1% deserved their lot. The answer would have to wait almost a century after Bentham's writings. In the meantime, the law, custom and the force of arms were decisive enough to settle the question in an anti-democratic age of imperialism and aristocracy. However, in an era of burgeoning democracy, increasing literacy and radical ideas about exploitation and inequality, the science could no longer wait. The first step was taken by three men interested in political economy and keen to bring a scientific gaze to questions of the economy: William Stanley Jevons

(1835–82), Léon Walras (1834–1910) and Carl Menger (1840–1921). The work of these three men eviscerated politics and power from political economy. It is unclear what motivated these men to do this, other than a desire to create a more exact 'science' rooted in mathematics. Their ideas, bizarre and distant from reality, would go on to form the neoclassical school of economics – the dominant school to this day. Known to us as marginalists, these early dissident economists combined the abstract deductive method of David Ricardo and others with Bentham's utilitarian calculus of pain and pleasure. In doing so they managed to create formal mathematical models of an imagined 'economy' existing separate from history, society and politics (Milonakis and Fine 2009: 91ff). Their chief focus was on the isolated individual spending a limited amount of funds in what they assumed to be perfectly competitive markets, where demand for goods and services equilibrated with the supply of them.[7] In their thinking, they employed the concept of marginal utility: the surplus satisfaction or happiness a consumer gains from consuming one more item of the good or service – with the added assumption that satisfaction will decrease as more is consumed (negative utility).[8] The goal of individuals is to maximise their pleasure given these constraints: a limited amount of money and diminishing marginal utility.

But the real problem started to emerge when the topic shifted to the distribution of wealth. It was clear to all early political economists that labour and land added to the wealth of nations, less so capital goods (Nitzan and Bichler 2009: 68ff). Of course, ever since Adam Smith, the idea that workers received wages, landlords received rents and capitalists received profits was well known. But to stay at this level of assertion would simply not do. It would not do because it was akin to saying that income

is the result of where you are on the class hierarchy – your position – not your contribution, productivity or skill. Early answers
to the question of the origin of profit are summarised by Nitzan
and Bichler and worth quoting at length:

> Chief among these theories were the notions of 'abstinence'
> as argued by Nassau Senior (1872) and of 'waiting' as stipu-
> lated by Alfred Marshall (1920). According to these explana-
> tions, capitalists who invest their money are abstaining from
> current consumption and therefore have to be remunerated
> for the time they wait until their investment matures. By the
> end of the nineteenth century, though, the huge incomes
> of corporate magnates, such as Rockefeller, Morgan and
> Carnegie, enabled them to consume conspicuously regardless
> of how much they ploughed back as investment (ibid.: 70).[9]

But as Nitzan and Bichler suggest, even if these explanations
were all true, 'the *magnitude* of their remuneration' remains
unexplained (ibid.: 70). For example, why do some capitalists
make a 5% return, others 10% and still others 1,000%? Just as
Bentham sought to overturn Rousseau's radical appeal to natural
rights, so John Bates Clark (1847–1938) stepped into the fray to
provide a convincing theory for the origin of profit. This would
become the main way in which typical economists explained
and justified the distribution of wealth: the production function.

The first step was for Clark to posit that capital goods, like
land and labour, made a distinct contribution to production.
As Nitzan and Bichler point out, this assumes we can observe
and measure the distinct contribution made by each factor of
production in the production process (ibid.: 70–1): for example,
in the production of automobiles we can observe and measure 10
units of labour, 20 units of land and 70 units of capital. If their

marginal contributions to the economic output can be known, Clark argued, then – under a perfectly competitive market – income will be proportionate to the marginal contribution made by each factor of production. Since capital goods are assumed to be productive goods and are owned by capitalists, then profit is the return on their specific contribution to economic output. Clark was not ambivalent about his goals. In the opening of his 1899 *The Distribution of Wealth*, he states:

> it is the purpose of this work to show that the distribution of the income of society is controlled by a natural law, and that this law, if it worked without friction, would give to every agent of production the amount of wealth which that agent creates (Clark 1965: 1).

In other words, since income is proportional to contribution, everyone gets their just deserts. So if the 1% draws ever greater portions of income to themselves, this must be because, according to the production function, they are contributing that much more to economic output.

There are many problems with the production function but one critique overrides them all: even if you could observe and measure each factor's contribution to production, it could exist only in a fantasy land of perfect competition. For economists, perfect competition means that no agent in the market has the power to set prices. But with the development of the large-scale corporation and big government, perfect competition became a chimera, if it ever existed at all. Readers who prefer reality over fantasy will find this intuitive. But it is worth mentioning a recent study carried out by three systems theorists from Switzerland. The theorists studied the network of ownership among firms 'which hold at least 10% of shares in companies located in more

than one country' (Vitali et al. 2011). *Forbes* nicely summarises
what they found:

> They discovered that global corporate control has a distinct
> bow-tie shape, with a dominant core of 147 firms radiating out
> from the middle. Each of these 147 own interlocking stakes of
> one another and together they control 40% of the wealth in
> the network. A total of 737 control 80% of it all. The top 20 are
> at the bottom of the post. This is, say the paper's authors, the
> first map of the structure of global corporate control (Upbin
> 2011).

What this summary of the study suggests is that there is sound
evidence that we should not search for a convincing explanation for the massive disparity of wealth between the 1% and
the 99% in fantasies such as perfect competition. Since mainstream economics cannot convincingly explain the distribution
of wealth, we will have to look elsewhere. A good place to start
is by considering the difference between business and industry.

### Veblen's political economy

Thorstein Veblen (1857–1929) had the advantage of research-
ing and writing at a time when the economic landscape of
the United States was being transformed by coal, oil and the
modern corporation. It was also the period of what Josephson
(1934) called the Robber Barons – men who accumulated some
of the largest fortunes in history by seizing control of oil, steel,
the railways and the creation of credit. To understand this vast
accumulation of capitalised income streams, Veblen argued for
a focus on ownership and the corporation. But to do so required
a knowledge of historical development.

For Veblen, human creativity and production (as for Marx),

are only possible within a community. As he claimed: 'the isolated individual is not a productive agent' (Veblen 1998: 34). What this means is that 'the phenomena of human life' take place only within the life history of human communities. But what is of particular note about these 'generational' or 'life-reproducing' communities, according to Veblen, is the common stock of knowledge, habits, customs and ways of life concerning production and reproduction held informally by the great body of the people involved in the community. This is what Veblen identifies as the 'immaterial equipment' or 'intangible assets' of the community. For example, over time Finns have built up a knowledge base of poisonous mushrooms they should avoid gathering for food. This knowledge on how to avoid getting sick or dying from eating a poisonous mushroom was developed by trial and error over time and communicated through a common language as Finnish history unfolded. The present population has the benefit of this compound knowledge.

Veblen suggests that as society advances and this 'technological stock' of 'immaterial equipment' grows larger and larger, it becomes increasingly difficult to identify – let alone trace – the connection between any given 'technological detail' and any specific individual of the community. This is most certainly one of Veblen's most controversial propositions because, from this point of view, the institution of ownership cannot be rationalised. That is, the productive and even destructive power of the species is not simply the result of individual initiative, but of a working community with a 'technological heritage' passed on through various ways and means of knowledge transfer and communication. In other words, anyone who creates a new invention or stumbles upon a new discovery owes an unpayable debt to the communities of the past and the present. From this standpoint, it is virtually impossible to advocate monopoly or oligopolistic control over any discovery, let alone contend that the individual is the rightful producer, and thereby the owner of a tangible or intangible asset. Historically, however, this point of view has never attracted enough attention for it to become a revolutionary idea because those in power have a keen interest in denying its veracity.

Now, according to Veblen, as human industry expands along the lines of a more thorough technological development, property rights start to take on a definite form, while the principles of ownership gain consistency. It becomes possible, argued Veblen, through force and fraud, for individuals to engross or corner the 'immaterial assets' of the community through legal title. More to the point, there comes a time in human development when the 'ownership of industrial equipment' becomes an 'institution for cornering the community's intangible assets' (Veblen 1919: 35). Thus, for Veblen, ownership, while having a basis in the power relations of material reality, is nothing more than an outright seizure of a given portion, element or fraction of the 'immaterial equipment' of humanity and has virtually nothing to do with individual productivity per se. It is a legal fiction, sanctioned by law and backed by the coercive powers of the police and governmental apparatus. As Tigar and Levy remind us:

> legal change is the product of conflict between social classes
> seeking to turn the institutions of social control to their
> purposes, and to impose and maintain a specific system of
> social relations ... Any social system preserves and maintains
> itself against its enemies, and regulates its internal affairs,
> through power – and thus in the last analysis through force
> and the threat of force. Its formal rules rest on the premise

that if one does not obey the commands of the state – the institution with a public force specially appointed to enforce laws and commands – sooner or later one will be either forcibly constrained to obey or punished for not obeying. Any group that wants to make a radical change in a society – and the early businessmen wanted such change – first tests the existing institutions of power to see how far they will bend, and then attacks the institutions of state power directly, setting up its own apparatus of public force, with new laws and commands designed to secure its own interests (Tigar and Levy 1997: xiii, xv).

Businessmen took over from the old aristocracy they challenged and now use the legal apparatus, when it is convenient, as one of the key tools of their enrichment. As Mills noted in his study of elite power: 'The general facts, however, are clear: the very rich have used existing laws, they have circumvented and violated existing laws, and they have had laws created and enforced for their direct benefit' (Mills 2000: 99). With this in mind, we turn now to Veblen's conceptualisation of industry and business.

For Veblen, industry is a synonym for human potential or creativity. It is identified with the community, workmanship and human interdependence – it is the materialisation or the application of a heritage of human knowledge to nature. Broadly conceived, it represents a matrix of interdependent points, each reliant to a greater or lesser degree on other points or branches in the industrial system. As the industrial process matures, Veblen claimed, it results in a tendency towards standardisation, itself concomitant with the fact that mass industry requires planning and coordination. Without this uniformity of coordination and planned synchronisation of industrial activity, the industrial system could not develop with any degree of sophistication. In other words, a break or major factor difference in any one branch of the industrial process threatens the entire system, or a great part of it, with collapse. Imagine, for example, what chaos would be created if all dwellings of a nation had different electrical sockets. Left to its own devices, however, the industrial system, Veblen argued, would be extremely productive and has the capacity to flood the world market with a diversity of goods and services. The livelihood of the community, then, is best served by an uninterrupted, planned and balanced functioning of the industrial process.

The business enterprise or modern corporation, however, superintends and sabotages industry. While the industrial process has material and structural priority, it is not in the ascendancy. Business enterprise, with its motives, methods and aims, has come to drive the industrial process in pursuit of ever-expanding pecuniary gains – gains determined primarily by the expected or future earning capacity of each individual firm. The businessmen in control of each individual firm have this goal in common, although they find themselves in competition for market share. The competition for market share and profits, combined with the growing complexity and interconnectedness of the industrial system, forces each business enterprise to seek out differential advantages. For Veblen, this process manifests itself chiefly through the strategic control of industry. Thus, it is not that firms produce for the sake of production, which would be in the interests of the community, but rather they do so for the sake of profit. The products of material goods and services are supplied to the community only insofar as the businessman can calculate the saleability of his product and realise a reasonable rate of profit. As Veblen put it:

By virtue of this legal right of sabotage which inheres as a natural right in the ownership of industrially useful things, the owners are able to dictate satisfactory terms; so that they come in for the usufruct of the community's industrial knowledge and practice, with such deductions as are necessary to enforce their terms and such concessions as will induce the underlying population to go on with the work. Without the power of discretionary idleness, without the right to keep the work out of the hands of the workmen and the product out of the market, investment and business enterprise would cease. This is the larger meaning of the Security of Property (Veblen 1923: 67).

Sabotage is a requisite of business and the chief way in which dominant owners accumulate money. Indeed, it can be shown that many business actions have actively harmed society in their drive to accumulate more money: the slave trade, the arms industry, pollution and global climate change are all evidence. One of the reasons why this is so is that capitalist societies – whatever their cultural differences – do not produce for livelihood but for profit, and profit is limited by the ability of people to purchase the goods and services produced: by their income and their access to credit. So while we may have the capacity and potential as a species to provide clean water to everyone, enjoy nutritious food, increase leisure time, improve public transport networks, and ensure healthcare and life insurance for all, as well as transition away from fossil fuels, corporations and much of our political leadership are all directed towards enriching the few. With our examination of Veblen's ideas complete, we can now turn to how modern heterodox economists have conceptualised the growing disparity between the rich and the rest of us.

**Unjust deserts**

One book that will surely be greeted as kryptonite by the 1% is *Unjust Deserts* by Alperovitz and Daly (2008).[10] Alperovitz and Daly canvass the growing body of literature that purports to demonstrate precisely what Veblen discussed at the turn of the century: that an isolated individual is not a productive unit and that the creation of wealth and its current magnitude are largely due to a past store of accumulated *social* knowledge that has grown at an increasing rate. What they miss is that this explosion in social knowledge, or what Joel Mokyr calls the 'industrial enlightenment', would have likely been impossible without the surplus energy provided by abundant and affordable fossil fuels. The authors marshal considerable evidence to advance their conservative argument that the top wealth-holders do not truly deserve their wealth. Conservatives or politicians on the right wing of the political spectrum are typically the first to cry out that those at the bottom of the social hierarchy do not really 'deserve' public hand-outs, and in many cases they do their best to frustrate or stymie programmes aimed at helping the less fortunate. So if it can be demonstrated that the rich do not really deserve their fortunes and indeed have taken a disproportionate share of society's wealth, then it follows that something must be done to right this wrong. What that something is is up for debate, but let us reflect on the evidence.

In order to consider the unequal distribution of wealth and income, Alperovitz and Daly survey a great deal of literature on the sources of wealth creation. I summarise only some of their key points here since their study should be read in its entirety. The question they begin with is this: could it really be that individuals – by themselves – are the primary source of wealth? Their answer is an emphatic no and they support this claim in a number of ways. First, while our societies have a tendency to reward those who come up with inventions first – typically by being first to file a patent – history demonstrates that any scientific community tends to be working with the same knowledge base. What this means is that certain discoveries would be arrived at regardless of an individual 'genius'. The historical record is replete with examples of people who arrived at the same discovery or scientific conclusion at roughly the same time. Hence, when asked who 'invented' the telephone, most would answer Alexander Graham Bell, but he just happened to be first to file for a patent (and for a non-workable phone). He also had very good lawyers to fend off other potential claimants. Five years before he became the legal 'inventor' of the telephone, Antonio Meucci had designed such a device, but, due to lack of money, he could not file the full patent. There is also evidence to suggest that Meucci's designs were later stolen (ibid.: 59–60).

Second, those who come up with discoveries are completely dependent on the accumulated knowledge of the past. Alperovitz and Daly use Newton to make their point:

> If Newton, in his lifetime, had to learn everything humanity had learned from the time of the caveman to the late seventeenth century – if he had no knowledge inheritance whatsoever to work with – he could not have contributed much more than an insightful caveman could in his lifetime (ibid.: 144).

And we have become better and better at storing ever more knowledge outside our brain (in computers, for example). Third, those in a position to discover or invent new goods or services have a positionality in a social system that supports their endeavours. If inventors were worried about obtaining food, clothes and shelter, there would be considerably less time to focus on scientific discoveries. But because there is a social structure where other people work producing food, clothes and shelter, among other things, the division of labour can be further extended by people not engaged in these activities. Moreover, Alperovitz and Daly point to the vital role public spending has had on successive discoveries. The internet is perhaps the most prominent example but there are countless others, such as public education, pharmaceuticals and computers. This public or social spending has fed into the private fortunes of the 1%. Last, the authors use the work of Nobel laureate Robert Solow, who focused on productivity growth in the United States. After crunching the numbers, what he found was that 88% of the increase in productivity growth from 1909 to 1949 was not due to added inputs of capital or labour but to what is broadly understood as 'technical change' (ibid.: 25–6). In sum, there is mounting evidence to suggest that wealth is socially created but its distribution has been privately appropriated by the few.

Two other thought experiments can demonstrate the point. First, if individuals were the crucial factor in wealth generation, then one might assume that the death of the wealthy would significantly wound the capitalisation of the firms they own, run or control. Take, for example, the revered Steve Jobs. When he died, Apple shares were worth US$422 in October of 2011. Rather than plummet in value, shares actually appreciated to a high of US$691.28 in September 2012. We can also consider Sam Walton, the founder of Walmart and Sam's Club. Walton passed away in April 1992, when Walmart's share price was US$12.93. Rather than nose-diving upon his death, Walmart's capitalisation has exploded. In November 2013, shares traded at their highest – US$81.37 – a 529% increase in monetary value in just over 20 years.

If the individual superhuman theory of wealth is correct, then it would appear that the deaths of Sam Walton and Steve Jobs were actually beneficial to the bottom line of their companies. Clearly, wealth generation has little to do with one particular individual.

A second example is to imagine which billionaires would still be billionaires if they were stripped of their ownership of income-generating assets. As Mills suggested:

> If we took the one hundred most powerful men in America, the one hundred wealthiest, and the one hundred most celebrated away from the institutional positions they now occupy, away from their resources of men and women and money, away from the media of mass communication that are now focused upon them – then they would be powerless and poor and uncelebrated (Mills 2000: 10).

Many of the very rich are loath to admit it, but there are some who recognise that living in a society of immense wealth and talent along with the past practices of their ancestors, such as colonialism and slavery, have contributed significantly to their pool of wealth. For example, Katrina Browne traced her family's wealth back to the transatlantic slave trade. Her ancestors constituted one of the largest slave-trading families in history and she argues that she currently benefits from that original accumulation of wealth.[11] Anyone who still wants to believe in the superhuman theory of wealth should also consider the testimonials compiled to the contrary by United for a Fair Economy (Collins et al. 2004).

## The distribution of wealth and capital as power

Alperovitz and Daly have provided a great service to the growing community of people concerned with mounting inequality by synthesising the economic literature on the sources of wealth.

Their chief shortcomings, other than the failure to see the connection between growth and surplus carbon energy, are twofold: 1) ownership and power are largely in the background of their presentation; and 2) economic growth and the ways in which it has taken place are assumed to be unproblematic. Our view, following Nitzan and Bichler, but also recognising an ecological dimension, is different.

First, from the perspective of capital as power, the distribution of income and wealth is wholly and fully a matter of institutionalised power rooted in ownership. Dominant owners are not rich because of special talents or superhuman traits but because they own income-generating assets that do not come from their labour. They capitalise expected future profits and the magnitude of their earnings relates not to productivity, as we saw in Chapter 2, but to a corporation's power, alongside that of various government bodies, to shape and reshape the terrain of social reproduction *writ large*. Briefly, by social reproduction we mean the concrete ways in which any society produces, consumes and reproduces its life and lifestyles.

Second, production for profit rather than for livelihood (and for the livelihood of future generations) is far more worrying and contradictory than Alperovitz and Daly countenance. At a time of immense wealth for some, rapid technological change and promises of a better future for those excluded from the present benefits, a refusal to accept that the path we are on is unsustainable is somewhat understandable. Some, indeed, are doing very well, even if they are not dominant owners. But the evidence is mounting that the capitalist mode of power is ruining the very biosphere we all depend upon for a dignified and fulfilled life – not to mention the lives of future generations. McMurtry (1999) calls this the 'cancer stage of capitalism'.

Perhaps the most worrisome thing about this is that it is not that the science isn't forthcoming or available. We know about global climate change. We know about the acidification of our oceans. We know about pollution in our waterways and air. We know that our agriculture and food regimes are dangerously reliant on fossil fuels for energy inputs. We know that fossil fuels are non-renewable. We know that we are overworked and do not have enough time to spend with our loved ones. We know that species are becoming extinct at a terribly rapid rate. We know all of this and more and yet virtually nothing is done to halt this 'progress'.

The fact that we are not changing course is not due to a lack of knowledge or even a lack of ideas. It is the logic of differential accumulation held by the ruling class of owners, combined with the capture of our political and cultural systems, that represents the greatest risk to our lives and the lives of our children. The aim of capitalists is for their logic to be all-encompassing, all-embracing. There have been attempts to curtail and even thwart this power, but in a world where money represents the power to command and where the 1% have appropriated most of it, the needs, desires and even the demands of the 99% have been actively suppressed – often with considerable violence. Again, this is not to suggest that these individuals and their families are evil. However, we have to recognise that they are slaves to the logic of differential capitalisation just as much as the pharaohs were slaves to their own logic of pleasing the gods in the hopes of gaining their favour. Differential capitalisation is the ritual that gives them the *illegitimate* power to control humans and natural resources in an effort to accumulate ever more money and power. It is illegitimate because it is undemocratic and in no way earned on the basis of individual skill or talent. It is the

appropriation of social wealth pure and simple. And here Marx
was right on the money:

> [the purpose of accumulation is] not to satisfy the personal
> needs of its owner, but to give him money, abstract social
> riches and capital, more power over the labor of others, i.e., to
> increase this power (Marx 1978: 464–5).

# 6 | THE PARTY OF THE 99%: RESISTANCE AND FUTURE PROSPECTS

There's class warfare, all right, but it's my class, the rich class, that's making war, and we're winning. (Warren Buffet of Berkshire Hathaway quoted in Stein 2006)

Power concedes nothing without a demand. It never did and it never will. Find out just what any people will submit to, and you have found out the exact amount of injustice and wrong which will be imposed upon them; and these will continue till they are resisted with either words or blows, or with both. The limits of tyrants are prescribed by the endurance of those whom they oppress. (Frederick Douglass 1857)

The passivity of the majority is what allows the powerful to rule.[1] (Raj Patel 2009: 118)

The emergence of the 1%, and the imposition of its ruling logic, has always confronted resistance of some kind. Originally this resistance was isolated and localised as the price system of the market crept into rural or tribal life. With the price system now dominant virtually everywhere, resistance is far more global in scope, facilitated by the telecommunications revolution and often coordinated across borders. The Occupy movement was just the latest example in the long history of resistance movements in both the Global North and the Global South. Using the theme of the 99% and resistance, this chapter concludes our study of the 1%.

**Occupy in context**

The Occupy movement's pedigree can be traced back to the first struggles against the imposition of capitalist markets and the formation of a small class of dominant owners. The eminent political economist Karl Polanyi (1957) called this the double movement. What Polanyi meant by this term was that the idea of free market industrialisation was not broadly accepted and had to be imposed – often with considerable violence – on an unwilling population by business and state agents. This was one side of the movement. The other side of the movement consisted of social forces struggling against the imposition of capitalist markets because they destabilised their traditional ways of living and treated them as commodities to be bought, sold and discarded when profits suffered. These were the forces of social self-protection struggling for a decent livelihood against dominant owners and their functionaries. Polanyi believed that the double movement was the primary cause of the World Wars and the Great Depression in the capitalist heartland. He thought, as did many at the time, that cooler heads would eventually prevail and 'in a truly democratic society, the problem of industry would resolve itself through the planned intervention of the producers and consumers themselves' rather than of the 'elites and aristocracies' and their corporations (Polanyi quoted in Dahms 2000: 150). And while business was to some degree tempered by democratic governments after World War II, the logic of differential accumulation was never questioned or touched, merely frustrated by national regulation. Indeed, there is a prevailing myth that class war somehow ended in the West with the rise of the welfare state. Yet, in a society divided by class, where the 1% effectively own all of society's productive assets and control the money supply, class war never sleeps. If the prevailing rationality of the system is perpetual differential accumulation in the attempt to accumulate ever more money and power relative to others, class war is also perpetual. This war cannot be stopped without pursuing a different logic with a different social purpose. As long as the current rationale remains intact, any policy changes will be marginal and largely ineffective.

Still, many think of the post-war period as a time of economic growth and prosperity when benefits were widely shared with workers in industrialised countries. An unwritten compromise between workers, capitalists and the government seemed to be at hand. Workers received higher pay commensurate with pro-ductivity and better benefits in return for not striking. Capitalists avoided potentially costly strikes and the government achieved civil peace for overseeing the relationship. This, of course, is a highly stylised image of the period, but, at any rate, many scholars believe that this compromise started to unwind in the 1970s and 1980s as more right-leaning governments came to power and unions were targeted for elimination. These governments started to reconfigure the welfare state in favour of what Gill (1995) has called disciplinary neoliberalism. Disciplinary neoliberalism is a set of policies, such as privatisation, the liberalisation of trade and investment and deregulation. The policies are essentially designed to increase the power of dominant owners and their corporations. Although many have called these initiatives 'free market reforms', they have had nothing to do with creating a 'free' market anywhere or at any time (Nitzan 2001). In fact, these policies augmented corporate power, enriched the owners of dominant capital and lessened the power of workers globally. Apart from declining unionisation and stagnant wages, one of the major indications is the rash wave of transnational mergers and acquisitions that started in the late 1980s and really took off in the 1990s and 2000s. Between 1981 and 2012, the number of global mergers and acquisition deals increased by 2,000%. Hundreds of thousands of deals were made to concentrate ownership. The value of these transactions also increased, by 4,700% from 1981 to 2007, when US$4.8 trillion in deals were made. Mainstream economists justify these mergers and acquisitions by arguing that they must create more efficiency by encouraging 'synergy' and reducing transaction costs (Harding et al. 2014). As Nitzan (2001) points out, the evidence for this argument is flimsy and this is probably not the main point of corporate amalgamation.

In the 'capital as power' approach, the purpose of mergers and acquisitions is greater power. First, by merging instead of creating new capacity (called greenfield investment), corporations do not inject any additional productive capacity into the economy. Second, combining with other corporations increases the power of a particular firm to collect additional income streams. For example, Facebook has acquired over 40 companies since 2005; the more it acquires, the more it collects real or potential income streams and increases its power over other corporations by virtue of expanding what it can control through ownership. It can do this because a corporation is a legal fiction capable of owning a series of income-generating assets. Put differently, corporations merge and acquire in order to decrease competition and increase their differential earnings in relation to the average rate of return for their industry.

As corporate power concentrated in one of the largest merger and acquisition waves in history, the bamboo and iron curtains came down. China and the former Soviet Union were now open for transnational business, effectively adding 1.5 billion more people to the global workforce and providing one of the major reasons given for the declining power of workers. If workers ask for too many demands, or the wrong ones, corporations can threaten relocation. At the same time as the corporate assault on standards of living intensified, so too did the rise of personal debt in many countries. This took the form of high-interest-rate credit cards, student loans, home equity loans, mortgages and various other debt instruments. Since money can expand only through loans, this has had the effect of injecting liquidity into the system, and, for a time, boosting demand for goods and services. The problem, of course, is that there are limits to how much debt households can afford, and by March 2001 that limit appeared to be reached. The United States, the largest economy in the world, went into recession for eight months.

The solution to this problem was to create more debt. Alan Greenspan, then chairman of the United States Federal Reserve and either duplicitous or a fool, slashed interest rates to encourage borrowing and spending. With most of the middle class suffering from high household debt to disposable income ratios, mortgage loans were offered to people who could scarce afford to repay them on the faulty premise that house prices always go up. As we have already discussed, mortgage debt is a leading way in which money is created in most economies, but personal and business debt are also growing massively. These subprime loans were then securitised by Wall Street banks and given investment grade status by the oligopoly of rating agencies. Fraud, corruption and deceit ran throughout the supply chain of credit but, with a strong seal of approval from the rating agencies, the securitised loans were sold on to global investors or kept as income-generating assets on the books of financial institutions. These loans added over a trillion dollars to the money supply of the United States and temporarily boosted the economy. However, as more and more people failed to meet their mortgage payments due to inadequate incomes, the sub-prime mortgage market began to crash. The loans went from being assets to non-performing loans on bank balance sheets. In addition to this crisis, increasing prices for food and petroleum further squeezed working-class budgets, adding to the problem of insufficient disposable income and insufficient diets for many in the 99%. This perfect storm of conditions – millions of in-debted people without the ability to service their loans, rising oil and food prices and sinking housing prices – dampened the mood of global investors and global capitalisation plummeted. The market value of virtually every company was chopped. As reported by the World Federation of Exchanges, global capitalisa-tion went from a high of US$63 trillion in October 2007 to US$29 trillion by February 2009 (Di Muzio 2014: 29). Within the span of months, investors slashed the value of global companies by over half. Unemployment soared and, according to the International Labour Organization (ILO), the problem continues to get worse:

> What began as a crisis on the financial markets has become a global jobs crisis. The risk of increased unemployment has augmented, and the crisis is a direct threat to decent work across the globe. Responses to the crisis cannot be restricted to fiscal stimulus packages, and the social dimension of the crisis should not be ignored.[2]

As was the case during the Great Depression, there are now plenty of people who want to work but there appear to be fewer and fewer jobs. The youth have been the most affected by the crisis of unemployment. Currently, in 2013, the ILO places the total number of unemployed at 202 million, with that number expected to rise in the coming years (ILO 2014: 3).

As the financial crisis deepened, governments were forced to step in and rescue the financial institutions and the economy. Once again, the solution was the creation of more debt. As national debts mounted to pay for stimulus packages and the fraud of reckless bankers, the political class promised to take measures to curtail government spending to please the very financial markets they had bailed out! Organised financial crime, accelerating inequality, widespread political corruption, a fear of future prospects and policies of austerity inspired the Occupy movement to fight for the 99%.

According to the *Guardian*'s detailed corroborated database, there were 750 Occupy movements in cities around the world,[3] with the majority in North America and Europe. The fact that the movement was so widespread in the heartland of global capitalism demonstrates the degree to which the 99% have come to realise that they are on the wrong road into the future and that this is because the 1% effectively own the economy and have used the political system to further their own narrow goals. As global as the movement became, it was started by a group of anarchist New Yorkers who organised a call to action published by *Adbusters*:

> On September 17, we want to see 20,000 people flood into lower Manhattan, set up tents, kitchens, peaceful barricades and occupy Wall Street for a few months. Once there, we shall incessantly repeat one simple demand in a plurality of voices.[4]

The 'one demand' was modelled after the success of Mubarak's ousting by protesters in Tahir Square in Egypt. Occupy Wall Street suggested that their one demand should focus on the removal of money from US politics, the reinstatement of the Glass–Steagall Act, the dissolution of corporations found to have broken the law three times, or the dismantling of the many thousands of US military bases around the world. The movement aimed to have a democratic and horizontal power-sharing structure so that decisions could be made in consensus. However, it appears that the New York movement turned from repeating 'one simple demand in a plurality of voices' to repeating a plurality of demands in a babel of voices.[5] As admirable as the original encampment was for its energy, its concern for democracy and its collective desire to found a social order centred on people and the planet rather than on the symbolic accumulation of power, its tactics and strategies doomed what could have been a far more powerful movement. To be fair, had the pressing need for an income combined with displacement by the police been non-issues, the movement could have developed a stronger political programme out of its experiment with direct democracy. Either way, one thing is for certain: Occupy Wall Street and the Occupy movement more generally have drawn so much attention to the growing divide between dominant owners and the rest of society that the idea of 'the 1% versus the 99%' will not go away any time soon.

## Five reasons why present trends will likely continue

It is also highly likely that current trends in gross inequality will only be exacerbated for at least five immediate reasons. First, as Polanyi suggested, dominant owners have:

> no organ to sense the dangers involved in the exploitation
> of physical strength of the worker, the destruction of family
> life, the devastation of neighborhoods, the denudation of
> forests, the pollution of rivers, the deterioration of craft
> standards, the disruption of folkways, and the general

degradation of existence including housing and arts, as well as the innumerable forms of private and public life that do not affect profits (Polanyi 1957: 133).

The most important indicators used by the 1% are virtually all financial and tied in with profit as the chief measure of success. We should never forget that the politics and the purpose of the 1% are to make ever more money – this trumps all other sentiments and political leanings. Each member of the 1% may not hold this view directly, but their money managers, who must obey the iron law of differential accumulation, certainly do. And when all these things harm society, there is always charity – a secular confession akin to the rich being forgiven their sins by the Catholic Church. Both involve the exchange of money; the only difference is that the latter exchange is given to enter extra-terrestrial Heaven, the former to gain more status and power. We would also do well to recall that finance does not develop as some neutral science disconnected from power and designed to better planetary life. It does not emerge to conquer a general risk encountered by humanity. The evidence is that the majority of humanity lives in a constant state of risk – risk of being thrown out of work, risk of not being able to afford food, risk of not being able to fund an education, risk of suffering indignities from a boss and so on. Even those who appear to have secure jobs are in constant fear of losing them. Finance emerges as a rationality of power to capitalise the control of humans and the natural world for the differential accumulation of dominant owners. It is the chief reason why we have a 1% at all. Moreover, as we have seen in Chapter 4, the rich have built their own virtual world relatively free from the 99%, except where and when we serve them. The history of human sociality since the agricultural revolution has demonstrated that no constituted power gives up its power willingly, despite evidence of illegitimacy or its destructive nature. In examining once complex and rich societies that have collapsed, Jared Diamond, like Polanyi, makes a prescient observation about those at the top of the social hierarchy:

> A further conflict of interest involving rational behavior arises when the interests of the decision-making elite in power clash with the interests of the rest of society. Especially if the elite can insulate themselves from the consequences of their actions, they are likely to do things that profit themselves, regardless of whether those actions hurt everybody else. All of these examples in the preceding several pages illustrate situations in which a society fails to try to solve perceived problems because the maintenance of the problem is good for some people (Diamond 2005: 431, 432).

The fact that the 1% currently benefit from differential accumulation and the widespread destruction of nature for profit is thus extremely worrying in light of the history of our species. It could very well be that extreme forms of hierarchy and the lust for power over creativity and cooperation threaten our survival – particularly in the age of fossil fuel energy, extreme climate change and nuclear weapons.

Second, we have entered an era of expensive oil – what Huber (2013) has called the lifeblood of our modern societies. The costs of this increase, as well as the abject failure to transition away from oil, are being felt most acutely by the 99% in rising transportation costs and rising prices for food. The 1%, however, can continue to live their energy-intensive lifestyles and barely take note of the price. All the while, unless there is some sort of public intervention, the dominant owners of oil and gas companies will collect a fortune from declining supplies and relatively inelastic demand. The inequality produced by the 1% is also the inequality energy access, use and profit.

Third, as long as the banks control the extension of credit and therefore make the bulk of investment decisions, we will have a system of debt slavery and unequal access to money from which bank owners profit. Until money comes under democratic control and is produced debt-free, the 99% will continue to give a portion of their income to bankers who create money credit out of thin air. Any country that has a banking system owned by a small minority cannot properly be called a democracy. The great financiers of European bloodbaths – the House of Rothschild – understood this all too well (Ferguson 1998). The sentiment was also noted by Bill Clinton's former professor at Georgetown University, Carroll Quigley:

> the powers of financial capitalism had another far-reaching aim, nothing less than to create a world system of financial control in private hands able to dominate the political system of each country and the economy of the world as a whole. This system was to be controlled in a feudalist fashion by the central banks of the world acting in concert, by secret agreements arrived at in frequent private meetings and conferences. The apex of the system was to be the Bank for International Settlements in Basle, Switzerland, a private bank owned and controlled by the world's central banks which were themselves private corporations (Quigley 1966: 324).[6]

The fact that most people have no idea how money is created today provides considerable evidence of the early men of finance's success in setting up their global operations. If money is power, what should we call the power to create it?

Fourth, the 1% effectively control the apparatus of violence. While the majority of the police and soldiers worldwide are in the 99%, their pay cheques come from being able to do their jobs and their jobs are contingent on what orders they receive from governments desirous of maintaining 'stability'. Outright slaughter of protesters or rioters is much more difficult to accomplish now with the means of communication more readily available to the general population. State forces killing people en masse would be a public relations nightmare both at home and internationally. The Pentagon learned this during the television broadcasts of the Vietnam War, and this knowledge probably spread to other armed forces through military-to-military cooperation. Since then, and given the many protests against elite social forces, for example at the G8 or G20, a new category of weapons has been in constant development and refinement: non-lethal weapons. While these less-than-lethal weapons have been used internationally, it appears that the arms industry in the US plays a special role:

> The US is at the forefront of an international arms develop-
> ment effort that includes a remarkable assortment of techno-
> logies, which look and sound like they belong in a Hollywood
> science fiction thriller. From microwave energy blasters and
> blinding laser beams, to chemical agents and deafening sonic
> blasters, these weapons are at the cutting edge of crowd
> control. The Pentagon's approved term for these weapons
> is 'non-lethal' or 'less-lethal' and they are intended for use
> against the unarmed. Designed to 'control crowds, clear
> streets, subdue and restrain individuals and secure borders,'
> they are the 21st century's version of the police baton, pepper
> spray and tear gas (Khalek 2011).

The ability to control crowds by inflicting pain from a distance is a powerful tool of the 1% and the political leadership they largely sponsor. Demonstrations may still take place, but they could be easier to control. Compounding this inequality of force and violence is the growing market for private security. Peter Singer, one of the first to chronicle this worrying phenomenon, noted that:

> the military privatization phenomenon means that military resources are now available on the open market, often at better prices and efficiencies than could be provided by individual clients. So, contrary to predictions about the divorce of military and economic power, power is more fungible than ever ...
> The ability to transform money into force returns the international system to the dangers of lowered costs of war. A new international market of private military services means that economic power is now more threatening (Singer 2003: 171, 174).

Fifth, as long as the 99% remain fragmented and disorganised, the 1% will continue to rule by advancing their interests in accumulating more symbolic power. We have just witnessed a major financial crisis when it became blatant (once again) that bankers cannot be trusted with the money supply. Evidence of fraud, corruption and insider trading abounded (Ritholtz 2009).[7] Still, bankers walked away with enormous bonuses many times the size of an average worker's salary. But the largest market crash since the Great Depression did nothing to overturn the capitalist mode of power or the policies that support differential accumulation: it merely intensified them. One glaring example is the intensification of mergers and acquisitions post-crisis – which, again, only serve to intensify corporate power and consolidate ownership. Moreover, if we rely on traditional political parties we are likely to experience much of the same. Not only are these parties beholden to business interests and influenced by money but they all seem willing to accept the fundamental premise of differential accumulation – the very root cause of this increasing inequality between dominant owners and the 99%. To stop this trend, in each country I would argue that the 99% organise themselves into a visible and effective political party with clear goals for social transformation and the end of capital as power. This will require a wholly new apparatus of number indicators to coordinate society quite different from gross domestic product, interest rates and capitalisation. These indicators should be concerned with people, future generations and the environment, not profit. A return to the so-called golden era of Keynesianism, which some are wont to revisit, should not be pursued for two main reasons. First, Keynesianism never challenged the dominant ownership of the world's money supply by private individuals and families; in fact, it *encouraged more government debt*, a key source of profit for bank owners. As Rowbotham perceptively pointed out: 'What Keynes unwittingly provided was a theoretical framework for the exercise of government power and banking profit, dressed up in the guise of support for the economy' (Rowbotham 1998: 240). Second, the ecological and energy challenges we currently confront have intensified since the time of Keynes. These have to be addressed with immediacy and this cannot be done by advancing policies that continue to encourage ruinous economic growth premised on debt money and fossil fuels (Heinberg 2011).

**Ten priorities**

Confronting the destructive power-seeking nature of the 1% is the political project of our times. Our job is not to inherit the old system and somehow run it better, as neo-Keynesians

would like to do, but to found a new one. There will be much
to do and there is little doubt that anything progressive must
be done collectively. Many are already organised and working
towards a future form of sociality and economy that is con-
structive, inclusive, cooperative and democratic. I am familiar
with many of these projects but I would still argue that little
can be advanced to challenge the *systemic nature* of differential
capitalisation without a modern political party of the 99%. As
long as we remain fragmented we will continue to be ruled –
and perhaps ruled into oblivion. After my examination of the
1%, a few things have become clear to me; for what it is worth,
I single out ten priorities that I think an effective party of the
99% should strive for if a future society is to take shape based
around the creativity of humans rather than the power of capital.
These ten priorities are certainly not the only things to pursue,
but getting them right would go a long way to putting us all on
a more sustainable and progressive path to supporting decent
livelihoods and planetary health.

First, a party of the 99% should be organised around the
reform of its country's monetary system.[8] The current system
of creating money through debt benefits only the owners of
the banks.[9] The rest of us, with insufficient incomes for what
the economy can produce, get mounting debt that pushes up
prices (inflation) and an economy that is effectively controlled
by whether bankers feel confident to lend at profit (Rowbotham
1998: 292). For those who are confused about why prices must
increase with mounting debt, consider the following example.
When a bank creates money by making a loan, it creates all
of the money and charges interest (which it does not create).[10]
While businesses can typically cut wages and try to cut other
production costs, the one thing they cannot cut is their debt and

interest payments. The cost of servicing their debts to lenders is passed on to customers, pushing up prices. For example, at the end of 2013, business debt in the United States stood at US$13.4 trillion. To put this in perspective, the national debt at that time was US$15 trillion (Federal Reserve 2014). If financial lenders charged a 5% interest rate on this sum, within a year they would generate a little over a whopping US$670 billion. To put this into even greater perspective, let us imagine that the US$13.4 trillion is owed not by United States businesses as a whole but by one firm. Suppose this firm produces and sells bottled water and went into debt to expand its facilities. We know that, at the end of the year, US$670 billion has to be paid to the owners of the bank as interest – and they haven't even started to pay back the principal! Since the debt now becomes part of the cost of production of the bottled water, the firm will have to increase its prices to service its debt. You can start to understand why the banking industry is the second most capitalised industry on the planet after oil and gas. You can also start to understand that inflation is not about too much money chasing too few goods, as in the standard account, but, as Rowbotham (1998: 17) has convincingly argued, most inflation is the result of money created as debt. In other words, our banking system is purposely designed to benefit whoever owns the banks first and foremost. We might do well to find out who they are.

Of course, we might have some sympathy for the banks if they actually acted as intermediaries between those who wanted to save money and those who wanted to borrow, but this is clearly not the case. As already stated, bankers create money out of thin air whenever they make a loan. Since credit is now just numbers in a computer, there is no reason whatsoever why a few dominant owners should get rich thanks to everyone else's hard work and their need for money in a market-driven society. So any party of the 99% has to go straight to the heart of the matter and reform the monetary system. This is the most important task and it can begin with a worldwide education campaign to notify the publics of the world about the dangers of debt money, after which a democratically controlled debt-free money system can be created. The party of the 99% should fight to constitutionalise the fact that the public is in control of its own money supply and can create it debt-free. There are a number of proposals for how exactly to accomplish such an ambitious task, and each party of the 99% should debate which plan is the most suitable for their country. For example, in the UK, Positive Money is currently making headway educating the public about the corrosive nature of the monetary system. They have also made a number of interesting proposals for the creation of debt-free money.[11] So let us be clear: until we get our money right by taking it out of the hands of for-profit bankers who have the power to create it as debt, we will have higher prices for goods and services, mounting debt, more economic crises, more unemployment, more social unrest and an economy dictated to us by the dominant owners of banks and their managers. The current monetary system is a fraud pure and simple and it must be completely reformed.

Whatever the exact technical details, the party of the 99% should introduce a public bank to issue debt-free money. The main investment objectives a public bank should pursue are any mix or any one of the following: 1) investments that create jobs in the local community; 2) investments that encourage the production of the most durable goods; 3) investments in research and development to enhance the quality of life; 4) investments in renewable energy; 5) investments in sustainable public infrastructure; and 6) investments in local sustainable agriculture.

The bank will also have responsibility for funding other social goals noted in the paragraphs below. A final thing a party of the 99% might do as it starts out is to ensure that its citizens cannot hide their money offshore to evade taxes. This can be done by banning correspondent banking with the new publicly owned banks and increasing transparency.

Second, education, healthcare and childcare should be universal and free. Once again, there are a number of ways in which this can be accomplished and each party of the 99% will have to orchestrate its own path to implementation. This will be easier to accomplish in some countries than in others, since many of the most civilised countries already provide non-profit healthcare and education up to and including post-secondary education. All three concerns should be run at cost, with salaries clearly negotiated, made public and commensurate with skill and years of service. These services should be accessible to all and paid, debt-free, from the new public banking system. All knowledge produced by these institutions – particularly the universities and hospitals – should be available publicly for free online. Obviously, there will be different ways of setting these goals in motion, but a party of the 99% should ensure their implementation.

Third, a party of the 99% should ban all money from politics. Instead, politicians should be given a reasonable set of public funds to run their campaigns. Such funds will only be released at the beginning of the election cycle if a political party achieved 3% or more of the popular vote in a previous election cycle and if it has a clear political programme. A new political party should be eligible for reasonable start-up money as long as it meets certain criteria, such as a certain number of supporters. This will help eliminate fringe or less serious parties. Campaigns should be short in duration so money can be used for other priorities.

Businesses and non-profit organisations should be banned from making political advertisements during the election campaign. Individuals who wish to make campaign videos or posters must attach their names to the work to ensure accountability. Where possible, every effort should be made to move away from representative forms of democracy to more direct forms of democratic decision making. The internet can help facilitate such a project.

Fourth, a party of the 99% should aim to abolish the wasteful and innovation-killing patent system. Patents were the original way in which a monarch granted a monopoly to private interests – typically for an invention. Some believe that patents are the only way to encourage innovation: they reason that 'inventors' invent only if they can profit from their discovery. This might be so for a few individuals, but on a societal level where research and development funding can now be offered debt-free, this is highly unlikely. People will be rewarded for their contributions, but no one will be able to claim 'ownership' over a discovery. Since knowledge and language are social products and patents are a way of privately claiming a monopoly over knowledge, they should be abolished. This may sound like a radical step to some but it is also the position of researchers at the Federal Reserve Bank in St Louis:

> A closer look at the historical and international evidence
> suggests that while weak patent systems may mildly increase
> innovation with limited side-effects, strong patent systems
> retard innovation with many negative side-effects. Both
> theoretically and empirically, the political economy of govern-
> ment-operated patent systems indicates that weak legislation
> will generally evolve into a strong protection and that the
> political demand for stronger patent protection comes from
> old and stagnant industries and firms, not from new and

innovative ones. Hence the best solution is to abolish patents entirely through strong constitutional measures and to find other legislative instruments, less open to lobbying and rent-seeking, to foster innovation whenever there is clear evidence that laissez-faire under-supplies it (Boldrin and Levine 2012).

We have the best chance of uncovering new knowledge, creative work and inventions where people are able to work together cooperatively and share knowledge without the threat of being sued for infringing someone's income stream. Anyone who is in doubt about this should do themselves a favour and Google 'Jack Andraka' and 'knowledge democracy'. At the age of 15, Mr Andraka found a promising new early detection test for pancreatic (and other types of) cancer. The biggest obstacle he faced was not his own intelligence but accessing information, due to the high paywalls of academic journals. He is a strong advocate of the internet and argues for a knowledge democracy. A party of the 99% should propel this idea forward.

Fifth, a party of, by and for the 99% should make insurance public and not for profit. Insurance works on the principle of the law of large numbers: the larger the number of people involved in the insurance scheme, the less likely it is that everyone will experience the same calamity. People who do suffer an injury or accidental death are paid out of the contributions provided by those who do not experience an accident or injury. There is no reason whatsoever why insurance provision should be owned by private individuals making money out of the misfortune of others. This is the capitalisation of our injuries, accidents, mis-fortunes and death. Private insurance provision also violates the law of large numbers through exclusion. From a risk reduction and mathematical point of view, it makes much more sense to put the entire population of a country under an insurance scheme that can provide benefits when unfortunate events occur. Once again, the publicly run banking system can provide for this debt-free, with no premiums required. In other words, everyone is covered by virtue of being a member of the political community.

Sixth, a party of the 99% should fund retirement at a democratically agreed-upon age. Those who want to continue to work should be able to but those who want to retire can. There should be a basic yearly amount given to those who choose to retire that is in accordance with the general standard of living. It can be adjusted as need be. Since the aim is to have no debt money in the economy pushing up prices, funding retirement will also be done through the publicly owned banking system. This will be a big change from the many pension systems that act as large capitalists capitalising firms and government debt. Pension fund managers are also concerned with better than average returns for their clients or differential accumulation. Since one of their concerns is the share price of corporations, pension fund managers have in many cases exerted their influence over the economy to the detriment of workers (Harmes 2001).[12] The party of the 99% should abolish current pension fund schemes and return the funds directly to the individuals who made contributions or had contributions made on their behalf. This is because pensions will now be guaranteed by the public bank through the creation of debt-free money.

Seventh, a party of the 99% should provide each adult individual with a guaranteed income through the public bank.[13] The income should be set at a level that secures a basic standard of living. Critics will immediately cry out that this will lead to universal laziness. It will not. A guaranteed standard of living produces important social goals by taking the power of the sack away from employers. First, it establishes a rule of greater freedom than is currently enjoyed by the majority of workers. The idea is premised on the fact that we are creative, productive beings and work is a large part of our subjectivity or identity. Most people want to work but they want to work in employments that are meaningful to them. With a secure income, we can be sure that those who work for added income will be doing so because they want to contribute to society in some way. Second, a guaranteed income solves the problem of unemployment and does not create any new interest payments. Third, with a guaranteed income, people will likely choose to work less, increasing their leisure time and potentially leading to a drop in the consumption of goods and services. This is a worthwhile goal not only because leisure time is valued by all, but also because people will probably consume less. Without doubt, some will be up in arms about this proposal in such a materialistic economy where social status is connected to possessions and shaped by advertising and marketing. But, from a sane point of view, we know from studies that after a certain threshold of wealth, individuals are no happier having more and more stuff. It seems that acquiring more and more possessions is not about happiness but about power and the demonstration of it. If we displace the logic of differential accumulation and stop creating debt money, no one will make enough money to acquire an inordinate amount of goods in the first place.

Eighth, a party of the 99% should seek every way possible to transition away from fossil fuels. There are no quick fixes here, but time is of the essence if we want the transition to be relatively painless and peaceful. Three important studies have convincingly demonstrated that there is no way to socially reproduce current patterns of high-energy consumption in rich countries with alternative energy (Heinberg 2009; Trainer 2007; Zehner 2012). Of course, a party of the 99% should invest in renewable energy and implement renewable energy schemes wherever possible, but the party should also have a programme to reduce material consumption and promote low-energy leisure activities. As suggested, a guaranteed income should help in this pursuit.

Ninth, all parties of the 99% should work together to demilitarise the world. The military industry is also capitalised by dominant owners and they profit from conflict or the threat of conflict. Most of the bill is paid for by taxpayers and future generations, not to mention with the lives of soldiers and innocents. This is wasteful expenditure and we should not have our scientists working on solutions for how to kill people more effectively. In a social order where everyone is guaranteed a decent standard of living and there is no chance of gaining excessive power over others, there will be no need for a military. Some may recoil at this suggestion and believe it unrealistic, but the idea has deep roots in the liberal tradition. Concerned with the potential for a military dictatorship, people always feared standing armies. It was only with the rise of the capitalist mode of power that professional militaries became a cornerstone of Western states. As the capitalist mode of power withers, so too will the need for wasteful expenditure on an apparatus of violence, surveillance and death.

Tenth, a party of the 99% should ensure that the only income stream available other than the guaranteed income from the public bank comes from a person's direct labour. What this means is that no one will be able to capitalise the labour power of another or take undeserved rewards. Individuals will be free to form producing associations and, if they require investment, they can issue a proposal to the public bank. Provided that it meets the objectives of the public bank, the money can be created for the project. All projects funded by the bank should be transparent: this means that the entire entrepreneurial plan is made public. All businesses will be run on a not-for-profit basis and the 99% should design a salary schedule for each employment with strict caps at the top. Should some jobs that are necessary for the reproduction of society fall into abeyance because no one wants to do them, the government can offer special inducements where these jobs are necessary to support a decent quality of life for all. It could very well be that those working in sanitation and health end up making the most money – but, of course, always within democratically decided reason.

These ten points are not a magical panacea for a perfect world free of all social ills and of the vast ecological problems we face. There will be much more to do and debate, of course. For example, we need to abolish the debt of developing countries and reclaim the unearned gains of leaders who have stolen much of this money. But I would argue that the measures above would increase human happiness and human security while pushing us on a more sustainable path for future generations. Their implementation would also go a long way in ridding the world of an illegitimate system of power and control that is leading us in the direction of civilisational ruin. The problem is differential capitalisation based on a debt money system owned by the few. In a more democratic and less hierarchical order, no one would be allowed to capitalise the labour of another or of society as a whole for their sole benefit, just as no one is presently allowed to legally own another human being as chattel.

### Creativity, power and the meaning of life

I began this book with Braudel's observation:

Conspicuous at the top of the pyramid is a handful of privileged people. Everything invariably falls into the lap of this tiny elite: power, wealth, a large share of surplus production

... Is there not in short, whatever the society and whatever the period, an insidious law giving power to the few, an irritating law it must be said, since *the reasons for it are not obvious*. And yet this stubborn fact, taunting us at every turn. We cannot argue with it: all evidence agrees (Braudel 1983: 466, my emphasis).

Braudel considered the period from the fifteenth to the eighteenth century and found this law to be an extremely accurate portrayal of the era. As we have seen, the evidence presented in this book only confirms Braudel's observation for our own time. But unlike Braudel, who argued that the reasons for this gross inequality of wealth and power are 'not obvious', we have uncovered exactly why it is so: the capitalisation of income-generating assets and the logic of differential capitalisation rooted in ownership. Most people on the Earth do not follow this logic even though they are ensnared by it in their everyday lives. The 99% are far more concerned with having a decent livelihood and secure employment than with pursuing power or trying to control and capitalise the labour of others. They work, search for work, and, if they are lucky in this system, have one income stream from their labour. Only a very small fraction of the planet's inhabitants pursues the logic of differential accumulation, and, as we saw in Chapter 2, the goal of this logic is to achieve greater inequality of income and assets (Nitzan and Bichler 2009). The corporation and ownership are their biggest weapons, and, in order to accumulate, corporations must, as going concerns, exert their power over the entire social process and control and limit human potential and creativity. As we have already discussed in the opening of this book, we know we have the capacity to ensure a decent quality of life for everyone on the planet (our technology and knowhow are there), but this does not happen. It does not happen because we are being held hostage by a logic whose ransom is profit and whose goal is the increasing inequality of power.

The proposal for a party of the 99% and the ten-point plan sketched above are designed to break this logic. The only major way of doing this is to de-capitalise the economy and for the public to take control of creating its own money and to decide how to spend it democratically. In a society in which the only additional income one can gain is from one's own direct labour, salaries are democratically decided based on merit, and top salaries are capped, no one will be able to dominate the social order or consume wastefully. With a debt-free monetary system we will no longer have to be slaves to interest and economic growth. We will be free to pursue other, more worthwhile goals that enhance our well-being and happiness. The major fetter on our creativity will be removed and people will be able to self-organise in free associations to pursue their dreams – so long, of course, as they do not harm other people. The system described by Smith will be abolished:

> The labour and time of the poor is in civilized countries sacri-
> ficed to the maintaining of the rich in ease and luxury. The
> landlord is maintained in idleness and luxury by the labour of
> his tenants. The moneyed man is supported by his exactions
> from the industrious merchant and the needy who are obliged
> to support him in ease by a return for the use of his money
> (Adam Smith quoted in Perelman 2000: 211).

Making it socially unacceptable and illegal to *privately* cap-italise the work of society is one of the key challenges of our time, as is reforming our monetary system. Private property should be for personal possessions, not for additional income streams, as it is now. But the deeper philosophical question is our legacy as a species. At the end of his reading of the collapse of nineteenth-century civilisation, Karl Polanyi argued that the biggest philosophical question of the twentieth century was how to think about freedom in a complex society. He argued that 'institutions are embodiments of human meaning and purpose' and that 'no society is possible in which power and compulsion are absent, nor a world in which force has no function' (Polanyi 1957: 254, 257). We can agree with Polanyi that power and its exercise can sometimes be legitimate. We can also agree that it would be impossible to evacuate power from our societies. But ours is a question of legitimate power. For the last 5,000 years or so, since human beings formed more complex societies, we have been steadily losing our more egalitarian nature:

> At that time [5,000 years ago], people were beginning to live increasingly in chiefdoms, societies with highly privileged individuals who occupied hereditary positions of political leadership and social paramountcy. From certain well-developed chiefdoms came the six early civilizations, with their powerful and often despotic leaders. But before twelve thousand years ago, humans basically were egalitarian (Knauft 1991). They lived in what might be called societies of equals, with minimal political centralization and no social classes. Everyone participated in group decisions, and outside the family there were no dominators (Boehm 2001: 3–4).

As the statistics bear out, we can be very sure that we have a small class of dominators who profit from their ownership of virtually everything. This is not legitimate power rooted in productive contributions to society but domination based on past violence and current relations of power over individuals and society in a debt- and price-denominated system. Given this knowledge, the ultimate question may be whether we really want our creativity subjugated and subject to the accumulation of symbolic power by the few, or whether we want to have a better world for us and our children – a world of democratic decision making, cooperation and creativity, where we combat disease, illiteracy, malnourishment, homelessness, dire poverty, indignity, global climate change and a looming energy crisis. Wouldn't that make us all happier? And isn't that the meaning of life?

The tiny minority pathologically chasing ever more money will not yield in the present environment. They will tell us that a party of the 99% is politically impossible. We must tell them that it is politically necessary. We will not be able to solve all our problems, but a world of legitimate power and creative cooperation would be far superior to the rule of the 1% and their pathological pursuit of money at the expense of future generations and the planet.

# NOTES

## Introduction

1 I would like to thank Ashley Waterman for helping with research and Hanna Kivistö, Stephen Gill, Silke Trommer, Taavi Sundell, Natasha Popcevski, Leonie Noble and Adam Harmes for reading portions of the manuscript; Matthew Dow for his comments and compiling the index. All errors are, of course, my own.

2 At the time of writing, Piketty's *Capital in the Twenty-First Century* is receiving much fanfare for its detailed empirical study of growing inequality. Piketty, however, shows little indication that he understands how money is created and therefore his solution to the problem (a wealth tax) does not go far enough.

3 Petras (2008: 324) has recently argued that in the case of multimillionaires and billionaires, the key to their growth has been a 'deep supply of cheap capital and land and vast armies of low paid labor'. This is certainly part of the answer for the rise of the billionaire 1%.

4 On the question of addiction to money, see Polk (2014).

5 See, for example, CNBC's *Dangerously Rich: Billionaire super security*, currently available on YouTube. Stephen Gill (in Bakker and Gill 2003: 190–208) points to the paradox of securing wealth: the richer one tends to be, the more paranoid one becomes about security and the more one spends on protection. In other words, the more money someone has appears to be correlated to how insecure they feel.

6 I define the logic of livelihood as the pursuit of a decent and dignified standard of living versus the logic of differential accumulation, which is the pathological addiction to accumulating money as an end in itself.

## 1 The unusual suspects

1 The website www.globalrichlist. com/ was used to calculate the professor's position by astute commentators.

2 Britain abolished the slave trade in 1807 and, with some exceptions, slavery throughout the empire in 1833.

3 Of course, this simply stands for Mill's definition of wealth. After some preliminary remarks on wealth, Mill promises his reader: 'we shall next turn our attention to the extraordinary differences in respect to it, which exist between nation and nation, and between different ages of the world; differences both in the quantity of wealth, and in the kind of it; as well as in the manner in which the wealth existing in the community is shared among its members' (Mill 2004: 11).

4 See www.investopedia.com/ terms/w/wealth.asp (accessed 24 October 2013).

5 See www.wealthx.com/about/ introduction/ (accessed 29 October 2013).

6 Robert Frank of the *Wall Street Journal* suggested a fourfold taxonomy based on household net worth for what he calls 'Richistan' or the virtual country the wealthy inhabit. Lower Richistan consists of individuals with US$1 million to US$10 million in net worth, Middle Richistan consists of individuals with US$10 million to US$100 million, and Upper Richistan consists of households with a net worth of US$100 million to US$1 billion. The upper ceiling is what he calls Billionaireville (Frank 2007: 5–12).

7 In its UBS-sponsored report, Wealth-X estimated the *ultra*-high-net-worth population far higher at 199,235 (Wealth-X 2013: 9). This is because it uses total net worth rather than investable assets.

8 From 2011 to 2012, the growth rate was 9.2%, suggesting that it may be quite a while before HNWIs reach anywhere close to 1% of the global population.

9 *The Mayfair Set* (1999) by Adam Curtis is a four-part documentary that demonstrates how the process worked in the UK.

10 To remind the reader: ultra-HNWIs are those with US$30 million or more by net worth.

11 Numbers have been rounded.

12 See www.forbes.com/sites/luisa kroll/2013/03/04/inside-the-2013- billionaires-list-facts-and-figures/ (accessed 9 November 2013).

13 See www.bloomberg.com/billionaires/2014-01-17/cya (accessed 17 January 2014).

14 The G7 includes Canada, France, Germany, Italy, Japan, United Kingdom and the United States, while the BRICs are Brazil, Russia, India and China.

## 2 Capital as power

1 See also the brief exchange at *Dissident Voice*: dissidentvoice.org/2013/11/can-pensions-afford-recovery/ (accessed 27 February 2014).

2 Smith's conceptualisation of capital begins with 'stock', which is never clearly defined. Stock then gets divided into 'capital', which generates a revenue, and 'immediate consumption', which does not. He then moves on to say that this revenue can be generated in one of two ways: 1) circulating capital, which is more or less merchant capital where goods change masters; and 2) fixed capital, or the improvement of land or machines and instruments of trade that do not change masters (Smith 2005: 224).

3 Marx writes: 'As a matter of history, capital, as opposed to landed property, invariably takes the form at first of money; it appears as moneyed wealth, as the capital of the merchant and of the usurer. But we have no need to refer to the origin of capital in order to discover that the first form of appearance of capital is money. We can see it daily under our very eyes. All new capital, to commence with, comes on the stage, that is, on the market, whether of commodities, labour, or money, even in our days, in the shape of money that by a definite process has to be transformed into capital' (Marx 1996: 102).

4 Marx's big promise comes in Chapter 6: 'Accompanied by Mr. Moneybags and by the possessor of labour-power, we therefore take leave for a time of this noisy sphere, where everything takes place on the surface and in view of all men, and follow them both into the hidden abode of production, on whose threshold there stares us in the face — No admittance

except on business. Here we shall see, not only how capital produces, but how capital is produced. We shall at last force the secret of profit making' (Marx 1996: 121).

5 For the full critique of the Marxist approach to explaining capitalist profit in the labour process, see Chapters 5 and 6 in Nitzan and Bichler (2009).

6 This was a 'scholarly' return to its old meaning as a fund of money values for investment or money already invested in an income-generating enterprise. Of course, it should be noted that the process of capitalisation, the primary act of capitalists, dates further back than the emergence of corporate America.

7 See www.crmz.com/Directory/ (accessed 17 November 2013).

8 See databank.worldbank.org/data/download/GDP.pdf (accessed 17 November 2013).

9 JPMorgan Chase lists its business practices here: www.jpmorganchase.com/corporate/About-JPMC/client-solutions.htm (accessed 23 August 2013).

10 See www.marketwatch.com/investing/stock/jpm/financials (accessed 18 November 2013).

11 See www.opensecrets.org/orgs/summary.php?id=d000000103 (accessed 18 November 2013).

12 See www.alexa.com/topsites and Hern (2013).

13 Fuchs (2012: 143) attempts to demonstrate how Facebook exploits its user base from a Marxist perspective. He fails to realise that Facebook's earnings are contingent on many more factors than Facebook workers and its worker bee user base.

14 A list of issues that Facebook has paid lobbyists working

on can be found here: www.opensecrets.org/lobby/clientissues.php?id=D000033563&year=2013 (accessed 20 November 2013).

15 See www.sipri.org/research/armaments/production/Top100 (accessed 20 November 2013).

16 The amount of government debt increases by the second. At the time of writing, government debt stood at US$52 trillion and counting. Figures on Japan and the debt of the United States were taken from the *Economist*'s debt clock: www.economist.com/content/global_debt_clock (accessed 22 November 2013).

17 Given the tumult over the size of government debt in the United States and the sovereign debt crises in Europe, Tett (2011) asked whether or not the sovereign debt of Western governments could indeed be considered 'risk-free'.

18 See www.goldmansachs.com/what-we-do/investment-banking/industry-sectors/municipal-finance/ (accessed 22 November 2013).

19 See www.hardassetsinvestor.com/hard-assets-university/18-hard-assets-101-an-introduction-to-commodities/431-types-of-commodities.html?Itemid=4 (accessed 28 November 2013).

20 Competitors make up the remaining 5%.

21 Quoted from the 'Credit Rating Agencies and the Financial Crisis' hearing before the Committee on Oversight and Government Reform, House of Representatives, 22 October 2008 (serial no. 110-155). See house.resource.org/110/org.c-span.281924-1.pdf (accessed 23 January 2014).

22 See www.icifactbook.org/fb_ch2.html (accessed 23 January 2014).

23  See www.barclayhedge.
com/research/indices/ghs/mum/
Hedge_Fund.html (accessed 23 January 2014).

24  See www.newyorkfed.org/
aboutthefed/fedpoint/fed22.html
(accessed 27 January 2014).

25  At 5 May 2014 prices, the gold would be worth US$4,945,920,000 billion.

26  See www.bankofcanada.ca/
about/educational-resources/faq/
(accessed 25 January 2014).

27  Of course, this claim should be subject to further treatment but debates leading up to and during the American Civil War suggested that slaves were actually better cared for than waged industrial workers of the north. The key difference here was that slaves were owned and therefore taken care of to some degree. Wage workers are rented and can be let go as the employer pleases (with some difficulty for protected workers), creating considerable insecurity for the working population – an argument used by plantation owners and slave drivers.

## 3  Wealth, money and power

1  See Marx on estranged labour at www.marxists.org/archive/marx/
works/1844/manuscripts/labour.htm
(accessed 4 February 2014).

2  Christianity (a Middle Eastern religion) came to England on the heels of the Roman Empire.

3  Marx famously critiqued Malthus for failing to consider the distribution of wealth and how this affected the distribution of food (he also believed Malthus to have plagiarised previous authors). Radically unequal social property relations were probably the main cause of starvation during Malthus' time, just as they are today. The evidence is that we can produce enough food to feed the present population but many still go hungry, starve or are malnourished because they do not have money to buy food – and in a capitalist system, food is a commodity produced for profit first, not nourishment (Albritton 2009; George 1988; Patel 2008).

4  Of course, hunger was not enough in Britain either – the lower orders of society were subject to grossly terroristic laws to encourage labour and protect property, as Marx identified in Chapter 28 of *Capital*, Volume 1 (1996). E. P. Thompson also discusses the Black Acts in his *Whigs and Hunters* (1990), and Hay et al. (1975) provide further evidence to corroborate Marx's original point. Other than a new series of punishments to induce the poor to work or to penalise them in some way (such as transportation), more fanciful schemes were proposed such as Bentham's Panopticon: a capitalised (for profit) workers' prison efficiently designed to encourage worker self-discipline through low-cost surveillance (Foucault 1975).

5  I thank Adam Harmes for recommending Fioramonti's wonderful, must-read book.

6  I recognise that to some this may seem quite Eurocentric: that political economy was born in Europe and spread and was modified by others outside Europe. This seems to be borne out by the facts. However, this is very different from saying that capitalism was endogenous to Western Europe in general and England in particular (Wood 2002). For challenges or problematisations of this view from the perspective of

combined and uneven development and international interconnections, see Hobson (2004), Bhambra (2009; 2010) and Anievas and Nisancioglu (2013).

7 See socserv.mcmaster.ca/econ/ugcm/3ll3/petty/taxes.txt (accessed 26 December 2013).

8 In his *Theories of Surplus Value* (1861–63), Marx traces this back to Hobbes. See www.marxists.org/archive/marx/works/1863/theories-surplus-value/add1.htm#s1 (accessed 5 February 2014).

9 Taken from Henry George's *The Science of Political Economy* (1898) at www.politicaleconomy.org/spell_3.htm (accessed 5 December 2013).

10 Marx does say that: 'The public debt becomes one of the most powerful levers of primitive accumulation. As with the stroke of an enchanter's wand, it endows barren money with the power of breeding and thus turns it into capital' (Marx 1996: 529). Still, even if Marx understood what was happening in the monetary sphere, the consequences of creating money by extending loans is never fully theorised in his system. Put simply, there is no discussion of the private capitalisation of money.

11 When a bank makes loans, it creates only the principal, not interest. This means that there is always more debt in the system than there is the ability to repay it.

12 The creation of the national debt was without doubt the master stroke of the early bankers. But as Brewer (1989: 14) reminds us, 'the fiscal demands of the crown also prompted the sale of trade privileges and monopolies' in the reign of Elizabeth I. Brewer quotes Hurstfield, who described this as 'putting up for auction the machinery of government itself'. Monopolies were granted on 'starch, coal, salt and soap' and raised £80,000 a year for the Crown in the 1630s and 'between £200,000 and £300,000 for the monopolists'.

13 In his *Theories of Surplus Value* (1861–63), Marx traces this back to Hobbes. See www.marxists.org/archive/marx/works/1863/theories-surplus-value/add1.htm#s1 (accessed 5 February 2014).

14 Hall and Klitgaard (2012) come closest and their study comes highly recommended.

15 The complaint of not enough money for even a basic livelihood seems ubiquitous in market culture. I recall asking my Pop (my Italian grandfather) why they emigrated from Italy to Canada. He was a peasant farmer but did have some land. His answer? No money!

16 Of course, some workers will have shares in banking corporations, but, given our knowledge of the distribution of wealth, there is no way in the world that they would ever come to own them outright or in a significant proportion. For example, Warren Buffet's Berkshire Hathaway owns about 8% of Wells Fargo but it is impossible to tell who all the owners of Berkshire Hathaway are. Either way, the owners of Berkshire Hathaway are getting wealthy from Wells Fargo's ability to create money as debt.

17 As I was making some revisions for publication, two telling articles appeared confirming what bankers already know – Wolf (2014b) and Graeber (2014). The documentary '97% Owned' should also be viewed by anyone who wants to understand modern money.

18 Each year I ask my students to do an exercise. I ask them to write down how they think money is currently created and then ask them to research how it is actually created. The myths of money could not be more divergent from the truth of its creation, as they soon discover.

19 See im.ft-static.com/content/images/a858f40e-ca80-11e1-89f8-00144feabdco.pdf (accessed 9 February 2014). Banks appear to be the leading sector of capitalisation in this list, but it is misleading. The majority of oil is owned by state-run oil companies; if we added their projected market value to the existing value of firms on the list, oil and gas companies would rank highest (Di Muzio 2012).

20 Strangely, scientists discovered nuclear fission two decades before they came to understand the process of photosynthesis (Smil 1994: 2).

21 I am not suggesting here, as do Hall and Klitgaard (2012: 95), that the expansion of debt money corresponds in an exact way with energy consumption. What I merely suggest is that we can observe that countries with greater outstanding debts – national, commercial and private – will be larger consumers of energy.

22 I cite Arrighi here for his work on hegemonic transitions and less for his focus on energy as a key determinant of credit growth and capitalisation.

## 4 Differential consumption

1 I treat differential consumption as being synonymous with conspicuous consumption, and I thank James McMahon for pressing me on this at the Capital as Power conference in 2012.

2 It is never made entirely clear what they mean by 'overseas conquests'. At one point, the report also suggests that dopamine levels in the population may have something to do with the 'successes' of plutonomies (Citigroup 2005: 9).

3 The index represents 6,000 global stocks and is typically understood to be a benchmark for global securities.

4 See information on the MSCI Index's performance at www.mscibarra.com/products/indices/international_equity_indices/gimi/stdindex/performance.html (accessed 20 February 2013).

5 To put this in perspective for the majority of wage or salaried workers, suppose your annual income is the median salary of a plutonomy, roughly US$45,000. Now, imagine that your employer gave you a raise of 2,548%. Your new annual income would be US$1,146,600 in addition to your median salary.

6 While it may not be definitive, there is significant evidence for this claim in three recent popular studies. Two consider the newly affluent in the United States: Frank (2007) and Taylor et al. (2009). The study by Taylor et al. is the most generous to the global wealthy and found through surveys that many of the super-wealthy prefer 'stealth wealth' or to have their wealth go under the radar. These people are assumed to avoid displays of conspicuous consumption. Whether there is a difference between what they say and what they do is unknown. A third study has a slightly more global focus: Freeland (2012). An additional study from the Center on Wealth and Philanthropy at Boston College entitled 'Joys and dilemmas of wealth' suggests much

the same. The study was reported on in *The Atlantic* but unreleased (see Wood 2011).

7 Frank notes that about half the wealth in the United States was owned by 'the richest 1 percent of families' (Frank 2007: 38).

8 The population figure is an estimate based on the censuses of 1890 and 1900. See www.census.gov/ (accessed 20 January 2013).

9 As will be discussed further below, this is now surpassed in size and value by the Indian petrochemical tycoon Mukesh Ambani's billion-dollar home in Mumbai. Called Antilia, the 27-storey home dwarfs Biltmore with 400,000 square feet of living space (Hanrahan 2012). As a reference point, consider that the Great Pyramid of Giza, once the world's tallest structure, was 181,818 square feet.

10 See www.census.gov/const/ C25Ann/sftotalmedavgsqft.pdf (accessed 22 January 2013).

11 See www.biltmore.com/ our_story/our_history/ (accessed 22 January 2013).

12 The fall of the 'Bamboo' and 'Iron' curtains in the 1990s doubled the global workforce (Freeman 2010). The fact that by 1991 communism no longer posed a serious ideological threat to the private ownership of power and wealth can also be viewed as a chief characteristic of this age.

13 Data are from the World Bank Development Indicators; GDP is expressed in current US dollars: data. worldbank.org/indicator/NY.GDP. MKTP.CD (accessed 9 December 2012).

14 See www.forbes.com/sites/ seankilachand/2012/03/21/forbes-history-the-original-1987-list-of-international-billionaires/ (accessed 9 December 2012).

15 The growth in the number of ultra-HNWIs is also increasing the desire for intelligence on the behaviour of the wealthy and the willingness to service them. As a recent notice from Wealth-X notes: 'Having seen significant growth in 2012 on the back of a surge in global demand for Ultra High Net Worth intelligence, Wealth-X announced its plans to accelerate expansion in 2013. With over 160 researchers covering 35 languages, the global research team plans to recruit another 150 new employees worldwide.' See www.wealthx.com/ articles/2013/wealth-x-announces-aggressive-expansion/ (accessed 12 February 2013).

16 See www.forbes.com/sites/ luisakroll/2013/03/04/inside-the-2013-billionaires-list-facts-and-figures/ (accessed 17 February 2014).

17 Could it also be a law of history: the less you deserve your fortune, the more you aim to conspicuously consume? And if this 'rule' is in any way correct, what reasons might we give for it other than power and status-seeking?

18 The CLEWI for 2012 is at www.forbes.com/sites/scott decarlo/2012/09/19/cost-of-living-extremely-well-index-our-annual-consumer-price-index-billionaire-style/ (accessed 12 February 2013).

19 According to Frank, it is now commonplace for the uber-rich to have a fleet of yachts – some with shadow boats: 'At the Ft. Lauderdale boat show in 2005, I got a glimpse of the latest innovation in boater bling – the 170-foot Paladin, known as a "shadow boat." A shadow boat is a floating garage that tags along with the main yacht and carries all the extra "toys," like cars and

smaller boats. It's a kind of yacht for your megayacht. The Paladin, now owned by a Saudi, holds four to six cars, several motorcycles, jet skis, a submarine and a helicopter. It's also got a decompression chamber, a walk-in freezer, gym and night-vision cameras' (Frank 2007: 126–7).

20 See www.industrytap.com/worlds-largest-superyacht-comes-with-a-bullet-proof-master-suite-missile-defense-system/12014 (accessed 17 February 2014).

21 Frank (2007: 126) informs us that it costs 10% to 15% of the purchase price of a yacht to maintain it yearly.

22 See '*ShowBoats International* 2013 Global Order Book' at www.sanlorenzoamericas.com/photos/articleDocs/20.pdf (accessed 12 February 2013).

23 See www.ussubmarines.com/faq/luxury.php3 (accessed 14 February 2013).

24 See www.forbes.com/india-billionaires/ (accessed 12 February 2013).

25 See povertydata.worldbank.org/poverty/country/IND (accessed 12 February 2013).

26 The literature on this topic is too vast to consider here, but see Rockström et al. (2009) as well as Kempf (2008: 71) and Jackson (2009: 47ff), who demonstrate that material consumption puts extreme pressure on the environment and the myth that growth and environmental stress have been decoupled.

## 5 Society versus wealth

1 For a more comprehensive account of radical ideas during this time, see Hill (1991) and Kennedy (2008).

2 According to Wood and Wood (1997: 50), the right of resistance can be traced back to Ponet's *A Shorte Treatise of Politike Power* (1556).

3 The ensuing discussion draws on Locke's 'On Property' in *Two Treatises of Government*. I cite the text only when quoting it directly.

4 Macpherson notes: 'the structure Locke had built on his unhistorical postulate' read back 'into an original natural condition of mankind the later apparatus of money, markets, trade for profit, and wage-labour' (Macpherson 1978: 31).

5 In this sense, Bentham may be thought of as the originator of the private for-profit prison.

6 Bentham writes: 'Property is nothing but a basis of expectation; the expectation of deriving certain advantages from a thing which we are said to possess, in consequence of the relation in which we stand towards it' (quoted in Macpherson 1978: 51).

7 Nitzan and Bichler (2009: 72–3) demonstrate why perfectly competitive equilibrium is an impossibility.

8 We will not dwell on this concept, but to provide an example for those unfamiliar with the term, consider a chocolate bar. The first chocolate bar you buy and eat will likely give you a great deal of satisfaction. Having an additional chocolate bar will probably still be quite satisfying but less so than the first. A third, still less, and by the fourth chocolate bar you may start to feel sick. In simple terms, this means that you should stop eating chocolate after your third bar. This, of course, does not seem to be the case with accumulating money. If the satisfaction of owners with money obeyed this law of diminishing marginal utility, we would have far fewer capitalists!

9 The authors also note the biological explanations of Herbert Spencer, William Graham Sumner and Ayn Rand.

10 See Chapters 5 and 6 of McQuaig and Brooks (2012) for an enlightened discussion on the same theme.

11 Katrina Browne has made a documentary of her discovery called 'Traces of the Trade'; see www.pbs.org/pov/tracesofthetrade/. Her story is detailed in the document in footnote 126.

### 6 The party of the 99%

1 To which we add that it is not passivity alone, but a lack of knowledge concerning the operations of the 1%. Ignorance is just as much a breeding ground for passivity as despair.

2 See www.ilo.org (accessed 18 February 2014).

3 See www.theguardian.com/news/datablog/2011/oct/17/occupy-protests-world-list-map (accessed 18 February 2013).

4 See www.adbusters.org/blogs/adbusters-blog/occupywallstreet.html (accessed 18 February 2013).

5 I would like to thank Adam Harmes and Art Piatek for the Warsaw conversations on this matter at the shacks.

6 Perhaps not surprisingly, Quigley's book was suppressed by his publishing house.

7 On rampant insider trading in the United States, see www.pbs.org/wgbh/pages/frontline/business-economy-financial-crisis/to-catch-a-trader/preet-bharara-insider-trading-is-rampant-on-wall-street/ (accessed 19 February 2014).

8 One thing that might be pursued is a law that stipulates that every lending institution has to reveal its owners – down to the individual.

9 After this book was submitted for review, an important article appeared on this matter: see Graeber (2014).

10 For example, suppose you take a $100 loan at 5%. The bank creates the $100 out of thin air and puts numbers into your account on a computer. You have to pay back the initial $100 plus $5 in interest, or $105. Since banks charge but do not create interest, this is why there is always more debt in the system than there is money to pay it.

11 See www.positivemoney.org/ (accessed 21 February 2014).

12 The documentary by the brilliant Adam Curtis – *The Mayfair Set* – also explores this relationship.

13 This idea appears to originate with the British engineer and founder of the Social Credit Movement C. H. Douglas and is discussed at length by Rowbotham (1998: 227ff). My thoughts in this paragraph were developed in dialogue with Rowbotham's work.

# BIBLIOGRAPHY

Albritton, Robert (2009) *Let Them Eat Junk: How capitalism creates hunger and obesity*. London: Pluto Press.

Allianz (2013) *Global Wealth Report 2013*. Munich: Allianz. www.allianz.com/v_1380187782000/media/economic_research/publications/specials/en/AGWR2013e.pdf.

Alperovitz, Gar and Lew Daly (2008) *Unjust Deserts: How the rich are taking our common inheritance and why we should take it back*. New York, NY: The New Press.

— (2010) 'The undeserving rich'. *Dollars & Sense*, March/April.

Anderson, Richard (2011) 'Masters of the universe: meet the world's best-paid men'. *BBC News*, 2 February. www.bbc.co.uk/news/business-11942117.

Anievas, Alexander and Kerem Nisancioglu (2013) 'What's at stake in the transition debate? Rethinking the origins of capitalism and the "rise of the West"'. *Millennium: Journal of International Studies* 42(1): 78–102.

Arneil, Barbara (1994) 'Plantations, and property: John Locke and the economic defense of colonialism'. *Journal of the History of Ideas* 55(4): 591–609.

— (1996) *John Locke and America: The defence of English colonialism*. Oxford: Clarendon.

Arrighi, Giovanni (1994) *The Long Twentieth Century*. London: Verso.

Aspromourgos, Tony (1996) *On the Origins of Classical Economics: Distribution and value from William Petty to Adam Smith*. New York, NY: Routledge.

— (2005) 'The invention of the concept of social surplus: Petty in the Hartlib circle'. *European Journal of the History of Economic Thought* 12(1): 1–24.

Atwood, Margaret (2012) 'Our faith is fraying in the god of money'. *Financial Times*, 13 April.

Baines, Joseph (2014) 'Food price inflation as redistribution: towards a new analysis of corporate power in the world food system'. *New Political Economy* 19(1): 79–112.

Bakan, Joel (2005) *The Corporation: The pathological pursuit of profit and power*. New York, NY: Free Press.

Bakker, Isabella and Stephen Gill (eds) (2003) *Power, Production and Social Reproduction*. Basingstoke: Palgrave Macmillan.

Balzli, Beat and Michaela Schiessl (2009) 'The man nobody wanted to hear'. *Speigel Online*, 7 August.

Banner, Stuart (2005) *How the Indians Lost their Land: Law and power on the frontier*. Cambridge, MA: Harvard University Press.

Barry, David (2012) *The Politics of Actually Existing Unsustainability: Human flourishing in a climate-changed, carbon-constrained world*. Oxford: Oxford University Press.

Bartels, Larry M. (2008) *Unequal Democracy: The political economy of the new Gilded Age*. Princeton, NJ: Princeton University Press.

Beard, Patricia (2009) *After the Ball: Gilded Age secrets, boardroom betrayals, and the party that ignited the great Wall Street scandal of 1905*. New York, NY: HarperCollins.

Bernstein, Peter L. (2000) *The Power of Gold: The history of an obsession*. New York, NY: John Wiley & Sons.

Bernstein, William J. (2004) *The Birth of Plenty: How the prosperity of the modern world was created*. New York, NY: McGraw-Hill.

Bhambra, Gurminder K. (2009) *Rethinking Modernity: Postcolonialism and the sociological imagination*. Basingstoke: Palgrave Macmillan.

— (2010) 'Historical sociology, international relations and connected histories'. *Cambridge Review of International Affairs* 23(1): 127–43.

BIS (2013) *Triennial Central Bank Survey: Foreign exchange turnover in April 2013: preliminary global results*. Basel: Bank for International Settlements (BIS). www.bis.org/publ/rpfx13fx.pdf.

Blackburn, Robin (2010) *The Making of New World Slavery: From the baroque to the modern, 1492–1800*. London: Verso.

Boehm, Christopher (2001) *Hierarchy in the Forest: The evolution of egalitarian behavior*. Cambridge, MA: Harvard University Press.

Boldrin, Michele and David K. Levine (2012) 'The case against patents'. St Louis, MO: Research Division, Federal Reserve Bank of St Louis. research.stlouisfed.org/wp/2012/2012-035.pdf.

Borger, Julian (2005) 'Tapes reveal Enron's secret role in California's power blackouts'. *Guardian*, 5 February.

Bottigheimer, Karl S. (1967) 'English money and Irish land: the "adventurers" in the Cromwellian settlement of Ireland'. *Journal of British Studies* 7(1): 12–27.

Braddick, Michael J. (1996) *The Nerves of State: Taxation and the financing of the English state, 1558–1714*. Manchester: Manchester University Press.

— (2009) *God's Fury, England's Fire: A new history of the English Civil War*. London: Penguin Books.

Braudel, Fernand (1977) *Afterthoughts on Material Civilization and Capitalism*. Translated by Patricia M. Ranum. Baltimore, MD: Johns Hopkins University Press.

— (1983) *The Wheels of Commerce: Civilization and capitalism, 15–18th century*. New York, NY: Harper and Row.

Brennan, Jordan (2012) 'The power underpinnings, and some distributional consequences, of trade and investment liberalization in Canada'. Preprint. *New Political Economy*. No. iFirst, pp. 1–33.

Brenner, Robert (2003) *Merchants and Revolution: Commercial change, political conflict and London's overseas traders, 1550–1653*. London: Verso.

Brewer, John (1989) *The Sinews of Power: War, money and the English state, 1688–1783*. London: Unwin Hyman.

Brown, Ellen Hodgson (2007) *The Web of Debt: The shocking truth about our money system and how we can break free*. Baton Rouge, LA: Third Millennium Press.

Budden, Robert, Emily Steel and April Dembosky (2013) 'Facebook looks to new video ads as it seeks new revenue stream'. *Financial Times*, 6 May.

Campbell, Colin (1995) 'Conspicuous confusion? A critique of Veblen's theory of conspicuous consumption'. *Sociological Theory* 13(1): 37–47.

Cannan, Edwin (1921) 'Early history of the term capital'. *Quarterly Journal of Economics* 35(3): 469–81.

Canny, Nicholas P. (1973) 'The ideology of English colonization: from Ireland to America'. *William and Mary Quarterly* 30(4): 575–98.

Capgemini and Merrill Lynch (2011) *World Wealth Report 2011*. New York, NY: Capgemini and Merrill Lynch Global Wealth Management. www.capgemini.com/insights-and-resources/by-publication/world-wealth-report-2011/.

Capgemini and RBC (2013) *World Wealth Report 2013*. New York, NY: Capgemini and RBC Wealth Management. www.worldwealthreport.com/.

Carlisle, Rodney P. (2009) *The Gilded Age, 1870–1900*. New York, NY: Facts on File.

Carroll, William K. (2010) *The Making of the Transnational Capitalist Class: Corporate power in the 21st century*. London: Zed Books.

Chossudovsky, Michel (2003) *The Globalization of Poverty and the New World Order*. Pincourt: Global Research.

Citigroup (2005) 'Plutonomy: buying luxury, explaining global imbalances'. Industry Note, 16 October. New York, NY: Citigroup.

— (2006) 'Revisiting plutonomy: the rich getting richer'. Industry Note, 5 March. New York, NY: Citigroup.

Clark, John Bates (1965 [1899]) *The Distribution of Wealth*. New York, NY: Augustus M. Kelley.

Cochrane, D. T. (2011) 'Castoriadis, Veblen and the "power theory of capital"'. In I. S. Straume and J. F. Humphreys (eds) *Depoliticization: The political imaginary of global capitalism*. Aarhus and Copenhagen: Aarhus University Press, pp. 89–123.

Cohan, William D. (2012) 'The credit card for the 1 percent of the 1 percent'. *Bloomberg*, 29 February. www.bloomberg.com/news/2012-02-29/the-credit-card-for-the-1-percent-of-the-1-percent-the-ticker.html.

Cohen, William (1969) 'Thomas Jefferson and the problem of slavery'. *Journal of American History* 56(3): 503–26.

Collins, Chuck, Mike Lapham and Scott Klinger (2004) *I Didn't Do It Alone: Society's contribution to individual wealth and success*. Boston, MA: Responsible Wealth, a project of United for a Fair Economy.

Collins, Josh-Ryan and Tony Greenham, Richard Werner and Andrew Jackson (2011) *Where Does Money Come From? A guide to the UK monetary and banking system*. London: New Economics Foundation.

Cornelius, Janet (1983) '"We slipped and learned to read": Slave accounts of the literacy process, 1830–1865'. *Phylon* 44(3): 171–86.

Cox, Robert W. (1981) 'Social forces, states and world orders'. *Millennium: Journal of International Studies* 10(2): 128.

Credit Suisse (2013) *World Wealth Report 2013*. Zurich: Credit Suisse. resistir.info/varios/global_wealth_report_2013.pdf.

Dahms, Harry F. (ed.) (2000) *Transformations of Capitalism: Economy, society, and the state in modern times*. New York, NY: New York University Press.

Dauvergne, Peter (2008) *The Shadows of Consumption: Consequences for the global environment*. Cambridge, MA: MIT Press.

Davies, Glyn (2002) *A History of Money from Ancient Times to the Present Day*. Cardiff: University of Wales Press.

Davies, James B., Susanna Sandstrom, Anthony Shorrocks and Edward N. Wolff (2006) 'The world distribution of household wealth'. Helsinki: UNU-World Institute for Development Economics Research. www.globalpolicy.org/images/pdfs/1206unufull.pdf.

Davies, Stephen (2003) *Empiricism and History*. Basingstoke: Palgrave Macmillan.

Davis, David Brion (1999) *The Problem of Slavery in the Age of Revolution 1770–1823*. Oxford: Oxford University Press.

De Botton, Alain (2005) *Status Anxiety*. London: Penguin Books.

de Soto, Hernando (2003) *The Mystery of Capital: Why capitalism triumphs in the West and fails everywhere else*. New York, NY: Basic Books.

Di Muzio, Tim (2007) 'The art of colonization: the capitalization of the state and the ongoing nature of primitive accumulation'. *New Political Economy* 12(4): 517–39.

— (2012) 'Capitalizing a future unsustainable: finance, energy and the fate of market civilization'. *Review of International Political Economy* 19(I.3): 363–88.

— (ed.) (2014) *The Capitalist Mode of Power: Critical engagements with the power theory of value*. London: Routledge.

— and Richard Robbins (2015) *Stark Utopia: Debt as a technology of power*. London: Bloomsbury.

Diamond, Jared (2005) *Collapse: How societies choose to fail or succeed*. New York, NY: Penguin Books.

Dickson, P. G. M. (1967) *The Financial Revolution in England: A study in the development of public credit, 1688–1756*. New York, NY: St Martin's Press.

Domhoff, G. William (2006) *Who Rules America? Power, politics and social change*. New York, NY: McGraw-Hill.

Douglass, Frederick (1857) 'An address on West India emancipation'. Delivered at Canandaigua, New York, 4 August. www.lib.rochester.edu/index.cfm?PAGE=4398.

Ehrlich, Paul R. and Anne H. Ehrlich (2008) *The Dominant Animal: Human evolution and the environment*. Washington, DC: Island Press.

Einstein, Albert (2009 [1949]) 'Why socialism?' *Monthly Review* 61(101): May. monthlyreview.org/2009/05/01/why-socialism.

Engelbrecht, H. C. and F. C. Hanighen (1934) *Merchants of Death: A study of the international armaments industry*. New York, NY: Dodd, Mead & Company.

Engerman, Stanley (1999) *Terms of Labor: Slavery, serfdom and free labor*. Stanford, CA: Stanford University Press.

Federal Reserve (2014) *Federal Reserve Statistical Release: Z.1. Financial Accounts of the United States*. Washington, DC: Board of Governors of the Federal Reserve System. www.federalreserve.gov/releases/z1/current/z1.pdf.

Ferguson, Niall (1998) *The House of Rothschild: Money's prophets 1798–1548*. New York, NY: Penguin Books.

Ferro, Marc (1997) *Colonization: A global history*. London: Routledge.

Fioramonti, Lorenzo (2013) *Gross Domestic Problem: The politics behind the world's most powerful number*. London: Zed Books.

Foreman, John and Robbie Pierce Stimson (1991) *The Vanderbilts and the Gilded Age: Architectural aspirations, 1879–1901*. New York, NY: St Martin's Press.

Forstater, Matthew (2005) 'Taxation and primitive accumulation: the case of colonial Africa'. *Research in Political Economy* 22: 51–65.

Foucault, Michel (1975) *Discipline and Punish: The birth of the prison*. Translated by Alan Sheridan. New York, NY: Random House.

— (1977) *Power/Knowledge: Selected interviews and other writings 1972–1977*. New York, NY: Pantheon Books.

— (2003) *"Society Must be Defended". Lectures at the Collège de France, 1975–76*. Edited by Mauro Bertani and Alessandro Fontana. Translated by David Macey. New York, NY: Picador.

Fox, Adam (2009) 'Sir William Petty, Ireland and the making of a political economist 1653–87'. *Economic History Review* 62(2): 388–404.

Frank, Robert (2007) *Richistan: A Journey through the 21st century wealth boom and the lives of the new rich*. London and New York, NY: Piatkus Books.

Freeland, Chrystia (2012) *Plutocrats: The rise of the new global super-rich and the fall of everyone else*. London: Allen Lane.

Freeman, Richard (2010) 'What really ails Europe (and America): the doubling of the workforce'. *The Globalist*, 5 March. www.the globalist.com/storyid.aspx?Story Id=4542.

Fuchs, Christian (2012) 'The political economy of privacy on Facebook'. *Television New Media* 13(2): 139–58.

Galbraith, John Kenneth (1977) *The Age of Uncertainty*. London: BBC.

Garnett, George (2009) *The Norman Conquest: A very short introduction*. Oxford: Oxford University Press.

George, Susan (1988) *How the Other Half Dies: The real reasons for world hunger*. London: Rowman & Littlefield.

— (2010) *Whose Crisis, Whose Future: Towards a greener, fairer, richer world*. London: Polity.

Gilens, Martin (2005) 'Inequality and democratic responsiveness'. *Public Opinion Quarterly* 69(5): 778–896.

— and Benjamin I. Page (2014) 'Testing theories of American politics: elites, interest groups, and average citizens'. Forthcoming in *Perspectives on Politics*. www.princeton.edu/~mgilens/ Gilens%20homepage%20 materials/Gilens%20and%20 Page/Gilens%20and%20Page% 202014-Testing%20Theories%20 3-7-14.pdf.

Gill, Stephen (1995) 'Globalization, market civilization and disciplinary neoliberalism'. *Millennium: Journal of International Studies* 24(3): 399–423.

— (2008 [2002]) *Power and Resistance in the New World Order*. Basingstoke: Palgrave Macmillan.

— (ed.) (2011) *Global Crises and the Crisis of Global Leadership*.

Cambridge: Cambridge University Press.

— and Claire Cutler (eds) (2014) *New Constitutionalism and World Order.* Cambridge: Cambridge University Press.

— and David Law (1988) *Global Political Economy: Perspective, problems and policies.* Baltimore, MD: Johns Hopkins University Press.

Goldstone, Jack A. (2002) 'Efflorescences and economic growth in world history: rethinking the "rise of the West" and the Industrial Revolution'. *Journal of World History* 13(2): 323–89.

Gordon, Greg (2013) 'Industry wrote provision that undercuts credit-rating overhaul'. *McClatchy*, 7 August.

Graeber, David (2014) 'The truth is out: money is just an IOU and the banks are rolling in it'. *Guardian*, 18 March.

Hager, Sandy Brian (2013) 'America's real "debt dilemma"'. *Review of Capital as Power* 1(1): 41–62.

— (2014) 'What happened to the bondholding class? Public debt, power and the top one per cent'. *New Political Economy* 19(2): 155–82.

Hall, Charles A. S. and Kent A. Klitgaard (2012) *Energy and the Wealth of Nations: Understanding the biophysical economy.* New York, NY: Springer.

Hamilton, Clive (2004) *Growth Fetish.* London: Pluto Press.

Hanrahan, Mark (2012) 'Antilia: inside Mukesh Ambani's 27-story Mumbai residence, world's first $1 billion home'. *Huffington Post*, 21 May.

Harding, David, Karen Harris, Richard Jackson and Phil Leung (2014)

*The Renaissance in Mergers and Acquisitions: What to do with all that cash?* Boston, MA: Bain & Company. www.bain.com/Images/BAIN_BRIEF_The-renaissance-in-mergers-and-acquisitions-2-what-to-do-with-cash.pdf.

Häring, Norber (2013) 'The veil of deception over money: how central bankers and textbooks distort the nature of banking and central banking'. *Real-World Economics Review* 63: 1–18.

Harmes, Adam (1998) 'Institutional investors and the reproduction of neoliberalism'. *Review of International Political Economy* 5(1): 92–121.

— (2001) *Unseen Power: How mutual funds threaten the political and economic wealth of nations.* Toronto: Stoddart.

Harris, Paul (2013) 'Plans for Titanic replica set sail'. *Guardian*, 26 February.

Hay, Douglas (1980) 'Crime and justice in eighteenth- and nineteenth-century England'. *Crime and Justice* 2: 45–84.

— Peter Linebaugh, John Rule, E. P. Thompson and Calvin Winslow (eds) (1975) *Albion's Fatal Tree: Crime and society in eighteenth-century England.* London: Allen Lane.

Hazlett, Hugh (1938) 'The financing of the British armies in Ireland, 1641–9'. *Irish Historical Studies* 1(1): 21–41.

Heinberg, Richard (2001) *The End of Growth: Adapting to our new economic reality.* Gabriola Island: New Society Publishers.

— (2007) *Peak Everything: Waking up to a century of declines.* Gabriola Island: New Society Publishers.

— (2009) *Searching for a Miracle: Net energy limits and the fate of industrial society.* Santa Rosa, CA: Forum on Globalization and Post-Carbon Institute. www.postcarbon.org/report/44377-searching-for-a-miracle.

— (2011) *The End of Growth: Adapting to our new economic reality.* Gabriola Island: New Society Publishers.

Henry, James S. (2003) *The Blood Bankers: Tale from the global underground economy.* New York, NY: Four Walls Eight Windows.

— (2012) *The Price of Offshore Revisited.* Chesham: Tax Justice Network. www.taxjustice.net/cms/upload/pdf/Price_of_Offshore_Revisited_120722.pdf.

Henwood, Doug (1997) *Wall Street: How it works and for whom.* London: Verso.

Hern, Alex (2013) 'The faces of Facebook app shows all 1.2 billion users'. *Guardian*, 1 October. www.theguardian.com/technology/2013/sep/30/faces-of-facebook.

Hill, Christopher (1991 [1972]) *The World Turned Upside Down: Radical ideas during the English revolution.* Harmondsworth: Penguin Books.

— (ed.) (2006) *Winstanley: The law of freedom and other writings.* Cambridge: Cambridge University Press.

Hobbes, Thomas (1651) *Leviathan or the Matter, Forme, & Power of a Common-wealth Ecclesiasticall and Civill.* London: The Green Dragon in St Pauls Churchyard.

Hobson, John M. (2004) *The Eastern Origins of Western Civilization.* Cambridge: Cambridge University Press.

Huber, Matthew T. (2013) *Lifeblood: Oil, Freedom and the Forces of Capital.* Minneapolis, MN: University of Minnesota Press.

IAASTD (2009) *Agriculture at a Crossroads: Synthesis report.* Washington, DC: International Assessment of Agricultural Knowledge, Science and Technology for Development (IAASTD).

ILO (2014) *Global Employment Trends 2014: Risk of a jobless recovery.* Geneva: International Labour Organization (ILO). www.ilo.org/wcmsp5/groups/public/---dg reports/---dcomm/---publ/documents/publication/wcms_233953.pdf.

IMF (2000) *Offshore Financial Centers.* IMF Background Paper, 23 June. Washington, DC: International Monetary Fund (IMF).

Jackson, Tim (2009) *Prosperity without Growth.* London: Sustainable Development Commission.

Jahn, Beate (2013) *Liberal Internationalism: Theory, history, practice.* Basingstoke: Palgrave Macmillan.

Jevons, William Stanley (1866) *The Coal Question: An inquiry concerning the progress of the nation, and the probable exhaustion of our coal-mines.* London: Macmillan and Co.

Josephson, Matthew (1934) *The Robber Barons.* New York, NY: Harcourt, Brace and Company.

Kempf, Hervé (2008) *How the Rich are Destroying the Earth.* Translated by Leslie Thatcher. Totnes: Green Books.

Kennedy, Geoff (2008) *Diggers, Levellers and Agrarian Capitalism: Radical political thought in seventeenth century England.* Lanham, MD: Lexington Books.

Khalek, Rania (2011) '6 creepy new weapons the police and military use to subdue unarmed people'. *AlterNet*, 1 August. www.alternet.org/story/151864/6_creepy_new_weapons_the_police_and_military_use_to_subdue_unarmed_people.

Kikeri, Sunita and Aishetu Fatima Kolo (2005) *Privatization: Trends and recent developments*. Washington, DC: World Bank. openknowledge.worldbank.org/handle/10986/8494.

Kingsley, Patrick (2012) 'How credit ratings agencies rule the world'. *Guardian*, 16 February.

Kirkaldy, Adam C. (1920) *Wealth: Its production and distribution*. London: Methuen.

Knight Frank (2012) *The Wealth Report 2012: The global perspective on prime property and wealth*. London: Think for Knight Frank.

— (2013) *The Wealth Report 2013: The global perspective on prime property and wealth*. London: Think for Knight Frank.

Kolbert, Elizabeth (2014) *The Sixth Extinction: An unnatural history*. New York, NY: Henry Holt.

Komisar, Lucy (2003) 'Offshore banking: the secret threat to America'. *Dissent*, Spring: 45–51.

Korten, David C. (2001) *When Corporations Rule the World*. 2nd edition. Bloomfield, CT: Kumarian Press.

Kroll, Louisa (2005) 'Why so many new billionaires'. *Forbes*, 10 March. www.forbes.com/2005/03/10/cz_lk_lg_0310commentary_billo5.html.

Kucera, Danielle (2011) 'Facebook hires Burson-Marsteller to pitch story on Google'. *Bloomberg*, 12 May. www.bloomberg.com/news/2011-05-12/facebook-enlists-pr-firm-burson-marsteller-to-pitch-google-privacy-story.html.

Landes, David (1998) *The Wealth and Poverty of Nations: Why some are so rich and some so poor*. New York, NY: W. W. Norton & Company.

Lebor, Adam (2013) *Tower of Basel*. New York, NY: Public Affairs.

Litterick, David (2002) 'Billionaire who broke the Bank of England'. *Daily Telegraph*, 13 September.

Locke, John (2005 [1690]) *Two Treatises of Government*. Project Gutenberg e-book. www.gutenberg.org/ebooks/7370.

Macpherson, C. B. (ed.) (1978) *Property: Mainstream and critical positions*. Toronto: University of Toronto Press.

Mallaby, Sebastian (2010) *More Money than God: Hedge funds and the making of a new elite*. New York, NY: Penguin Books.

Malthus, Thomas Robert (1992) *An Essay on the Principle of Population*. Edited by David Winch. Cambridge: Cambridge University Press.

Mankiw, N. Gregory (2005) *Macroeconomics*. 7th edition. New York, NY: Worth Publishing.

Manning, Richard (2004) 'The oil we eat'. *Harper's*, February: 37–45.

Marx, Karl (1978) *The Marx–Engels Reader*. 2nd edition. Edited by Robert C. Tucker. New York, NY: W. W. Norton & Company.

— (1996 [1887]) *Capital: A critique of political economy. Volume 1*. Translated by Samuel Moore and Edward Aveling. Moscow: Progress Publishers.

— and Friedrich Engels (1848) *Manifesto of the Communist Party*. Translated by Samual Moore. www.marxists.org/archive/

marx/works/1848/communist-manifesto/.

McKinsey (2009) *Global Capital Markets: Entering a new era.* New York, NY: McKinsey Global Institute. www.mckinsey.com/insights/global_capital_markets/global_capital_markets_entering_a_new_era.

— (2011) *Mapping Global Capital Markets 2011.* New York, NY: McKinsey Global Institute. www.mckinsey.com/insights/mgi/research/financial_markets/mapping_global_capital_markets_2011.

— (2013) *Financial Globalization: Retreat or reset?* New York, NY: McKinsey Global Institute. www.mckinsey.com/insights/global_capital_markets/financial_globalization.

McMahon, James (2013) 'The rise of a confident Hollywood: risk and the capitalization of cinema'. *Review of Capital as Power* 1(1): 23–40.

McMurtry, John (1999) *The Cancer Stage of Capitalism.* London: Pluto Press.

McQuaig, Linda and Neil Brooks (2012) *Billionaires' Ball: Gluttony and hubris in an age of epic inequality.* Boston, MA: Beacon Press.

Mellars, Paul (2006) 'Why did modern human populations disperse from Africa ca. 60,000 years ago – a new model'. *Proceedings of the National Academy of Sciences of the United States of America* 103(25): 9381–6.

Michie, Ranald (2008) *The Global Securities Market: A history.* Oxford: Oxford University Press.

Mill, John Stuart (2004) *Principles of Political Economy.* Edited by Stephen Nathanson. Indianapolis, IN: Hackett Publishing.

Mills, C. Wright (2000 [1956]) *The Power Elite.* Oxford: Oxford University Press.

Milonakis, Dimitris and Ben Fine (2009) *From Political Economy to Economics: Method, the social and the historical in the evolution of economic theory.* New York, NY: Routledge.

Minority Staff of the Permanent Subcommittee on Investigations (2001) *Correspondent Banking: A gateway for money laundering.* Washington, DC: US Government Printing Office. www.imolin.org/pdf/imolin/CPRT-107SPRT69919.pdf.

Mintz, Sidney W. (1986) *Sweetness and Power: The place of sugar in modern history.* London: Penguin Books.

Moore, Barrington Jr. (1974) *The Social Origins of Dictatorship and Democracy: Lord and peasant in the making of the modern world.* New York, NY: Penguin Books.

Neeson, J. M. (1993) *Commoners: Common right, enclosure and social change in England 1700–1820.* Cambridge: Cambridge University Press.

Nef, John U. (1977) 'An early energy crisis and its consequences'. *Scientific American*, November: 140–50.

Newell, Peter (2012) *Globalization and the Environment: Capitalism, ecology and power.* Cambridge: Polity.

Nikiforuk, Andrew (2012) *The Energy of Slaves: Oil and the new servitude.* Vancouver: Greystone Books.

Nitzan, Jonathan (2001) 'Regimes of differential accumulation: mergers, stagflation and the logic of globalization'. *Review of International Political Economy* 8(2): 226–74.

— and Shimshon Bichler (2009) *Capital as Power: A study of order and creorder*. London: Routledge.

OECD (2001) *Financial Market Trends No. 79*. Paris: Organisation for Economic Co-operation and Development (OECD).

Orwell, George (1949) *Nineteen Eighty-Four*. New York, NY: Penguin Books.

Overton, Mark (1996) *Agricultural Revolution in England: The transformation of the agrarian economy 1500–1850*. Cambridge: Cambridge University Press.

Parmar, Neil (2013) 'The millionaire residency visa'. *Wall Street Journal*, 20 September.

Patel, Raj (2008) *Stuffed and Starved: From farm to fork, the hidden battle for the world food system*. London: Portobello Books.

— (2009) *The Value of Nothing*. Melbourne: Black Inc.

Perelman, Michael (2000) *The Invention of Capitalism: Classical political economy and the secret history of primitive accumulation*. Durham, NC: Duke University Press.

Perkins, John (2005) *Confessions of an Economic Hitman*. New York, NY: Plume.

Petras, James (2008) 'Global ruling class: billionaires and how they "make it"'. *Journal of Contemporary Asia* 38(2): 319–29.

Pettifor, Ann (2006) *The Coming First World Debt Crisis*. Basingstoke: Palgrave Macmillan.

Piketty, Thomas (2014) *Capital in the Twenty-First Century*. Translated by Arthur Goldhammer. Cambridge, MA: Belknap Press of Harvard University Press.

Pipes, Richard (1999) *Property and Freedom*. New York, NY: Alfred A. Knopf.

Polanyi, Karl (1957) *The Great Transformation: The political and economic origins of our times*. Boston, MA: Beacon Press.

Polk, Sam (2014) 'For the love of money'. *New York Times*, 18 January.

Powell, Betsy (2009) 'Money mart's rates "criminal," borrowers' lawyer tells court'. *Toronto Star*, 18 April.

Quigley, Carroll (1966) *Tragedy and Hope: A history of the world in our time*. New York, NY: Macmillan.

Rai, Milan (1993) 'Columbus in Ireland'. *Race and Class* 34(4): 25–34.

Remnick, David (ed.) (2001) *The New Gilded Age: The New Yorker looks at the culture of affluence*. New York, NY: Modern Library.

Ritholtz, Barry (2009) *Bailout Nation*. Hoboken, NJ: John Wiley & Sons Inc.

Robinson, William I. and Jerry Harris (2000) 'Towards global ruling class? Globalization and the transnational capitalist class'. *Science and Society* 64(1): 11–54.

Rockström, Johan et al. (2009) 'A safe operating space for humanity'. *Nature* 461: 472–5.

Rodney, Walter (1972) *How Europe Underdeveloped Africa*. Washington, DC: Howard University Press.

Roose, Kevin (2014) 'One-percent jokes and plutocrats in drag: what I saw when I crashed a Wall Street secret society'. *New York Times Magazine*, 18 February.

Rowbotham, Michael (1998) *The Grip of Death: A study of modern money, debt slavery and destructive economics*. Charlbury: Jon Carpenter Publishing.

Shaxson, Nicolas (2011) *Treasure Islands: Uncovering the damage of offshore banking and tax havens.* Basingstoke: Palgrave Macmillan.

Shilliam, Robbie (2004) 'Hegemony and the unfashionable problematic of "primitive accumulation"'. *Millennium: Journal of International Studies* 32(1): 59–88.

Sinclair, Timothy (2005) *The New Masters of Capital: American bond rating agencies and the politics of creditworthiness.* Ithaca, NY: Cornell University Press.

Singer, P. W. (2003) *Corporate Warriors: The rise of the privatised military industry.* Ithaca, NY: Cornell University Press.

Sklair, Leslie (2001) *The Transnational Capitalist Class.* Oxford: Blackwell.

Smil, Vaclav (1994) *Energy in World History.* Boulder, CO: Westview Press.

Smith, Adam (2005 [1776]) *An Inquiry into the Nature and Causes of the Wealth of Nations.* Electronic Classic Series. Hazelton, PA: Pennsylvania State University.

Sobel, Robert (2000) *The Pursuit of Wealth: The incredible story of money throughout the ages.* New York, NY: McGraw-Hill.

Solomon, Steven (2001) *Water: The epic struggle for wealth, power and civilization.* New York, NY: Harper Perennial.

Sparr, Pamela (1994) *Mortgaging the Lives of Women: Feminist critique of structural adjustment.* London: Zed Books.

Stanworth, Phillip and Anthony Giddens (1974) *Elites and Power in British Society.* Cambridge: Cambridge University Press.

Stavrianos, L. S. (1981) *Global Rift: The third world comes of age.* New York, NY: William Morrow and Company Inc.

Stein, Ben (2006) 'In class warfare, guess which class is winning'. *New York Times*, 26 November.

Stiglitz, Joseph E. (2011) 'Of the 1%, by the 1%, for the 1%'. *Vanity Fair*, May. www.vanityfair.com/society/features/2011/05/top-one-percent-201105.

Stijns, Jean-Philippe, Christopher Garroway, Vararat Atisophon, Jesus Bueren, Gregory De Paepe and Carlos Sanchez (2012) *Can We Still Achieve the Millennium Development Goals? From Costs to Policies.* Organisation for Economic Co-operation and Development (OECD).

Story, Louise, Landon Thomas Jr. and Nelson D. Schwartz (2010) 'Wall St. helped to mask debt fueling Europe's crisis'. *New York Times*, 13 February.

Syal, Rajeev (2009) 'Drug money saved banks in global crisis says UN advisor'. *Observer*, 13 December.

Tainter, Joseph A. (1988) *The Collapse of Complex Societies.* Cambridge: Cambridge University Press.

Taylor, Jim, Doug Harrison and Stephen Kraus (2009) *The New Elite: Inside the minds of the truly wealthy.* New York, NY: Amacom.

Tett, Gillian (2011) 'Sub-prime moment looms for risk free sovereign debt'. *Financial Times*, 3 November.

Thakur, Atul (2008) '33% of Indians live in less space than US prisoners'. *Times of India*, 25 November.

Thomas, Tim (2012) 'The world's biggest yachts and their billionaire owners'. *Forbes*, 25 March. www.forbes.com/sites/timthomas/2012/03/25/the-top-yachts-spot/.

Thompson, E. P. (1966) *The Making of the English Working Class*. New York, NY: Vintage Books.

— (1990) *Whigs and Hunters: The origin of the black act*. London: Penguin Books.

— (1991) *Customs in Common*. London: Penguin Books.

Tigar, Michael E. and Madelein R. Levy (1977) *Law and the Rise of Capitalism*. New York, NY: Monthly Review Press.

Tilman, Rick (2006) 'Colin Campbell on Thorstein Veblen on conspicuous consumption'. *Journal of Economic Issues* 40(1): 97–112.

Trainer, Ted (2007) *Renewable Energy Cannot Sustain a Consumer Society*. New York, NY: Springer.

Treanor, Jill and Dominic Rushe (2012) 'HSBC pays record $1.9bn fine to settle US money-laundering accusations'. *Guardian*, 12 December.

Trouillot, Michel-Rolph (1995) *Silencing the Past: Power and the production of history*. Boston, MA: Beacon Press.

Tverberg, Gail (2011) 'The shared fate of GDP and energy growth'. *Financial Sense*, 15 November. www.financialsense.com/contributors/gail-tverberg/2011/11/15/the-shared-fate-of-gdp-and-energy-growth.

Twain, Mark (1871) 'The revised catechism'. *New York Tribune*, 27 September.

UNDP (2000) *World Energy Assessment: Energy and the challenge of sustainability*. New York, NY: United Nations Development Programme (UNDP).

United States Congress (1973) *Energy Reorganization Act of 1973: Hearings, Ninety-third Congress, first session, on H.R. 11510*. Washington, DC: US Government Printing Office.

Upbin, Bruce (2011) 'The 147 firms that control everything'. *Forbes*, 22 October. www.forbes.com/sites/bruceupbin/2011/10/22/the-147-companies-that-control-everything/.

Vaggi, Gianni and Peter Groenewegen (2003) *A Concise History of Economic Thought from Mercantilism to Monetarism*. Basingstoke: Palgrave Macmillan.

van der Pijl, Kees (1998) *Transnational Classes and International Relations*. London: Routledge.

Veblen, Thorstein (1919) *The Place of Science in Modern Civilization and Other Essays*. New York, NY: B. W. Huebech.

— (1923) *Absentee Ownership: Business enterprise in recent times: the case of America*. New York, NY: Transaction Publishers.

— (1998) *Essays in Our Changing Order*. New York, NY: Transaction Publishers.

— (2005 [1904]) *The Theory of Business Enterprise*. New York, NY: Cosimo Classics.

— (2007 [1899]) *The Theory of the Leisure Class*. Oxford: Oxford University Press.

Vitali, Stefania, James B. Glattfelder and Stefano Battiston (2011) 'The network of global corporate control'. *PLOS ONE* 6(10): 1–36.

Ware, Norman J. (1931) 'The physiocrats: a study in economic rationalization'. *American Economic Review* 21(4): 607–19.

Wealth-X (2013) *World Ultra Wealth Report 2013*. Singapore: Wealth-X. www.wealthx.com/wealthxubs wealthreport/.

Weaver, John C. (2006) *The Great Land*

*Rush and the Making of the Modern World 1650–1900.* Montreal: McGill-Queen's University Press.

Webber, Carolyn and Aaron Wildavsky (1986) *A History of Taxation and Expenditure in the Western World.* New York, NY: Simon & Schuster.

Wedel, Janine (2009) *Shadow Elite: How the world's new power brokers undermine democracy, government and the free market.* New York, NY: Basic Books.

Weisdorf, Jacob L. (2005) 'From foraging to farming: explaining the Neolithic Revolution'. *Journal of Economic Surveys* 19(4): 561–86.

Wennerlind, Carl (2011) *Casualties of Credit: The English financial revolution, 1620–1720.* Cambridge, MA: Harvard University Press.

Wilkinson, Richard and Kate Pickett (2009) *The Spirit Level: Why more equal societies almost always do better.* London: Allen Lane.

Williams, Eric (1984) *From Columbus to Castro: The history of the Caribbean, 1492–1969.* New York, NY: Vintage Books.

— (1994 [1944]) *Capitalism and Slavery.* Chapel Hill, NC: University of North Carolina Press.

Williams, Michael (2006) *Deforesting the Earth: From prehistory to global crisis.* Chicago, IL: Chicago University Press.

Wolf, Eric R. (2010) *Europe and the People without a History.* Berkeley, CA: University of California Press.

Wolf, Martin (2014a) '*Capital in the Twenty-First Century* by Thomas Piketty'. *Financial Times*, 15 April.

— (2014b) 'Strip private banks of their power to create money'. *Financial Times*, 24 April.

Wood, Ellen Meiksins (2002) *The Origin of Capitalism: A longer view.* London: Verso.

— (2012) *Liberty and Property: A social history of Western political thought from Renaissance to Enlightenment.* London: Verso.

— and Neal Wood (1997) *A Trumpet of Sedition: Political theory and the rise of capitalism, 1509–1688.* London: Pluto Press.

Wood, Graeme (2011) 'Secret fears of the super-rich'. *The Atlantic*, 24 February. www.theatlantic.com/magazine/archive/2011/04/secret-fears-of-the-super-rich/308419/.

World Bank (2013) 'The state of the poor: where are the poor, where is extreme poverty harder to end, and what is the current profile of the world's poor?' Economic Premise No. 125. Washington, DC: World Bank.

Wrigley, E. A. (2010) *Energy and the English Industrial Revolution.* Cambridge: Cambridge University Press.

Zanny, M. B. (2012) *For Richer, for Poorer.* London: Economist Intelligence Unit.

Zehner, Ozzie (2012) *Green Illusions: The dirty secrets of clean energy and the future of environmentalism.* Lincoln, NE: University of Nebraska Press.

Zeitlin, Maurice (1974) 'Corporate ownership and control: the large corporation and the capitalist class'. *American Journal of Sociology* 79(5): 1073–119.

# INDEX